PROVINCE-BUILDING AND THE FEDERALIZATION
OF IMMIGRATION IN CANADA

Province-Building and the Federalization of Immigration in Canada

MIREILLE PAQUET

Translated by Howard Scott

UNIVERSITY OF TORONTO PRESS
Toronto   Buffalo   London

Originally published as *La fédéralisation de l'immigration au Canada*
Édition Originale © 2016 Presses de l'Université de Montréal

© University of Toronto Press 2019
English-language edition
Toronto Buffalo London
utorontopress.com
Printed in the U.S.A.

ISBN 978-1-4875-0140-2

∞ Printed on acid-free paper with vegetable-based inks.

Library and Archives Canada Cataloguing in Publication

Paquet, Mireille, 1981–
[Fédéralisation de l'immigration au Canada. English]
Province-building and the federalization of immigration in Canada / Mireille Paquet ; translated by Howard Scott.

Translation of: La fédéralisation de l'immigration au Canada.
Includes bibliographical references and index.
ISBN 978-1-4875-0140-2 (hardcover)

1. Canada – Emigration and immigration – Government policy. 2. Federal government – Canada. I. Scott, Howard, 1952–, translator II. Title. III. Title: Fédéralisation de l'immigration au Canada. English.

JV7233.P36513 2019   325.71   C2018-903878-0

This book has been published with the help of a grant from the Federation for the Humanities and Social Sciences, through the Awards to Scholarly Publications Program, using funds provided by the Social Sciences and Humanities Research Council of Canada.

University of Toronto Press acknowledges the financial assistance to its publishing program of the Canada Council for the Arts and the Ontario Arts Council, an agency of the Government of Ontario.

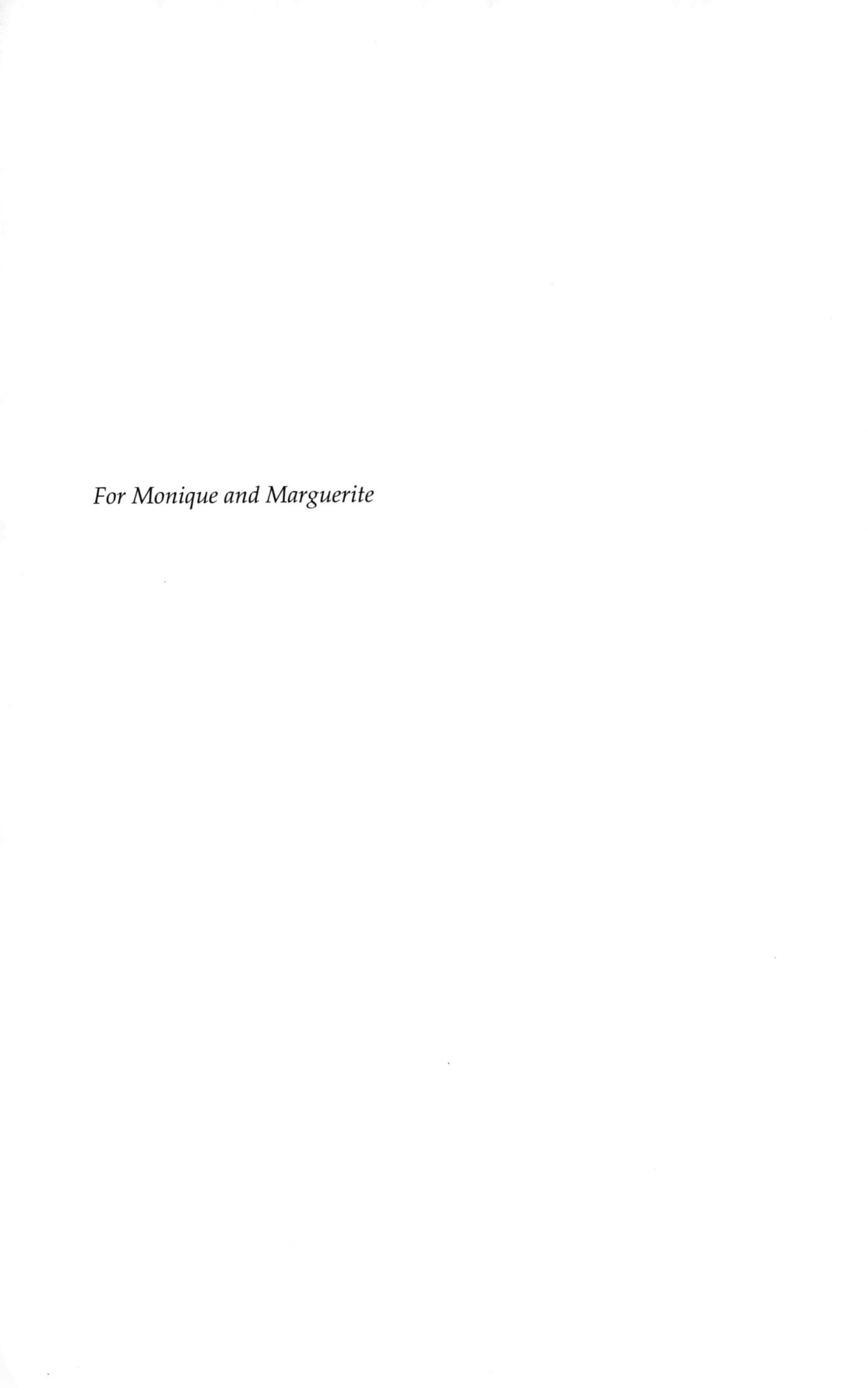

For Monique and Marguerite

Contents

Acknowledgments

This book does not represent the work of a single author; it is the result of dialogue and debate within a close circle of colleagues and friends. My professors and mentors at the Université de Montréal and the University of Ottawa contributed both directly and indirectly. The members of the Canada Research Chair in Citizenship and Governance have provided me with invaluable support. The holder of the Chair, Jane Jenson, has been (and remains) a mentor, an inspiration, and a generous, demanding, and formidable colleague. My colleagues at Concordia University welcomed me enthusiastically and have given me priceless support. Beyond these institutions, the list of individuals who have contributed to this book in one way or another could fill pages and would include people who have no idea how much they have inspired me. The list, in no particular order, includes Catherine Ellyson, Martine Hubert, Laura Madokoro, Melissa Thornton, Ted Rutland, Julie Cunningham, Rosemary Collard, Dimitrios Karmis, Martin Papillon, Caroline Andrew, Noemi Kreif, Nora Nagels, Alain Noël, Audrey Lespérance, Sean Mills, Marie-Ève Bélanger, and so many others. Bastien Castagner made everything perfectly better. I also have to mention the generosity and invaluable advice of Robert Young. Meyer Burstein, John Biles, and Leslie Seidle helped open doors that were sometimes a little rusty. Of course, in spite of everyone's help, all errors and omissions are my own.

The research presented in this book was carried out with the financial support of the Social Sciences and Humanities Research Council of Canada (SSHRC) and the Université de Montréal. In addition, the publication process was supported by the Research Support Program on Intergovernmental Affairs and Québec Identity of the Secrétariat aux affaires intergouvernementales canadiennes (SAIC), as well as by the Aid to Research Related Events program (ARRE) of Concordia University. This book was first published in French as *La fédéralisation de l'immigration au Canada* with Presses de l'Université de Montréal (PUM). I am extremely grateful for their support in the preparation of the original version of the book and for their participation in the translation project. The translation of the manuscript was made possible by the generous support of the SSHRC Awards to Scholarly Publications, of the Centre de recherche interdisciplinaire sur la diversité et la démocracie (CRIDAQ) and by the Aid to Research Related Events program (ARRE) of Concordia University. Howard Scott was an excellent and patient translator, with a formidable eye for details. At the University of Toronto Press, the enthusiasm of Daniel Quinlan for this translation project was always heartwarming. It is a real privilege to be able to share my ideas in *les deux langues officielles*; thank you for helping me make it a reality.

A substantial number of civil servants and people active in community organizations working with immigrants gave generously of their time in the course of the production of this book. By agreeing to meet me, whether officially or unofficially, these people have made it possible for me to tell a story in which they are the heroes. Their generosity and passion for immigration and integration seem to me to be truly the magic ingredients of the "Canadian model."

List of Acronyms

ACOA   Atlantic Canada Opportunities Agency
APEC   Atlantic Provinces Economic Council
BCSAP   BC Settlement and Adaptation Program
BCSIP   BC Settlement and Immigration Program
CAP   Council of Atlantic Premiers
CHST   Canada Health and Social Transfers
CIC   Citizenship and Immigration Canada
COFI   Centres d'orientation et de formation des immigrants
CP   Conservative Party (generic)
CRS   Comprehensive Ranking System
EI   Employment insurance
ESL   English as second language
LP   Liberal Party (generic)
MICC   Quebec Ministry of Immigration and Cultural Communities
MID   Quebec Ministry of Immigration, Diversity, and Inclusion
MISA   Metropolitan Immigrant Settlement Association
MRCI   Quebec Ministry of Citizen Relations and Immigration
NDP   New Democratic Party (generic)
NLSIP   Newfoundland and Labrador Settlement and Integration
        Program
PNP   Provincial Nominee Program
PQ   Parti Québécois
TFWP   Temporary Foreign Worker Program
TRIEC   Toronto Region Immigrant Employment Council

PROVINCE-BUILDING AND THE FEDERALIZATION
OF IMMIGRATION IN CANADA

Introduction

Immigrants are the lifeblood of Canada. Ever since the first European settlers came to this country, international immigration has increased constantly, to the point that it is now the primary source of population growth. Compared to its neighbours to the south and to European countries, Canada projects a positive image with regard to intergroup relations, and few voices question whether immigration is contributing to society and the economy. The country's success in this domain is not so much the consequence of Canadians' particular predisposition. Rather, it is in large part the result of government decisions that established, starting in the 1960s, a regime of public policies on immigration and integration. This "Canadian model" is distinguished, internationally, by the leading role the government plays in managing immigration, liberal selection policies based on economic criteria, an official policy of multiculturalism, and relatively easy naturalization requirements (Bloemraad 2006; Kymlicka 2003).

In the contemporary period, the consolidation of this "model" is the most important change that has affected – with considerable durability – Canada's relationship with immigration. There has been a transformation of the racially selective and exclusionary approach that had characterized immigration policy in the first half of the twentieth century (Kelley and Trebilcock 2010). The government began actively disseminating various iterations of a discourse that presented immigration as an economic and social contribution to the country. This fostered a social climate conducive to the integration of newcomers; it also made it possible to maintain political support for growth in the numbers of immigrants to be welcomed annually.

Between 1990 and 2010, a second change transformed the Canadian state's relationship to immigration: a shift from a model dominated by the federal government to a model of immigration governance in which the ten provinces played an increasingly active role. In this book I identify this process as the "federalization of immigration," given that it corresponds to the emergence of new legitimate actors in the management of immigration under Canada's federal regime. This process unfolded gradually, without attracting much attention from citizens and researchers. Its discreet nature can be explained, among other things, by the fact that it did not result from a crisis or even a change in the Canadian approach to immigration. Despite this major shift, Canadian immigration and integration policies remain liberal and inclusive. However, federalization has called into question a key principle of the "Canadian model": domination by Ottawa with regard to immigrant selection and integration. Although it has gone largely unnoticed, federalization has fundamentally transformed the model by expanding the number of venues in which immigrants interact with governments and by increasing the number of actors who can influence immigration and integration policies in Canada.

This federalization process has affected both immigration and integration policies. In this book, immigration policies refer to government actions aimed at attracting, facilitating, or limiting the settlement of people of foreign origins on their territories. As they relate to sovereignty, these actions also include border controls and the management of temporary population movements. Integration policies, a more contemporary domain of public action, correspond to policies and programs that support the integration of immigrants into a new society. These include language courses and employment access programs. Governments usually distinguish between integration policies and immigrant settlement policies. The latter are related to the basic needs of newcomers (e.g., reception at the airport, then clothing, health care, housing), while the former serve needs that arise in the medium and long term. It is also important to distinguish diversity management policies, such as interculturalism, multiculturalism, and the various instruments designed to fight discrimination, from immigrant integration policies. Diversity management policies cover a broader spectrum than integration policies; they are intended for the entire population and not just for people who have recently immigrated to a country (Smith 2009). This book does not deal with diversity management policies, which serve different, albeit complementary policy objectives than immigration and integration policies.

This book argues that provinces have been and remain key agents of change within Canada's federal regime. More precisely, it is aimed at answering a key question: How has the governance of immigration become federalized since 1990, in the absence of any external immigration crisis and especially in the absence of a paradigm shift in the "Canadian model"? Through analysis of policy trajectories over a period of twenty years, this book shows that it was the provinces that triggered and kept in motion the process of federalization of the governance of immigration and integration. In the ten provinces, in response to changing political, ideational, and economic contexts, the political elites mobilized to have immigration recognized as a key resource for economic and social development. In doing so, the provincial governments have, one after the other, developed policies and programs related to immigration, and provincial political actors have claimed more and more powers and resources from the federal government. Although federalization has involved and affected Ottawa, it is therefore a process of change brought about by the Canadian provinces.

While this argument is of crucial interest for all observers of the dynamics that influence immigration in Canada and other liberal societies, it also has consequences for the study of Canadian politics. In particular, for analysts of federalism and intergovernmental relations, this study highlights additional elements to answer the essential question of *who governs* in Canada. In fact, the federalization of immigration shows that all of the provinces – not only Quebec – can bring about a gradual change in the federal policies or, quite simply, force Ottawa to act.

The provinces' crucial role in this process of change illustrates, more broadly, the importance of provincial societies and their autonomous political lives. The change described in these pages is the result of a contemporary iteration of a phenomenon already analysed in Canada: province-building. In the 1970s, province-building was largely about political and economic elites using natural resources as an engine of economic, political, and social development. The mobilization of provincial elites is now as concerned with immigration and immigrants as with natural resources, and this has transformed the governance of immigration in Canada. Analysis of federalization shows that it is impossible to understand contemporary Canadian federalism without paying close attention to political life in *all* of the provinces. This book is thus a plea that the role of the provinces as agents of change be recognized in Canadian federalism and Canadian political life.

Chapter 1

Provinces, Immigration, and Institutional Change

Since 1990, the Canadian provinces have become increasingly important actors in the institutional regime governing immigration and integration. The provinces are active in delivering integration services in their areas of jurisdiction (education, for example) and are now also highly proactive when it comes to selecting immigrants. They also mobilize over immigration in intergovernmental arenas. Many federal policies and institutions have been altered as a consequence of these developments, and this in turn has called into question the federal government's capacity to act unilaterally in the area of immigration.

This change is a major break with past practices in the Canadian federation. Immigration is one of two formally shared jurisdictions under the British North America Act of 1867 (section 95), a reflection of the British colonies' efforts to attract settlers before Confederation. Yet before 1990, and especially in the decades after the Second World War, the federal government had been almost totally dominant in the development and implementation of immigration and integration policies (Vineberg 1987). This reflected a broader lack of interest among the provinces, which, with the exception of Quebec, were reluctant to act with regard to selecting and integrating newcomers. Several factors explain this passivity, including fears of the costs associated with public action in immigration and concerns about public opinion within each province (Hawkins 1988). Accordingly, the provinces did not challenge Ottawa's dominance, and immigration remained largely the purview of the federal government, despite the shared constitutional jurisdiction.

The contemporary situation is entirely different: the provinces are openly active in the area; indeed, they are challenging federal dominance over immigration and integration. In the ten provinces, positive discourses on immigration have emerged. They present newcomers as assets for provincial economies and societies. By publishing official strategies on immigration, the provinces are positioning themselves to play pivotal public roles in the sector; and by funding programs, provincial governments are creating direct links with immigrants and community organizations, which have long been the "clients" of the federal government. In working to attract and select permanent and temporary immigrants, the other aim of the provinces is to meet the needs expressed by the economic actors in their jurisdictions.

These new provincial stances are being expressed institutionally. Since the early 1990s, the ten provinces have been partners in federal-provincial immigration agreements, which range from collaboration to devolution. These agreements have modified and codified how responsibilities are to be shared between the two orders of government. In certain cases, especially in Ontario, they have also assigned responsibilities to other governments or to private actors – to municipalities in particular (Seidle 2010a).

Except in Quebec, which has more sophisticated procedures, these agreements have codified the practices of collaboration in the area of integration and created instruments for direct action in immigration selection, through the Provincial Nominee Program (PNP). According to Citizenship and Immigration Canada, the PNP allows the nine provinces "to nominate potential immigrants whom they believe will meet particular provincial/territorial needs, and who intend to settle in the PT of nomination" (Canada 2011a, 1). The program functions much like the one that Quebec established 1991. Individuals file their applications directly with the province or territory; the provinces/ territories review those applications and decide whether to issue nomination certificates. These certificates are sent on to the federal public administration, which reviews the applications according "to local economic development needs" (Canada 2011a, 19) as well as criteria such as health status and criminal background as set out in the Canadian law on immigration and the associated regulations. After this review has been conducted, the applicant is accepted or rejected. Close to 96 per cent of provincial nominations are approved by Ottawa, which is comparable to the rate of approval of the nomination certificates issued by the Quebec government (Canada 2011a, 20). The PNP agreements include conditions for implementation (integrity and accountability) as well as a general condition in programmatic terms: the economic contribution of immigration is to be maximized. Beyond these conditions, however, the provinces have considerable manoeuvring room with regard to how they configure their programs and who they select as immigrants.

In many cases – Quebec, Ontario, British Columbia, and Manitoba – these agreements have involved substantial transfers of funds to the provinces, most often in the form of grants. These transfers have been made with few conditions and often with minimal accountability requirements (Seidle 2010b; Canada 2012a). Accordingly, these agreements have heightened the provinces' capacity to act without placing any real limits on their activities.

The creation of the PNP, the expansion of provincial activities supported by a positive discourse of immigration, and the implementation of diverse bilateral agreements in the area of immigration are a few of the key features of the federalization process. Another aspect of the recent evolution of the Canadian regime is particularly important: ongoing federal action in the face of increased engagement by the provinces.

The provinces' autonomous actions are carried out in their areas of jurisdiction and within the framework of shared jurisdiction over immigration. Immigration agreements have not limited the provinces' areas of action or those of the federal government. Except for the selection procedures for economic immigrants and their dependants, established for Quebec in 1991, the federal government retains the power to select immigrants throughout Canada. In addition, the transfer of responsibility for administering and delivering settlement services to BC and Manitoba did not explicitly prohibit the federal government from intervening, as is the case in Quebec. Rather than a zero sum transfer, the situation can be more appropriately described as a gradual overlapping of the actions of the two orders of government.

This change in the institutional regime of governance of immigration and integration thus corresponds to a process of *federalization*. In this book, federalization refers to the emergence of new actors and the modification of the status of those that have strong institutional or political legitimacy within an institutional regime.[1] This process is different from decentralization, which refers to a transfer of authority, resources, or capacity from one government to another. It is also different from deconcentration, which refers to the partial transfer of responsibilities from the central government to peripheral jurisdictions, with the latter becoming responsible for implementing public policies (Rocher and Rouillard 1998). Federalization, by contrast, involves an increase of the agency of provincial governments, without a diminishing of the role of the federal government. It also entails growing interactions between orders of government. The outcomes of federalization processes can vary from province to province and over time, ranging from increasing conflicts between political actors, to the revision of public policy orientations across an entire country.

The federalization of immigration and integration governance corresponds to the gradual development, over the past twenty years, of shared jurisdiction in immigration, as defined in section 95 of the Constitution Act, 1867. It constitutes a break with the federal paramountcy and provincial passivity that had prevailed since the 1960s. In observing this crucial shift, we can see how questions broadly related to immigration policy are interwoven with the dynamics inherent in Canadian federalism itself.

Change in the Federation

Confronted with complex political institutions as well as conflicts over the very nature of federalism, political scientists have developed a rich set of instruments for studying relationships among Canada's governments. In dialogue with these contributions and with the research on comparative federalism, this book shows that it is highly productive to refocus the analysis on processes of institutional change in order to understand the contemporary evolution of the Canadian federation. This book thus presents a different perspective on change in the federation: it focuses on gradual institutional change, coupled with an interactional understanding of federalism. This perspective is distinct from the three most common approaches to studying change in the literature on Canadian federalism.

The first approach focuses on describing the institutions arising from change. To properly understand the contemporary dynamics of governance and compare Canada with other countries, researchers have attempted to measure the degree of centralization or decentralization in the Canadian federation (Wallner 2008). This research has made it possible to document the gradual decentralization of the Canadian federal regime since Confederation (Russell 2004; Turgeon and Wallner 2013). In the same vein, the difference between formal institutions and practices and the actual capacities of governments (e.g., federal spending power) is constantly being examined and debated in order to ascertain the degree of decentralization that has taken place in the federation (Noël 2007; Pelletier 2008; Rocher and Rouillard 1998). At the same time, many authors are developing new concepts to describe changes affecting the Canadian federation. Multi-level governance, for example, has been used to describe the inclusion of cities and Aboriginal nations in analyses of intergovernmental institutions (Papillon 2012; Leo and August 2009).

The second approach to examining change within the federation is concerned with intergovernmental relations. Since the Second World War, political scientists have developed means to classify relationships between the federal government and the provinces. This has led to significant conceptual innovations. This research has given us concepts such as federal–provincial diplomacy, competitive federalism, cooperative federalism, collaborative federalism, non-constitutional renewal, and open federalism (Simeon 2006; Stevenson 1989; Cameron and Simeon 2002; Banting et al. 2006; Montpetit 2007). These studies focus mainly on the changing practices of governments and, when relevant, on intergovernmental institutions that have emerged from these changes.

There is a third approach that researchers of Canadian federalism have taken to examining change: the normative evaluation of its consequences. Research has examined the economic effectiveness or political legitimacy of evolving federal arrangements (e.g., Bakvis, Baier, and Brown 2009; Bakvis and Brown 2010). In the context of constitutional tensions and in light of the Quebec independence movement, these analyses have studied the degree to which the multinational nature of Canada has been recognized within federal institutions (Gagnon 2006; McRoberts 2001). Others have described the impacts of "asymmetrical" changes within the federation, viewing them as positive or negative (Gagnon 2001; Brock 2008; Maclure 2005). For these authors, federalism corresponds to a particular ideal and any change must be seen in terms of whether that ideal has been attained or abandoned.

These three trends have made it possible for political scientists to establish productive dialogues with comparative politics and, especially, with studies on federalism elsewhere in the world (e.g., Wallner and Boychuck 2014; Béland and Lecours 2007; Lecours 2017). This book proposes yet another way to address change in the Canadian federation: studying the processes of gradual institutional change. Instead of describing the results of the changes in terms of institutions or relationships, I will show here that processes of gradual institutional change are what most need to be explored by scholars of Canadian politics. Drawing from the work of others who have taken an institutional approach to the topic, this book focuses on *how* change occurs within the Canadian federation. This book is therefore not intended to describe the institutions or the relationships resulting from the process of federalization, and even less to judge their legitimacy, their fairness, or their validity. It is aimed instead at explaining how federalization came about. Only after that task has been completed will it be possible for societal actors and researchers to evaluate the impact of this significant change.

The emphasis on the processes of change makes it possible to consider theoretical developments while recognizing a key characteristic of the Canadian federal regime: the formal rigidity of Canada's institutions, which has historically forced actors to invent and experiment with strategies and informal practices in order to respond to the evolution of Canadian society. This characteristic was consolidated in the 1990s, after successive failures of projects to reform the Canadian Constitution to include Quebec. In a contemporary Canada where no one dares talk about constitutional amendments, analyses of processes of gradual institutional change are crucial if we are to theorize contemporary federalism.

An Interactional Approach to the Study of Federalism

The analysis of federalization presented in this book is also distinguished by an interactional approach to federalism. This approach, based on Quebec research on federalism and comparative research on provincial politics, involves analysing federalism as a set of interactions marked by the interdependence and autonomy of two non-subordinate levels of government (Rocher 2006). It does not imply making judgments about the legitimacy of one order of government over another. Rather, it calls on researchers to consider the impact of relationships between governments on the evolution of Canadian federalism. Moreover, it tasks analysts to account for the multiple forms, directions, and contents of these relationships. Although it requires constant attention to how the two levels of government relate to each other, the practical implication of this interactional reading of federalism is that it expands on the limited treatment accorded to the provinces in the study of Canadian federalism.

The approach presented in this book rejects the idea – implicit or sometimes explicit – that Canadian federalism is primarily a vertical, one-way relationship, from Ottawa towards the provinces. This view of political life in Canada is often the result of implicit normative concepts regarding federalism, especially of ideas related to the role the federal government should play in the management of the country. For others, it is a way to describe the inequalities in power, capacities, and resources between the orders of government – inequalities that favour the federal government in many policy areas.

This conception of the relationships between governments reflects a limited vision of the provinces' role in the development, maintenance, performance, and evolution of the federal regime. When Ottawa is viewed as the main site of decision-making, little attention is paid to the ways in which the provinces experience and negotiate federalism from day to day. This vertical vision supports many assumptions regarding the provinces – chiefly the idea that they are passive receivers of decisions and policies emanating from the federal government. More broadly, this approach implicitly limits our curiosity and our capacity to see the impact of the provinces on the content and management of national policies. When federalism is seen as a one-way vertical dynamic, it obscures and underestimates the multitude of ways in which the provinces can influence the interests of the federal government and modify the capacity of Ottawa (and other provinces) to act.

Furthermore, central to the interactional approach is the fact that provinces' political, social, and economic lives, as well as historical contexts, hold great importance for the study of Canadian federalism. This proposition is in line with many studies on provincial policy and, even more so, with work on the role and the place of Quebec in the federation. The approach adopted in this book is nevertheless distinguished from these studies in that it affirms that, in most cases, provincial influence is not the attribute of a single province. In this respect, the book can be contrasted with many research studies that focus – not without reason – on the central role played by Quebec in the transformation of Canadian federalism (Cameron and Krikorian 2002; Fafard and Rocher 2009). I maintain that it is important to seriously consider the roles played by all provinces, large *and* small, nationalist *or not*, in the evolution of the Canadian political regime. The aim, then, is to expand the spectrum of the analysis beyond case studies that focus on one province at a time (Tellier 2011). The interactional approach favours the comparative study of how the provinces have acted and reacted when faced with changes affecting all of Canadian society. In this regard, the book intervenes in studies of provincial and territorial politics, which are still often confined to case studies on public policies, culture, economics, or electoral politics (Dunn 2001).

As the following chapters will show, the interactional approach discredits the idea that federalization is solely the result of a desire for decentralization on the part of Ottawa, or mostly the result of actions taken by Quebec (as suggested, for example, by Banting [2012]). Indeed, it allows us to see that the ten provinces have played an active role in initiating change and that, through their interactions with Ottawa and with other provinces, they have kept the process of federalization moving forward. In short, I argue that provinces are the agents of change at the heart of the process of federalization. This conclusion is only possible if we take an approach that views federalism as a set of interactions marked by the interdependence and autonomy of two non-subordinate orders of government.

Federalization and Studies in Immigration

Even though the governance of immigration and integration in industrialized countries has evolved since the 1990s (Zicone and Caponio 2006), the study of federalism and immigration is relatively new in political science (Siemiatycki and Triadafilopoulos 2010). Emerging research has focused on the dynamics of multilevel governance, nationalist mobilization, and descriptions of local policies (e.g., Hepburn and Zapatero 2014; Caponio and Jones-Correa 2017; Baglay and Nakache 2014). The explanations offered for the increasing mobilization of constituent units – such as provinces or states – with respect to institutional changes related to immigration in the federation do not, however, adequately account for the changes that have been occurring in Canada since the 1990s.

In fact, provincial mobilization around immigration, and the demands that arise from it, differ considerably from the cases described in the international literature on the topic. As a general rule, the conflicts related to immigration in federations are the result of tensions between the central government's policies and the interests of the other orders of government (Newton and Adams 2009; Spiro 2001; Ramakrishnan and Gulasekaram 2013). For example, in the United States, the states have long mobilized in response to the federal government's failure to enact comprehensive immigration reform. By contrast, the movement observed in Canada is a mobilization of federal entities in keeping with existing policy and in line with liberal principles established since the 1960s. Provincial actions do not contradict the "Canadian model" but are aimed rather at the expansion and enlargement of that model's advantages for their jurisdictions and societies.

The Canadian case is also distinguished by the absence of social movements or political parties with anti-immigrant demands at the provincial level. Provincial demands, in fact, promote a positive view of immigrants and the value they add to society. They have as an objective the implementation of policies for increasing the number of immigrants and facilitating their inclusion in society.

Nationalism is also often cited as an engine of the activity of constituent governments in the area of immigration (Barker, 2015). The demands and activities of constituent units are presented as being primarily the result of a process of nation-building based on identity, or of the need to preserve the linguistic integrity of a territory; or they reflect a process of change in the citizenship regime (Rocher and Labelle 2010; Gagnon and Iacovino 2003; Jenson 1998). For political and practical reasons, control over migration flows and over the instruments for integrating immigrants has become a focus of mobilization for governments and nationalist movements.

The emphasis on nationalism and its consequences has been useful for understanding Quebec. While it is important to recognize the importance of nationalism, the mobilization of the provinces other than Quebec shows that it is crucial to consider other dynamics as well. For example, how can we explain the adoption, in 2009, of an immigration strategy by the Saskatchewan government (Saskatchewan 2009b)? After all, the province was then led by a party with conservative and certainly not nationalist tendencies – that is, the Saskatchewan Party (Rayner and Beaudry-Mellor 2009). The absence of a nationalist mobilization in the great majority of provinces outside Quebec,[2] coupled with the growing presence of discourses, actions, and demands for a *provincial* role in immigration and integration, suggests that nationalism is not the sole driver of the provinces' interests and actions.

Generally, federal actions on immigration can also reflect the opinions of the citizens of a territory, as can be the case at all levels of government (Hainmueller and Hopkins 2014). In Canada, this relationship has not yet been directly tested at the provincial scale, though there has been recent research on the opinions of citizens within the ten provinces regarding immigration and visible minorities. For example, Bilodeau, Turgeon, and Karakoç (2012) found that there was no growth in anti-immigrant feelings in the provinces between 1988 and 2008. Instead, a *decrease* in demands that the number of immigrants be restricted was observable over that period. While it is impossible to state unequivocally that public opinion within each province actually persuaded the government to pursue positive actions regarding immigration, these results do show that public opinion has not been an impediment to provincial mobilization.

Internationally, many research studies suggest a link between the number of new immigrants, the pace of their arrival, and the reaction of national and local governments (Marquez and Schraufnagel 2013;

Money 1997). Most often, the relationships explored show that the greater the number of immigrants or racialized immigrants in a territory, the more the government of that territory will react, most of the time anticipating electoral or public opinion dynamics. In most studies, government responses are aimed at limiting immigration or responding to public opinion that is more and more anxious about newcomers. In Canada, however, the movement of provinces towards more substantial intervention in immigration cannot be explained functionally as a response to the concentration of immigrants in a territory.

The distribution of immigration among the Canadian provinces has always been very uneven. In 2010, three provinces – Ontario, Quebec, and British Columbia – received the majority of new arrivals while the four Atlantic provinces together received only 2.78 per cent of immigrants. Figure 1 shows the distribution among the provinces of total immigration in 2010.

Figure 1: Distribution of permanent immigrants across provinces, 2010*

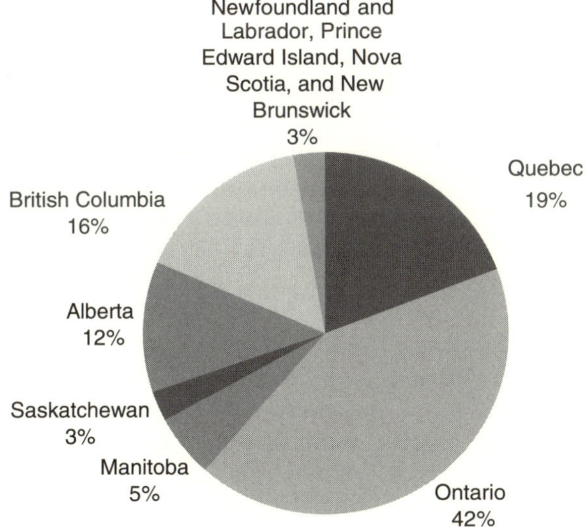

* Specifically, New Brunswick had 0.73% of total immigration (2,215 permanent residents), while Newfoundland and Labrador had 0.24% of total immigration (714 permanent residents), Nova Scotia had 0.83% (2,408 permanent residents), and Prince Edward Island had 0.89% (2,581 permanent residents). These numbers are proportionally small, but represent sizeable amounts for these small provinces.
Source: Canada (2011b).

It is easy to attribute provincial intervention to the presence of immigrants; however, the situation is more complex than that. Starting in the 1990s, we can see the evolution of responses in all the provinces, even those with only small numbers of international immigrants (e.g., Manitoba). In addition, the Ontario government's relatively belated interest in immigration illustrates the fact that the presence of a large immigrant population is not a precondition for provincial mobilization in this policy area.

Structured Variation and Similarity

The apparent lack of a correlation between significant immigrant population and provincial response has made federalization a difficult phenomenon to explain. This puzzle is also made more complex by the presence of structured variation among the provinces. While comparable, the Canadian provinces are distinguished from one another by political, economic, demographic, cultural, and structural differences (Imbeau et al. 2000). The general mobilization of all provincial governments towards immigration, coupled with the diversity of the provinces, suggests that federalization has occurred in ten idiosyncratic ways. Furthermore, we may predict a key distinction between a Quebec model, characterized at least in part by nationalist mobilization, and a Canadian provincial model in the nine other provinces. The reality, however, is far more intricate.

A visible result of the process of federalization has been the implementation of immigration and integration policies in the ten Canadian provinces, which in many cases were not very active in the area before 1990. In this book, these policies are referred to as *modes of intervention*. This concept, based on research on the development of the welfare state by Gøsta Esping-Andersen (1990), and on research on immigration policies by Keith Banting (2010) and Gary Freeman (2004), refers to the configuration of institutions, strategies, public policies, and policy instruments that are mobilized by a government to intervene in a given domain. The concept of mode of intervention makes it possible to go beyond general observations regarding the growth of interventions or public spending to take into account the interactions among various components of public policies as well as the dominant logic influencing public action.

A detailed comparison of the policies and programs implemented in 2010 points to notable contrasts among the modes of intervention of the ten provinces.[3] In contrast to the predictions of dualism (Quebec versus the nine other provinces) or idiosyncrasy (ten unique models), we can

Table 1: Four provincial modes of intervention in immigration and integration

	Holistic	Bridging	Reactive	Attraction–retention
	QC and MN	AB and SK	ON and BC	Atlantic Canada
Dominant logic	Immigration as part of society building	Immigration to respond to labour market demand	Response to the needs created by immigration	Immigration for provincial survival
Immigrant recruitment and selection interventions	Intense and exhaustive, based on economic and social criteria	Intense, based on labour market demands	Limited and targeted, based on highly skilled occupations	Moderate, based on large array of criteria aimed at demographic growth
Immigrant integration interventions	Global and based on a continuum approach	Limited, based on labour market access objectives	Dualistic, response to the needs of immigrants living on the territory and specific services for highly skilled immigrants	Limited, supplement to federal services and based on retention objectives

distinguish a limited structured variation among the provinces: four modes of intervention in immigration and integration can be observed. Table 1 summarizes this structured variation. These differences are sustained by various linkages between the actions of governments, and by variations with respect to the content of policies, as well as by divergences with respect to the roles attributed to the different actors.

The existence of these differences is in line with comparative research that identifies history, partisan configurations, and economic contexts as sources of variation among provincial public policies (e.g., Boychuk 1998; Haddow and Klassen 2006; Haddow 2015). However, the variations among the provincial modes of intervention are structured differently from what one would assume from traditional analyses in Quebec and Canadian political science. These variations reflect not an opposition between a Quebec model and a "Canadian provincial" model, but rather a richer diversity among the interventions of the nine other provinces. In addition, the four modes of intervention do not represent a precise copy of the structural elements that can affect provincial actions, especially the number of immigrants accepted or the type of immigration agreement. Rather, each of the modes of intervention reflects political dynamics characteristic of each group of provinces, dynamics that are still poorly understood.

The first provincial mode of intervention in immigration and integration is the *holistic mode*. In Quebec and Manitoba, government intervention is distinguished by its global orientation. In these two provinces, the dominant intervention approach entails constructing provincial society through the development of the population, the labour force, and the provincial social community. This mode is characterized by a significant role attributed to the provincial government in the administration and implementation of immigration activities and programs. It is also distinguished by substantial state interventions both in selection and integration, as well as by a strong relationship between these two fields of activity.

In contrast to the holistic mode of intervention, the policies promoted by Alberta and Saskatchewan primarily target access to employment for newcomers. These interventions are referred to collectively as the *bridging mode*, since government efforts, autonomously and in collaboration with economic actors, aim to serve as bridges permitting immigrants – most often selected on the basis of economic criteria – to enter the provincial labour market as quickly as possible. Under this framework, immigrants – who may be highly qualified or have technical skills – are viewed as necessary to sustain and accelerate the province's economic growth. As such, the provincial government's intervention in immigration is presented as part of broader efforts to support the economy. This mode of intervention assigns a substantial role to the market. The economic actors are mobilized in the selection *and* integration of new arrivals. There is significant provincial activity in the area of selection and recruitment; efforts in settlement and integration focus mainly on integration into the labour market.

Ontario and BC embody a third mode of intervention, the *reactive mode*. Given that these provinces receive significant flows of new arrivals without recruitment efforts, public action is dominated by responses to the needs generated by the presence of a large immigrant population. The objective is to ensure social cohesion and to maximize the benefits related to the presence of this population, by favouring participation in the labour market and preventing social exclusion. This mode of intervention is distinguished by a limited role for the provincial government and by substantial responsibility being given to civil society and, in some cases, to the market. Finally, the approach taken by

Ontario and BC is distinguished by explicit dualization between two target populations: highly qualified immigrants and newcomers in general.

The fourth provincial mode of intervention relates to the policies and strategies developed by the provinces of Atlantic Canada. The *attraction–retention mode* involves, as its name suggests, public actions focused on increasing the numbers of immigrants and then on retaining these newcomers once they have arrived. Provincial actions are all related to the dominant view that immigration is a lever for economic development and demographic survival. The economy and demography are presented as interdependent means for ensuring that provincial societies can be sustained. To that end, the *attraction–retention mode* identifies the government and the society as the key actors in immigration and integration. The policies and programs of these provinces are distinguished by strong efforts in recruitment and selection and by less intense integration policies aimed primarily at the retention of new arrivals.

Setting aside these differences, there is a high level of convergence among the four modes of intervention, based on a conception of immigration as a resource for the provincial society and for the provincial economy. The provinces all present their actions as pro-immigrant and as means to ensure the sustainability of their societies. This is demonstrated by the comparison made by the Alberta Progressive Conservative Premier Ed Stelmach during the debates of the legislative assembly of his province in 2006: "Another important area, Mr. Speaker, is gaining control of the tools to manage immigration policy. It could be as fundamental to Alberta's future prosperity as the affirmation in 1929 of constitutional jurisdiction over natural resources has been to our present prosperity" (Legislative Assembly of Alberta, 27 February 2006, 72).

In all ten provinces, immigrants are seen as providing necessary skills, human capital, demographic capital, or financial capital. Indeed, they are discussed as resources for the province. In 2010, Ontario's citizenship and immigration minister, Eric Hoskins (Liberal), made this emblematic declaration on the importance of immigration for his province:

> [I]mmigration is Ontario's lifeblood. It's our demographic future. It is fuel for our economic engine. With an aging population and a declining birthrate, Ontario's future prosperity depends on immigration. Attracting skilled newcomers, helping them to get settled and retaining them here in this province is an economic imperative for Ontario. This is especially

> important because within the next decade, newcomers will make up 100%
> of Ontario's net labour growth. To ensure that Ontario remains prosper-
> ous, we need immigrants for the skills and talents that they bring and for
> the richness that they add to the fabric of our society. (Legislative Assem-
> bly of Ontario, 27 September 2010, 2342)

These declarations are typical of the political discourses on immigration
in all provinces since 1990. Each mode of intervention in immigration and
integration presents an action plan for maximizing immigrants as a resource for enriching the economic and social fabric of a given province.

A detailed comparison of provincial policies and programs in immigration and integration demonstrates the presence of four dominant
modes of intervention. This structured variation reflects the existence of
room for provincial difference in the development of policy responses
in these policy sectors. However, the similarity of the ten provincial
discourses, including the Quebec discourse – all of them identify immigration as an essential resource – indicates the presence of a unique dynamic within the ten provinces, namely province-building centred on
immigration. The differences, which are not easy to define, coexist with
shared discourses, thus forming a puzzle for the analyst. Rather than
seeing these characteristics as idiosyncrasies peculiar to the Canadian
federal regime, this book maintains that they are key to understanding
the process of federalization.

Gradual Institutional Changes

Theories and approches associated with institutionalism are mobilized in this book. In particular, the central argument rests on accounts
foused on gradual institutional changes. In response to the main criti-
cism made against the return of analyses focusing on institutions in
political science – especially their inherent explanatory bias with
respect to stability – studies about the dynamism characteristic of formal and informal institutions have developed (Thelen 1999). This book
shares the position of historical institutionalist researchers who have
abandoned the typical concepts focusing on exogenous forces creating
changes, such as the critical juncture (Streeck and Thelen 2005; Benz
and Broschek 2013; Triadafilopoulos 2012). Here, instead, I examine
changes that are less abrupt, less succinct, and sometimes difficult to
identify after the fact. While recognizing the self-reinforcing tendencies of institutions, analyses of gradual institutional changes maintain

that institutions change significantly as much through small changes as through external shocks or major upheavals. This perspective is distinguished by the explanatory role it confers on the activities of actors within institutions as well as on temporality and the sequence of political processes.

The concept of *institutional regime* is central to this perspective. It emphasizes the role of actors, power relations, and practices in the maintenance, through performance, of political institutions. An institutional regime is expressed empirically as the relationships between actors who, through formal and informal rules, organize the distribution of resources and power (Mahoney and Thelen 2010b, 7–10). Institutional regimes comprise formal elements (the rules) and interactional elements (the actors and their relationships). From this perspective, institutional regimes are first and foremost instruments for distributing resources (power, legitimacy, money, etc.); also, they generate positions for actors and associated resources as well as capacities to act. Institutional regimes are the result of certain agreements, implicit or explicit, between actors and practices that are being constantly reproduced, primarily through respect or non-respect for rules and conventions. Note that these agreements can be the product of compromises between actors who have long left the regime. Moreover, the practices of actors can call into question the balance of power and organization of an institutional regime, be it deliberately or as the result of an incongruity with a new context. There is, in this sense, an inherent dynamism in institutional regimes, which can evolve in any number of ways over time. The relational nature of institutions thus makes them more subject to change than is suggested by theoretical contributions on institutional reproduction.

This perspective on gradual institutional changes permits us to analyse the processes of change in federations and, in the case of federalization, to explain the gradual nature of the change observed. Similarly, it makes it possible to explain the maintenance of the key principles of the "Canadian model" of immigration and integration established since the 1960s, despite federalization. What is more, it is consistent with the research that has analysed intergovernmental relationships in Canadian immigration. Analysts have identified two pivotal moments in the evolution of the governance of these policy areas. These moments do not constitute critical junctures; rather, they are periods that have had medium- and long-term structuring effects on the actors within the regime.

First of all, many authors contend that provincial demands changed after 1990 following the failure of the Meech Lake constitutional accord – which included a clause on bilateral agreements and provincial powers over immigration – and the subsequent conclusion of the Canada–Quebec accord on immigration in 1991 (e.g., Garcea 1991). Following this failure, the federal government promised more openness with regard to intergovernmental agreements in the area of immigration (e.g., Tessier 1995). Others point out that the Canada–Quebec accord, while it answered Quebec's demands, convinced the other provinces to make their own stronger financial demands. Authors also present the Provincial Nominee Program (PNP; see above); this response by the federal government to provincial demands regarding immigration meant it did not have to sign devolution agreements similar to the one agreed to with Quebec (e.g., Banting 2012; Tolley et al., 2011).

Regarding fiscal federalism, some authors have explained the change in the institutional regime in part with reference to the financial context of the 1990s. They point out that after the budgetary and fiscal crisis of that decade, the federal government had to cut public spending and modify its transfers to the provinces. In 1994, Ottawa launched a program review exercise aimed at reducing government spending with the goal of eliminating the federal deficit. At the time, Citizenship and Immigration Canada conducted its own review exercise, titled Settlement Renewal (Vineberg 2012), which included countrywide consultations with citizens, immigrant associations, organizations delivering services, and governments. The Settlement Renewal process was the basis for agreements to transfer settlement programs to BC and Manitoba.

With respect to financial resources, policies, and authority, the Settlement Renewal process and the failure of the Meech Lake Accord had serious consequences for distribution under the regime of immigration governance. This illustrates an important fact: the federal government contributed to the federalization of immigration through decisions that culminated in the decentralization of powers and resources. These decisions subsequently altered the preferences and actions of the provinces – both those that were directly affected by this decentralization of the governance of immigration and those that were not. Indirectly, these decisions also altered the interests and actions of the federal government because of its constant interaction with provinces.

Yet recognition of this federal role does not explain many other characteristics of the federalization process. It does not account for the involvement of all provincial governments in the area of immigration, not only the ones attracting the most new arrivals or the ones with early immigration agreements. Nor does it explain the pattern of structured variations where provinces cluster around four modes of intervention. In addition, a focus on the federal role does little to clarify the presence of common provincial discourses presenting immigration as a resource. These characteristics can only be explained by examining the interactions between these federal decisions and the dynamics characteristic of the provinces as actors within the institutional regime, starting in the 1990s.

The Mechanism of Province-Building

This book advances the argument that the mobilization of the provinces is the missing piece of the puzzle for understanding the federalization of immigration governance in Canada. This argument is in keeping with research that has identified provincial demands as the source of certain changes in federal immigration policies (Poirier 2006; Lewis 2010; Carter and Amoyaw 2011). This argument is directly related to the perspective on gradual institutional changes, insofar as it emphasizes the crucial role of the actors and their interactions as catalysts of institutional evolution.

In institutional regimes, the modification of typical interactions among actors – for example, between "rules makers" and "rules takers" – is a source of gradual institutional change (Mahoney and Thelen 2010b). Most often the evolution of these interactions is a result of the actions of actors who are not in a dominant position in an institutional regime, either because of the distribution of resources or because of their interests in relation to the institution. The preferences and behaviours of internal actors are not structured by exogenous shocks; rather, those actors are themselves the mediators of subtle changes in the broader contexts in which the institution and the actors are situated. These changes occur when the roles, functions, and boundaries of a regime are called into question, because they no longer conform to the society and to the interests of the actors who depend on them.

Applying this perspective, the following chapters show that in response to several forces affecting the Canadian federal regime, provinces began to mobilize around immigration, and that this mobilization rendered them agents of change. These forces included the evolution of fiscal federalism, changes in the sharing of responsibilities between governments, and the more general evolution of the Canadian economy. Four transformations of the federal context were felt particularly strongly by provinces, starting in 1990. These were changes to transfers to the provinces in the area of health and social services, the asymmetrical withdrawal of the federal government from labour market management policies, the renewal of the federal role in economic development, and modifications to the overall practices of intergovernmental relations. These changes reflected the repositioning and revitalization of the federal government's roles according to ideological and structural pressures starting in 1990 (Boismenu and Graefe 2004). The provinces faced the same pressures, in addition to changes in the interests and strategies of their key partner, the federal government. These changes created a context favourable to the reinvention of the provincial governments.[4] Faced with these disruptions, the provinces became agents of change by repositioning themselves, independently.

This repositioning took the form of a specific mechanism: province-building centred on immigration. An ambiguous and rather overused concept in Canadian political science, province-building refers primarily to the development dynamics of the provinces (Paquet 2014). This concept is rooted in a desire to explain the resilience of the provinces and the development of provincial governments, despite the modernization of the Canadian state, which was supposed to foster unification and centralization. It has also been used to assert the importance of provincial governments in the development of political and economic communities within Canada (Cairns 1977; Black and Cairns 1966; Stevenson 1980; Brodie 1990). The concept of province-building lost popularity during the 1990s, because of criticisms of equivocal uses and because of what some considered an overly economical and limited reading of the interests of the political actors related to it (Wilder and Howlett 2015). In particular, Robert Young, Philippe Faucher, and André Blais criticized the use of the concept on many fronts, including these: (1) conceptual stretching, (2) the differentiation between the indicators of the operation and the indicators of the results of province-building, and (3) the dearth of information regarding how province-building actually functions (Young, Faucher, and Blais 1984).

To address the criticisms associated with this concept, this book proposes a mechanismic definition of province-building: it involves a mobilization of the elite, centred on the establishment of strategies aimed at the development of provincial society (government, public service, economy, and population). This definition treats the interests and the motives of the elite as an empirical issue. In dialogue with the criticisms related to province-building, it should be assumed that these interests are much more complex than re-election or economic efficiency and that they can extend over various temporal scales. This definition makes no claims or hypotheses about the results of province-building. Instead it opens the door to an analysis of how this social mechanism operates.

This definition is rooted in an epistemological approach to the exploration of causality through mechanisms (Paquet 2014; Paquet and Broschek 2017). Social mechanisms are relational systems whereby outcomes are produced through the transmission of causal forces. In general, a mechanism is comprised of many components (actors and actions) representing the stages that are minimally sufficient to support its presence (Beach and Pedersen 2012, 39, 176). Social mechanisms need not be causal: it is impossible to predict a result from the observation of their presence in any given case (Falleti and Lynch 2009). It is better instead to view them as portable concepts that produce specific effects in accordance with a particular context and with their possible interaction with other mechanisms.[5] When it is conceptualized as a social mechanism, it becomes possible to identify province-building as the similar modality through which provincial interests and actions changed, starting in 1990. Though they shared much the same mechanism of mobilization, the provinces exhibited different policy outcomes, as demonstrated by the existence of four modes of interventions.

A mechanismic approach to the study of social and political phenomena is not meant to measure variables or develop general theories; rather, is intended to develop knowledge about social mechanisms by identifying them in various empirical contexts and by clarifying their internal functioning (Paquet and Broschek 2017). It proposes insight into "how" questions. This is similar to examining interacting gears and chains: the main objective of empirical research becomes the identification of the minimal components that make it possible to demonstrate the presence of a given mechanism.

The identification of the minimal components of a mechanism and the documentation of its operation are best validated through comparison. In this book, comparison is structured around propositions regarding the presence of a similar mechanism (province-building) in comparable contexts (provinces), and not in relationship to similarities with regard to dependent or independent variables, or results. By focusing part of the analysis on the general characteristics of the functioning of the mechanism of province-building, it is possible to show that this mechanism indeed functions according to a distinctive internal structure.

The interactional analysis used here shows that the mechanism of province-building has functioned in each of the ten provinces at different times and with various intensities since 1990. Comparison of provincial trajectories shows that this operating has taken place in three essential steps: activation, consensualization, and institutionalization.

Activation entails putting on the agenda a problem or a challenge that directly affects provincial society and its potential solutions. This is the task of the provincial elite: governments, politicians, senior civil servants, or economic actors. It can be preceded by period of reflection. It can also be a response to a changing context or, more rarely, come through direct pressure by a group of actors on the government. Activation corresponds to the identification of the crucial resource and decisions related to the need for the growth of government activities or institutions.

Consensualization begins once the issue is clearly on the agenda and once the government actors are promoting a specific discourse on the role of the resource for the provincial society. It also entails the diffusion of a discourse about the responsibilities of the government and society with respect to maximizing its benefits. As the mechanism is activated, these discourses gradually become established as a consensus beyond the government. Creating a consensus helps justify the growth of provincial governments and break down partisan divisions and societal cleavages with respect to the resource and the role of provincial governments in a given policy sector.

During the *institutionalization* stage, the provincial government sets up a public administration responsible for the resource as well as public policies directly related to it. Through these actions, the government consolidates the provincial repositioning with respect to the changing federal context, and embodies, through policies and institutions, ideas crucial to the emerging consensus.[6]

The mechanism of province-building helps account for two crucial characteristics of the federalization of immigration in Canada: the mobilization of the ten provinces, and their similar pro-immigrant discourses. The repositioning of the federal government that began in the 1990s affected all of the provinces, albeit in different ways, and province-building centred on immigration was their response. This response was set in motion at different times over twenty years and in diverse provincial contexts. Nevertheless, provincial trajectories are all characterized by the presence of a strong political discourse that presents immigration as a resource for the provincial society and economy. In each of the cases explored in this book, the discourse arose out of a mobilization of the elite aimed at the development of the provincial society, in a context of the repositioning of governments within the Canadian federation.

The role of the elite in this process is crucial, and this book proposes a broad concept of elite actors, based on Theda Skocpol's (1979) research in comparative historical sociology. The changes seen in the provinces with regard to immigration and integration were not the result of a social movement, of a shift in public opinion, or of electoral dynamics. The change, as I will show, was rooted in a group of actors who were relatively isolated from social pressures: provincial elected officials, in particular those with executive power, provincial civil servants as well as certain economic actors, and, very rarely, actors from the community sector working to deliver services to immigrants. Citizens and, especially in the case that concerns us here, immigrants as actors were absent from this process of change, even though it affected them significantly. Elite actors are capable of acting in ways that are relatively autonomous from society, be it in terms of the problem definition, agenda-setting, or decision-making. This situation is reinforced by the nature of the Canadian political system and by the relatively limited and positive attention given to immigration by citizens of the provinces. This autonomy is also consolidated by the bureaucratic and technical nature of the processes of developing immigration and integration policies in Canada (Hardcastle et al. 1994; Paquet 2015) and by the executive dominance that is characteristic of intergovernmental relations in the country (Watts 1989).

Elite actors have a general interest in maintaining their power and position, and this sometimes requires them to make political decisions in response to societal demands. However, they pursue their interest largely by developing new public institutions and implementing new government responses. In this way, elites are able to respond to major changes (economic, political, and social) that call into question their power and their centrality with respect to their society of reference (Skocpol 1979; Paquet 2014). Changes in the Canadian federation since the 1990s – whether a result of federal decisions or international pressures – are of a nature that calls into question the power and the centrality of the actors who are leading the social and political destiny of the provinces. While I consider that the actual content of provincial elite interests must be verified empirically, I propose that it is appropriate to suggest that province-building is the mechanism through which these actors responded to changes that had the potential to dislodge them and to call into question the place of their province in Canadian society as a whole.

The activities of this social mechanism have generated different political dynamics and public policies in each of the provinces. Because of their relational nature, social mechanisms are not determinants – that is, it is impossible to infer from their presence the attainment of a given result or a specific outcome. It is instead according to their interaction with a particular context – especially the temporal context, as well as the historical, economic, and political context of a province and, when applicable, their interaction with other mechanisms – that they generate results. This approach serves as the foundation for an explanation of the structured variation of the provincial modes of intervention in immigration and integration.

Between Province-Building and Decentralization

The identification of the mechanism of province-building as a source of change within the regime of governance for immigration and integration complements analyses focusing on the decentralizing impulses of the federal government. A refocusing on the provinces makes it possible to refine the analysis of the period under consideration – 1990 to 2010 – by presenting a detailed reading of provincial responses to these decentralizing impulses, and their impact, in the medium and long term, on provincial preferences and actions. The approach to federalism applied in this book – because it is rooted in a major interactional foundation – and its combination with a perspective on the gradual institutional changes will make it possible to show how provincial actions have, over time, affected the interests and the political responses of the federal government.

In retracing, over the medium term, how federalization occurred, this book shows that the agency of the provinces, embodied in the mechanism of province-building centred on immigration, was a decisive element in the initiation and implementation of changes to the Canadian institutional regime of governance for immigration and integration. By relating how the internal mobilization of each province in the area of immigration has been set in motion, it is possible to show how this mobilization has finally been transformed, at distinct moments, into external actions that have transformed parts of the federal regime.

The empirical evidence presented in this book demonstrates that Canadian provinces, as agents of change, have played two roles in the federalization process. First, they acted as *triggers* for that process by initiating two elements of the decentralization mechanism in the 1990s: (1) the presence of an immigration agreement with Quebec had significant fiscal consequences for the institutional regime of the governance of immigration, and (2) the successful pressures to create a new sub-national immigration selection program gave provinces the tools to implement their constitutional immigration powers. Further analysis of the federalization process will illustrate that the provinces acted as *maintainers* of that process from 1995 to 2010, for they were in large part the source of the forces that kept the decentralization mechanism in motion.

The "Canadian model" is now governed by an institutional regime that has been transformed by the federalization process. Without suggesting any formal or tacit equality between the levels of government, we should recognize that the ten Canadian provinces are now active in immigration and integration. A demonstration of the provinces' key role in triggering and maintaining in motion the federalization process will allow us to better grasp the actual nature of the governance of these matters. Because the provinces have shaped the current regime to address changes that have occurred in Canada and the world, they have real interests in the future of the "Canadian model" of immigration. These interests have been generated both by the distributional consequences of the institutional regime and by the political and societal impacts of the mechanism of province-building centred on immigration. Ottawa has witnessed this process of change without shedding its responsibilities, and as a result, any policy related directly or indirectly to immigration in Canada has now been federalized.

Methodological Considerations

Within the larger framework of a historical institutionalism, this book is based on a method of analysis called *process-tracing*, which focuses on identifying and documenting the activities of one or more mechanisms within a given process (Bennett and Elman 2006). Two variants of this method are used in this book: (1) outcome-explaining process-tracing, and (2) process-tracing for purposes of theoretical development.

First, process-tracing is aimed at documenting federalization for the purposes of understanding and explanation (Beach and Pedersen 2012). In practical terms, this involves reconstituting the process of gradual change from 1990 to 2010. In order to pay special attention to temporality, this reconstitution is carried through a sequential study of the process, with particular emphasis on the order of mechanisms and the connections that link them in the production of an explanation (Pierson 2004). This method is particularly useful for the study of a process that takes place over a period of medium duration (ten to twenty years) – rather than over a very long historical period – because this is a time scale in which the mechanisms and actors are more easily identifiable and in which it is possible to attain a certain degree of internal and external validity, as noted by Falleti (2010). At the national level, this time scale also makes it possible to isolate the potential impacts of the 2011 election of the Conservative Party as a majority government in Ottawa. An indicator of the complete recasting of the partisan system, this victory also initiated an era of reforms related to the principles of the "Canadian model" of immigration and integration (Andrew and Bradford 2011; Winter 2014). The relationships between these reforms and the federalization process will be explored in this book's conclusion.

Second, this book uses process-tracing for the purposes of theoretical development. Here, the objective is to identify one or more portable social mechanisms, based on empirical observation. Halfway between induction and deduction, this variant permits the development of theoretical contributions with respect to mechanisms, contributions that should be applicable beyond one or more case studies (Beach and Pedersen 2012). By treating each group of provinces as a case study regarding the activity of the mechanism of province-building centred on immigration, this variant of process-tracing makes it possible to identify the general characteristics of the mechanism and to differentiate contextual elements affecting it.

In the following chapters the mechanism of province-building in immigration is examined within each province. This sheds light on its relationships with the decentralization mechanism and to relate those relationships to the development of its mode of intervention. These case studies make it possible to better understand the functioning of the mechanism of province-building (and, to a lesser extent, the decentralization mechanism) by observing it in highly comparable contexts, that is, in the Canadian provinces.

The analysis in this book combines documentary sources with data drawn from interviews with elite actors. The documentary sources are various. First of all, I surveyed federal and provincial government publications related to immigration and integration, including annual activity reports, public accounts, studies commissioned or produced by governments, and government promotional materials. For each province, all the official publications of the ministries active in immigration and integration policies from the 1980s to the 2010s – either directly or indirectly – were systematically consulted and inventoried. The amount of information collected in this way is substantial and serves as the basis for the descriptions of policies and programs proposed by the provinces. To make the text more readable, the references to this material include only those excerpts that are particularly representative of provincial action at key moments.

The analysis then examined sources that could explain the political bargaining and the evolution of the stakeholders' concerns in the provinces and the federal government: the platforms and working documents of the parties, Speeches from the Throne, and Hansards and other parliamentary publications. Hansards – transcriptions of the debates in legislative assemblies – are particularly useful sources for the debates involving all elected members in the province, and not only members of the government. These debates are also invaluable for documenting the strategies of the provincial governments in the area of intergovernmental relations; they also make it possible to better understand how the economic and social context in each province affected the decisions of the executive. For each province, the Hansards from 1989 to 2010 were scoured for references to immigration and integration in speeches and debates. In the text, references to the Hansards of the provincial legislative assemblies are identified by the acronym "L.A.," followed by the province, the date, and the page number.

The research also involved a targeted review of the press coverage in order to document certain key episodes that are still poorly understood by political scientists. It also drew from many secondary sources, especially for descriptions of the political, economic, and migratory contexts in the provinces studied.

The analysis is also based on semi-structured interviews with elite actors conducted between September 2011 and December 2012. In total, seventy-one interviews lasting from thirty minutes to almost two and a half hours were conducted. The individuals interviewed included federal and provincial civil servants (some of them still in office, others retired), provincial, federal, and municipal elected officials, and representatives of organizations delivering services to immigrants. Throughout the book, the relevant interviews are cited in endnotes, with general information on the individual respondents. Many of the interviews were of confidential, and the relatively limited number of civil servants, elected officials, and representatives of community organizations involved in the federalization process required that the respondents not be identified. To respect the confidentiality of many stakeholders still active in current political processes, certain interviews are not cited in the book.

These interviews were indispensable to the analysis of the federalization process and have made it possible to more completely reconstitute the events in a context in which that process is still not well-documented and in which many government sources remain inaccessible. They were also very useful for verifying the proposed social mechanisms, insofar as these involve these civil servants, elected officials, and others. Finally, combining these two data sources allows the closest thing to a triangulation that can be achieved in this analysis and makes it possible to avoid, to some extent, the limitations inherent in the conducting of interviews aimed at reconstructing an earlier process (Davies 2001; Tansey 2007).

Organization of the Book

I have structured the book into chapters in such a way as to reflect the temporal sequence of the federalization process and to uncover the drivers of the various the modes of intervention in immigration and integration. Each chapter presents a case study of the activity trajectories of the mechanism of province-building centred on immigration and its interactions with the decentralization mechanism, in a changing federal context.

In chapter 2, readers will learn that in Quebec and Manitoba – the provinces with a *holistic mode* of intervention – the province-building mechanism centred on immigration was activated by the second Liberal government of Robert Bourassa, which came to power in 1986, and the Conservative government of Gary Filmon, which came to power in 1988. In approaching immigration as a resource for developing provincial society, both demographically and economically, these governments were innovative. Quebec has demanded an expanded role in immigration since the 1960s; however, the shift that occurred in the second half of the 1980s replaced the nationalist discourse on immigration with a discourse focused on province-building and on a concept of immigrants as a resource for the province. In Manitoba, the previous activation of the province-building mechanism centred on immigration in the early 1990s established the institutional, political, and societal bases on which the province could accept the federal government's offer to transfer to it the administration of settlement services for immigrants as part of the Settlement Renewal exercise that began in 1995. Similarly, the demands of Quebec and Manitoba served as the foundation of the 1991 Canada–Quebec immigration accord and the 1996 PNP. The former, strongly affected by constitutional tensions and by new ideas in public and fiscal governance, set the federalization process in motion.

Chapter 3 documents the later activation of the province-building mechanism centred on immigration in Ontario and BC. This activation occurred in a context marked by a decrease in federal transfers in the area of health and social services, and a decentralization of responsibilities in the area of labour market policies, as well as changes in federal policies on business immigration. In these two provinces, both with *reactive modes* of intervention, the activation of the province-building mechanism centred on immigration occurred in the 2000s, after the 2003 election of Dalton McGuinty and the 2001 election of Gordon Campbell. From that time on, the discourse presenting immigration as a resource benefiting the economy and provincial society replaced the former discourse on immigration and social justice and on immigration as a generator of excessive costs. To support province-building, BC and Ontario demanded that the federal government provide a fair share of immigration resources. These demands placed constant pressure on decentralization, which drove the federalization process forward, although the two provinces maintained different relationships with the federal government during this period.

Chapter 4 covers Alberta and Saskatchewan and the establishment of the *bridging mode* of intervention. Only with the end of political dynasties marked by fiscal austerity – with the Alberta government of Ralph Klein (Conservative Party [CP], 1992–2006) and the Saskatchewan government of Roy Romanow (New Democratic Party [NDP], 1991–2001) – was the mechanism of province-building centred on immigration really activated in these provinces. As part of a slightly more interventionist approach, and possessing abundant fiscal resources, their successors – Ed Stelmach in Alberta (CP, 2006–11) and Lorne Calvert in Saskatchewan (NDP, 2001–7) – emphasized strong connections between immigration and the economic destiny of their respective provinces. Province-building centred on immigration was set in motion in these provinces using already proven models and already developed tools, following the examples set by Quebec, Manitoba, Ontario, and BC. In addition, its activation in Alberta and Saskatchewan coincided with major changes at the federal level: increasing concerns about distributing immigrants throughout Canada, and the Conservative government of Stephen Harper coming to power. The encounter between the province-building mechanism and this new context would actively maintain the decentralization mechanism.

The four Atlantic provinces, which shared an *attraction–retention mode* of intervention, were the last to get involved in the federalization process, as we will see in chapter 5. The federal context was marked by increased concerns about regional inequality in the area of immigration and by the establishment of new policies to support economic development. Commitment to immigration by the Progressive Conservative governments of Pat Binns in Prince Edward Island (1996–2007), John Hamm in Nova Scotia (1999–2006), and Danny Williams in Newfoundland and Labrador (2003–10), as well as by the Liberal government of Shawn Graham in New Brunswick (2006–10), followed periods of societal reflection in these provinces, during which the idea of a provincial role in immigration was diffused in the region. In Atlantic Canada, the province-building mechanism centred on immigration was maintained by a consensus that presented immigration as a demographic and economic resource for provincial society and that favoured an interventionist role for government in the area of recruitment. The position of the Atlantic provinces in the federalization process and their traditional relationships with the federal government in the area of economic development and immigration meant it was only at the end of the period covered by this book that they played a part in the pressures that kept the decentralization mechanism in motion.

Chapter 6 returns to the federalization process and explores its impact on the current governance of immigration and integration in Canada. It documents the reconfigurations of the regime that the federal government carried out after 2010, as well as provincial reactions to those changes. These reconfigurations have included recentralization of settlement programs, the expansion of the federal Temporary Foreign Worker Program, a strengthening of the role of economic actors, and the formulation of a new model for selecting permanent immigrants based on job supply (the "Express Entry" system), implemented in 2015. This chapter will show that these reconfigurations are in part the federal government's responses to the decrease in its margin of manoeuvre resulting from the autonomous development of immigration policies in the provinces, a consequence of the federalization process. Using an interactional approach to federalism, chapter 6 also presents current issues and foreseeable tensions with respect to intergovernmental relationships related to immigration as we enter this new, reconfigured era. To the extent that the federalization process was the result of growing awareness among the provinces of the importance of immigration for their survival and development, it is possible to predict that this question will be added to the list of areas of tension within the federation, on par with health funding, trade, the environment, and social transfers.

Chapter 2

Quebec and Manitoba: Province-Building Centred on Immigration

Quebec and Manitoba were pioneers in the process of federalizing the governance of immigration and integration in Canada. This pairing may seem surprising, given that analyses of immigration and integration policies tend to view Quebec as distinct, but it reflects parallels in the holistic modes of intervention developed by the two provinces starting in the 1990s.

These similarities reflect the confluence of two elements. First, both provinces saw the establishment, in tandem with the federalization process, of a consensus regarding the role of immigration in the development of provincial society. This consensus broke with policy legacies as they related to immigration. Second, policy similarities were partly a consequence of the timing of the province-building mechanism within the federalization process. Indeed, this chapter demonstrates that Quebec and Manitoba played a foundational role in launching the federalization of immigration in Canada.

By retracing the political trajectories of Quebec and Manitoba, this chapter shows how a mechanism of province-building centred on immigration was set in motion after two new governments came to power in the late 1980s. These governments – Robert Bourassa's second Liberal government, elected in 1986, and Gary Filmon's Conservative government, elected in 1988 – brought new ideas regarding the governance of the state, of the economy, and of civil society. It was then that immigration was recognized by the political elite as a resource for developing provincial societies, both demographically and economically. In Quebec, this movement marked a new phase in the mobilization in favour of immigration, although the province had been active in this policy sector since the 1960s, in keeping with a logic of competitive nation-building. In Manitoba, the activation of the province-building mechanism centred on immigration in the 1990s was innovative but still in line with provincial interventions implemented since the 1960s.

The evolution of the interests and actions of Quebec and Manitoba took place against a backdrop of an extremely centralized immigration regime. Some institutional overtures were made between the end of the Second World War and the 1990s to permit a greater role for the provinces. Yet neither the federal government nor the provinces (except for Quebec) committed themselves to any real changes in their practices. Nevertheless, the provinces developed interventions related to immigration, if only to meet needs on the ground. Thus, prior to the activation of the province-building mechanism, Quebec and Manitoba were active in the area of immigration, albeit to a far lesser degree.

Quebec: At the Centre of Competitive Nation-Building

Starting in the 1960s, as part of a competitive nation-building dynamic with the federal government, the Quebec government broke with its historical inaction in immigration (Helly 1996). During the Quiet Revolution, the province's nation-building efforts were centred on gaining the allegiance of citizens and increasing the government's effective capacity for action. The nation-building mechanism is distinct from the province-building mechanism, which is analogous to that of state-building. These two mechanisms can coexist and even overlap "while remaining conceptually different" (Linz, Darviche, and Genieys 1997, 5; Linz 1993). Province-building aims to develop the provincial economy, government capacities, and population, whereas nation-building – whether it takes place at the national or sub-national level – aims at creating bonds between the citizens and a government that claims to represent a political community (Pierson 1995). Nation-building can take many forms, ranging from the establishment of assimilation policies to the political recognition of national minorities or ethnolinguistic groups. It can also be characterized by an increase in or a reorientation of government intervention, although this is not always the case. Just as with province-building, the mechanism of nation-building is relational; it depends on the interaction of two or more actors. This implies, among other things, that many dynamics can coexist at the same time on a single territory. This was the case when the federal government established the citizenship regime after the Second World War and when Quebec was experiencing the Quiet Revolution (Jenson 1998; 1997). The conjunction of these two efforts at nation-building has been referred to as "competitive nation-building" (Banting 1995). Beyond this prime example, Canada has experienced this phenomenon many times in its history. Once again, it is important to avoid a deterministic reading that automatically conflates nation-building with intergovernmental conflicts.

In 1968, in this context of competition, the Quebec government established a department specifically devoted to immigration (Pâquet 2005; Fontaine 1993). Before the 1990s, intervention in immigration and integration focused on gaining effective powers over immigration and establishing institutions capable of ensuring that immigration would not represent a threat to Quebec identity and to the French language.

Concerns about the linguistic integration of immigrants and the decline of the French language were central drivers of Quebec's first interventions in immigration (Behiels 1991). In the 1960s, political actors viewed Quebec as poorly served by federal immigration policy, which did not support the objective of integrating new arrivals into francophone society.[1] These concerns, explains Dominique Daniel (2006), reached their peak with protests against language legislation in St-Léonard in 1968. Faced with these tensions, the governments of Jean-Jacques Bertrand (Union nationale, 1968–70), Robert Bourassa (Liberal, 1970–76), and René Lévesque (Parti Québécois, 1976–86) each formulated political responses that were generally aimed at protecting the French language; these included laws targeting immigrants more specifically.[2] Through the 1970s and 1980s, the linguistic integration of immigrants continued to be a central concern for political actors in the province. It was also the main – if not *only* – perspective from which intervention in immigration was viewed by political actors in Quebec.[3]

The language question injected considerable energy into public policy development. In 1968 the province's immigration ministry established the Centres d'orientation et de formation des immigrants (COFI; Orientation and Training Centres for Immigrants). In 1977 the COFIs stopped providing English courses and the province became entirely responsible for language training, which was now provided only in French (Helly 1996). By the late 1960s the province had also set up front-line reception and settlement services. Key interventions included support for settlement and the creation of a reception service at Dorval airport in 1968. The Quebec government developed policy statements related to diversity management. The action plan of the period, *Quebecers Each and Every One*, was developed beginning in 1978 under the Parti Québécois government (Québec 1981). This document called for an explicit distancing of the Quebec model from the Canadian policy of multiculturalism (Gagnon and Iacovino 2003).

Quebec also requested greater immigrant selection powers from the federal government. This was closely linked to the province's demands for constitutional reform as well as to a broader dynamic of competitive nation-building. In the late 1960s the government of Daniel Johnson, Sr, demanded that the integration of immigrants be recognized as an exclusive provincial jurisdiction; that demand was later taken up by the government of Jean-Jacques Bertrand. During its first term (1970–76), the Liberal government of Robert Bourassa treated immigration as crucial to the recognition of Quebec's cultural rights if the Constitution was ever to be patriated. During the first term of the Parti Québécois, immigration was pushed aside in favour of other issues. Then from 1980 to 1985, following the failure of the first Quebec referendum and in the context of the patriation of the Canadian Constitution, immigration was one area over which the province demanded special powers within the framework of the federal regime.[4]

Outside the venue of constitutional wrangling, through successive bilateral agreements, Quebec gradually acquired powers with regard to the selection and integration of immigrants. The first agreement between the federal government and Quebec, the Lang–Cloutier Agreement, signed in 1971, gave the province the authority to assign Quebec agents to federal immigration missions abroad. The Andras–Bienvenue Agreement, signed in 1975 following negotiations begun by the Bourassa government, increased Quebec's involvement in the selection process by requiring that all Quebec-bound immigrants be met by provincial representatives. Finally, the Cullen–Couture Agreement, which endorsed a first devolution of powers to the province, was signed in 1978. The result of negotiations begun by the Liberal government but signed by the Parti Québécois, the agreement included, among other things, selection as a joint responsibility of the two levels of government while giving Quebec an effective veto over economic immigrants and refugees. It also permitted the province to establish the criteria for sponsoring new arrivals.

For Quebec, the consequences of this first phase of activity in immigration, which took place in a context of linguistic anxiety and constitutional tensions, were triple. First, a consensus had emerged among political parties and governments with respect to a provincial role in immigration, which was now viewed as a more or less important dimension of a broader societal project. Second, there was a gradual increase in Quebec's real powers in the area of immigration and integration. Finally, immigration questions were now included among

Quebec's constitutional demands. These three elements would serve as the foundations for a new mechanism of province-building centred on immigration, which, starting in the 1990s, would break from a logic of competitive nation-building.

Manitoba: The Foundations

Historically, Manitoba has relied on immigration to increase its population. The importance of immigration for the province can be seen in the fact that Manitoba had a Department of Agriculture and Immigration as early as 1890 and that until the 1910s, Manitoba immigration agents were responsible for most of the arrivals of settlers in the province. After the economic crises of the 1920s and 1930s, structural changes in its economy, and the Second World War, the province largely relinquished its activities in immigration in favour of a strong role for the federal government (Carter and Amoyaw 2011; Clement 2003).

The Manitoba government would again begin to show interest in immigration in the late 1960s, under the Progressive Conservative government of Walter Weir (1967–69). It demanded that Ottawa send a "fair share" of the total immigration to Canada to Manitoba. However, the question of a provincial role in immigration was the subject of a sharp partisan cleavage. The Progressive Conservative Party of the time tended to promote the idea of a provincial role in immigration, viewing it as a tool for economic development. Conversely, the New Democratic Party, and the government it formed from 1969 to 1977, resisted this idea and remained convinced that immigration was primarily a federal responsibility (Vanstone 1999; Hawkins 1988).

The return of the Progressive Conservatives to power in 1978 coincided with the enactment of the federal law on immigration (1976), which created increased possibilities for action by the provinces. Having mentioned immigration explicitly in its 1977 election platform as one solution to the demographic challenge faced by the province (Manitoba Progressive Conservative Association 1977), the Progressive Conservative government of Sterling Lyon (1978–81) showed strong interest in reaching an intergovernmental agreement on immigration and concluded, at the end of its term, a modest bilateral deal on the coordination of services for refugees. In 1978 the Lyon government created an administrative division specifically devoted to immigration. The return of the New Democrats to power in 1981 brought an end to provincial demands for more immigration powers, without at the same time stopping provincial intervention per se. Until its defeat in 1988, the New Democratic government of Howard Pawley showed no interest in negotiating further agreements on immigration – because of the costs associated with them, among other things (Adam 2008). A New Democrat MLA at the time recalled this lack of interest: "Before 1990, we weren't doing too much. We were in the government until 1988 [and] I don't remember anything about immigration coming to the caucus specifically."[5]

Before the 1990s, Manitoba's timid intervention in the area of immigration was spread through several departments responsible for labour, education, citizenship, and the family. Those ministries were active on three fronts: (1) research and analysis, (2) funding of certain settlement services, and (3) promotion targeting potential business immigrants (Manitoba Immigration and Settlement Branch 1986; Manitoba 1990).

Provincial interventions made it possible to increase Manitobans' support for immigration. However, this development was limited by changes of government, as well as by weak economic growth and the poor state of public finances in the province during the 1970s and 1980s. What is more, the existence of intermediate means to respond to provincial demands (e.g., the federal Immigrant Investor Program) limited the grievances of the province towards the federal government over this period. Nevertheless, during these years the foundations were laid to support the province-building mechanism centred on immigration, which would be activated in Manitoba starting in the 1990s.

The Activation of Consensualization and Institutionalization

In the 1990s a new approach to immigration emerged in Quebec and Manitoba, driven by the mechanism of province-building centred on immigration. In these two provinces the activation of this mechanism coincided with the election of new governments: the Liberal Party of Robert Bourassa in Quebec (1985–94) and the Conservative Party of Gary Filmon in Manitoba (1988–99). Activation came with the end of relatively long government tenures in both provinces, yet it had not been generated by campaign debates or by other electoral dynamics. Indeed, these two cases highlight an important characteristic of the activation of province-building centred on immigration: it is the result of an elite movement rather than public pressure. Furthermore, in both provinces the involvement of the premiers was crucial to setting in motion province-building centred on immigration. Following this activation, a new consensus on the role of immigration in provincial society emerged, and this led to interventions corresponding to the holistic mode of intervention.

Quebec

At the time Robert Bourassa was re-elected in 1985, the perception that immigration was an economic and demographic resource had started to develop in Quebec. Once the mechanism of province-building was activated, immigration went from an element to be controlled for the survival of the province to something to be harnessed for the development of Quebec. This can be explained in part by the emergence of new economic ideas and by the influence of new governance doctrines. It was also a function of the province's increased capacity – a result of past immigration agreements with Ottawa. More broadly, immigration powers also meshed with the distinct constitutional agenda of Bourassa's Liberal government.

New Concerns of the Elite

The final term of the Parti Québécois government (1981–85) led by René Lévesque was marked by a post-referendum slump, accompanied by a significant economic slowdown, tensions with the public sector, and the patriation of the Canadian Constitution without the consent of Quebec. When the Bourassa government came to power in 1985 it implemented a "vast reform program of the Quebec state [including] privatization of crown corporations, deregulation, and reorganization of the government" (Rouillard et al. 2008, 26), which some labelled a redefinition of the "Quebec model" (Bourque 2000, 137–67). The Liberal government developed strong alliances with the private sector, establishing the market rather than society or the community sector as the main engine of development for the province. This orientation would be reinforced after Bourassa was re-elected in 1989 and maintained until the end of that term, in 1994 (Lemieux 2008).

These ideas were strongly present in the Liberal Party's 1985 election platform as well as in Bourassa's Speech from the Throne. That platform was in line with the principles that had been driving provincial action in immigration since the 1960s: one of the conditions the

Liberal Party set out for Quebec to sign the Canadian Constitution was recognition of Quebec's jurisdiction over immigration (Liberal Party of Quebec 1985). This was a long-held position of the party and was not hotly debated during the election.

With regard to policies and programs, this period would see an increase in the resources allocated to Quebec's immigration ministry. More attention was being paid to provincial intervention in the area – a tendency that can be attributed, among other things, to the interest of the premier himself.[6] These concerns, which spread to the leadership of the Liberal Party, were centred on Quebec's demographic challenge and its economic impact, as well as on the province's role in the federation. In 1988 the Liberal Party published the document *S'ouvrir à demain* (Opening Up to Tomorrow), in which it highlighted the urgency for Quebec to re-establish its demographic balance. The observation is striking:

> Unless there is an immediate, dramatic turnaround, there will be a gradual depopulation of Quebec starting in the early twenty-first century. In addition to the falling birth rate, many other phenomena contribute to the demographic imbalance in Quebec: longer life expectancy, the aging of the population, and negative net migration. The predictable consequences of such a situation could be extremely difficult to deal with for Quebec: growing costs for health and social services, impacts on the markets and employment, the decreasing political weight of Quebec, and the role it plays not only within the Canadian federation, but in North America. (Liberal Party of Quebec 1988, 15)

In response to this potential crisis, the party proposed a policy based on boosting the birth rate and on greater openness to immigration. In particular, it called for provincial intervention with three pillars: (1) increasing the number of landed immigrants, (2) making energetic efforts to promote the province as an immigration destination, and (3) improving integration policies more generally.

The influence of these ideas on the party became abundantly clear in the 1989 Liberal platform. For the first time in Quebec, strong partisan commitments in the area of immigration were made during an election. These went beyond questions of language, identity, and constitutional powers. Under the titles "Infléchir puis renverser le déclin démographique" (Curb then reverse the demographic decline) and "Enrichir le Québec" (enrich Quebec), the platform called for the following: (1) an increase in immigration levels, to be brought about through adjustments to the selection grid, the relaxation of procedures, and more vigorous recruitment; (2) better financial support for community organizations active in immigration; and (3) an increase in the funds allocated to integration, including but not limited to francization (Policy Committee of the Liberal Party of Quebec 1989, 47, 50). In this regard, the texts of the party's policy committee detailing the platform were striking. They recast the province's needs in terms of immigration and proposed new concepts with regard to the responsibility of the state and of society in relation to it.[7] In the area of integration, the policy committee stated:

> While welcoming more immigrants, the Liberal Party of Quebec wants them to be able to completely integrate into Quebec society, both socially and economically. Consequently, knowledge of the French language is necessary to meet that objective. But it is not sufficient, they also need to know their host society. To achieve this, it will first of all be necessary to provide better support for the groups and non-profit organizations that provide assistance to immigrants when they arrive, that find them housing or jobs, and that facilitate their integration into our society. The francophone community is still considerably behind in this regard, and we will have to implement the necessary means to correct this ... Beyond the learning of French, we also need to provide new arrivals with the knowledge that will be indispensable to them to integrate more easily into our society. We recommend that the government create a new program for this purpose. We should also build on the dynamism of socio-economic or community groups and associations to facilitate implementation. (Policy Committee of the Liberal Party of Quebec 1989, 56)

During Bourassa's second term, beginning in 1985, the objective guiding provincial immigration intervention thus shifted from protecting Quebec language and identity to developing Quebec society by applying economic and demographic levers. These new objectives emerged primarily from elite actors rather than from social movements or public pressure. They were the first indication that province-building was replacing nation-building in the field of immigration.

The Consolidation of Quebec's Role

Casting immigration as a lever of development for Quebec society, rather than as a disruptive element to be regulated, would alter the

Liberal provincial government's constitutional and intergovernmental demands. With regard to immigration, these demands had once been in line with those of the Parti Québécois. From this period on, though, the Quebec Liberals' objective would be to acquire the powers necessary to control immigration on its territory (as opposed to simply holding a right of veto over federal decisions). The Bourassa government also began to show more interest in the selection of refugees – a growing group because of the rising political instability around the world.[8]

All of this motivated the Bourassa government to undertake negotiations intended to increase Quebec's powers relative to the federal government. Those talks culminated in a project to revise the 1978 Cullen–Couture Agreement. In 1987 the broad outlines were announced for a new bilateral agreement on immigration. This agreement would include the following: (1) the maintenance of Quebec's roles and responsibilities in the area of immigrant selection, as defined by the Cullen–Couture Agreement; (2) the creation of procedures assigning a significant role to Quebec in decisions regarding the volume of immigration directed to the province; and (3) the transfer to the province of responsibilities for settlement services for new arrivals, accompanied by financial compensation. Then in 1986, the Bourassa government declared that the constitutional entrenchment of Quebec's powers in immigration agreements would be a precondition for Quebec's acceptance of the new Canadian Constitution (Garcea 1994; McRoberts 1999).

At the time, Quebec's new demands regarding immigration did not make waves with other provinces. Many of those demands were also acceptable to Ottawa. The desire of the federal Progressive Conservative government of Brian Mulroney to mollify Quebec and to demonstrate that Canadian federalism was able to accommodate the province opened a unique door to Quebec demands on immigration. It was in this context that negotiations were undertaken for the Meech Lake constitutional accord.

Subtantiating Quebec's Interventions

The activation of the province-building mechanism did not reverse pre-existing policies in Quebec; rather, policies were adjusted to reflect the emerging new consensus. For example, the Bourassa government was very active in the implementation of *Quebecers Each and Every One,* a plan that had been developed by the Parti Québécois government

(Québec 1981). Under the Liberal government, however, there was a considerable increase in the number of immigrants received starting in 1985. This was the result of stronger government efforts to promote immigration to Quebec (Policy Committee of the Liberal Party of Quebec 1989). In this period the number of immigrants arriving in Quebec began to rise steadily. Between 1987–88 and 1989 the immigration ministry's budget increased significantly, from $33.1 million to almost $40 million. In addition, a budget increase was allocated to implement an action plan for francization (Black and Hagen 1994; Québec 1990b). Also implemented were new programs in the area of integration, going beyond francization, and including programs to fight racism and to raise public awareness about immigrants.

At the same time, the government replaced the Quebec Ministry of Immigration with the Ministry of Immigration and Cultural Communities (MICC) and established a Conseil des communautés culturelles et de l'immigration (Council of Cultural Communities and Immigration), a reflection of its growing interest in the civic and cultural integration of newcomers. The government also assigned a greater role to community organizations in the delivery of services and explicitly recognized their contribution to the integration process. It also made provisions for public consultations, which opened the door to greater citizen participation in integration. These policy developments are remarkable when viewed in the context of the Bourassa government's approach to public spending and public policy. At a time when the provincial government was implementing strict limits on provincial spending and state intervention, immigration and integration policy saw a huge expansion in Quebec (Black and Hagen 1994).

Key to this reorientation was Quebec's first comprehensive policy statement on immigration, issued in 1990. By 1985 the government recognized the importance of establishing a global policy "in order to orient and structure the intervention of the government from the perspective of an increase in immigration levels" (Québec 1990b). Published in 1990, the *Énoncé de politique en matière d'immigration et d'intégration: Au Québec pour bâtir ensemble* (Policy Statement on Immigration and Integration: In Quebec to Build Together) would remain, until 2016, the key document produced by the Quebec public service on the subject.

The statement boldly presented immigration as a "factor for development in Quebec" and identified how the province could respond to its four major development challenges: (1) correcting the demographic imbalance, (2) fostering economic prosperity, (3) ensuring the sustainability of the French language and culture, and (4) being open to the world. With the goal of ensuring that immigration "contributes to development of a French-speaking society and a prosperous economy" (Québec 1990a, 19), the statement recommended increasing the proportion of francophone immigrants received, creating instruments to maximize the economic benefits of independent and temporary immigration, supporting family reunification and international adoption, maintaining and better targeting the reception of refugees, and increasing immigration levels based on Quebec's needs and receptive capacity. The statement highlighted the importance of expanding the provision of francization courses; it also underscored the crucial importance of government action to foster socio-economic inclusion and economic integration. Finally, the statement called for action in the areas of equality policy and inter-community relations, and for the pluralization of institutions.

As Denise Helly rightly points out, in this document "immigration is defined by its usefulness, i.e., as an asset for Quebec's response to the challenges it faces, demographic, economic, linguistic, and international challenges" (Helly 1996, 40). The consensus central to province-building in Quebec developed along the lines of immigration's contribution to the province, rather than in relation to language politics. With the support of elite actors, this new relationship between Quebec and immigration would become institutionalized.

Manitoba

In Manitoba, the province-building mechanism centred on immigration was activated after a Conservative minority government led by Gary Filmon was elected in 1988, and particularly, after it was returned to power as a majority government in 1990. The Conservative victory in 1988,[9] after seven years of NDP government, can be explained in large part by internal tensions in the government as well as by a growing deficit, a series of policies that were unpopular with the electorate, and opposition to the NDP's economic development strategy.

The successive mandates of the Manitoba Conservatives (which would eventually extend to 1999) were an opportunity for significant policy reorientation marked by a gradual shift from "Keynesian conservatism" (a Manitoba tradition) to a model inspired by the new right (Wesley 2011). Confronted with poor economic performance, faltering public finances, and increased cuts to federal transfers, the Manitoba

Conservative government would incrementally implement new austerity measures, including the restructuring of social policies and industrial relations and a large wave of privatizations of public enterprises. At the same time, the province began placing more demands on the federal government, especially with respect to fiscal federalism (Thomas 2010). The efforts of the Filmon governments, coupled with an economic recovery, eventually allowed the province to get its finances under control. In fact, in 1995 the government ran a budget surplus for the first time in twenty-two years (Netherton 2001).

As a sign that the province's elite had activated the province-building mechanism, Filmon's Conservative government during its first term emphasized its interest in immigration and begun to reorient its interventions (L.A., MN, 2 October 1989, 1830–4). Mentioned for the first time in the history of the province in a Speech from the Throne, immigration was no longer just a social and humanitarian issue – it was also an economic one. Under the heading "Opportunity for All," the government declared that

> [i]mmigrants and refugees who come to our country with skills and expertise to share often find themselves unable to work in their chosen field because their credentials are not recognized. My Government is committed to establishing a means to assess new Canadians' trade, technical, and professional credentials. As part of this commitment, my Government will provide further assistance to businesses that place a landed immigrant in new, permanent positions of a professional or technical nature. (L.A., MN, 18 May 1989, 5)

The election of the Conservatives to their second term in 1990 as a majority government would finally activate Manitoba's province-building mechanism centred on immigration. Immigration thus became a component in the Conservatives' development toolbox. This is illustrated by Filmon's promise, during the 1990 election campaign, to begin negotiations with the federal government to reach a bilateral agreement on immigration for the purposes of economic development (L.A., MN, 5 December 1991, 5).

This interest in intervening more strongly in immigration came from the political elite – especially Gary Filmon and the Conservative cabinet – and, to a lesser extent, from the province's economic elite. Indeed, senior civil servants of the period point out that the cabinet independently expressed an interest in provincial intervention in immigration, especially in order to stimulate economic growth.[10]

This commitment by the political elite was strengthened by the return of economic growth in the province in the mid-1990s. That recovery generated strong demand for skilled workers in specific industries (e.g., in clothing and food processing); more broadly, it also mobilized the province's economic actors in favour of immigration (L.A., MN 5 December 1995, 3). From 1990 to 1995, the provincial government encountered increasing pressure from the business community and representatives of specific industries, as well as from declining rural communities.[11] This strengthened the Conservatives' political commitment on the issue; it also increased pressure on the government to reach an immigration agreement with the federal government.[12]

The Emergence of a New Consensus

The elite's interest paved the way for a new consensus on the importance of immigration for Manitoba. With it reappeared demands for tools that would permit the province to receive a "fair share" of immigration. In 1993 the Minister of Culture, Heritage and Citizenship, Bonnie Mitchelson, summarized the government's position in the Legislative Assembly:

> Mr. Speaker what we want to do in Manitoba is get our fair share of immigrants, and we all know by the numbers that Manitoba's numbers of immigrants have been decreasing and that, proportionately, our fair share should be around 4 percent of those who immigrate to Canada. Mr. Speaker, we want to ensure through an immigration agreement that we have some control over expeditiously allowing those to come to fill job shortages, with job skills that are not here in Manitoba, and we also want to expeditiously try to accommodate those who are coming here for family reunification. (L.A., MN, 27 July 1993, 1355–1400)

Immigration was thus presented as a tool for the province's economic development. It would provide workers and investment and thereby ensure the demographic sustainability of Manitoba.

This new consensus was based on the assessment that federal immigration policy had failed to meet the province's needs or that federal actors had been unwilling to meet them. This was compounded by the ineffectiveness of the federal immigrant investor program in Manitoba. This feeling of being poorly served by federal policies strengthened fears that the province was in demographic decline, particularly with regard to population loss in rural communities.[13] As a civil servant responsible for the immigration file in 1990 declared, Filmon's cabinet was well aware of these concerns:

> What had been happening in the province of Manitoba was that ... our population was not keeping pace ... and there was interest and concern for the depopulation of rural areas and we had a number of labour shortages that had been identified ... Again we did this kind of graphic for cabinet saying "all right, these are the areas we have issues in and here are potential ways to solve these issues." So, we had a lot of discussion with rural areas to see if there were ways that we could position the immigration movement to actually end up having a movement in the rural areas.[14]

A consensus thus formed in the early 1990s, across partisan lines, on the need for the province to act directly and independently in the area of immigration.

The Reorientation of Provincial Activities

Province-building in Manitoba would have the effect of reorienting and expanding provincial activities. In 1990, all services related to immigration and the integration of immigrants were centralized in a new division of the Ministry of Culture, Heritage and Citizenship. That ministry combined, for the first time, responsibility for settling immigrants, training adult immigrants, and teaching second languages, as well as for business immigration, recognition of immigrants' credentials, the combating of racism, and immigration-related policy development (Manitoba 1993; 1992).

Despite a policy of limiting public spending, the government invested resources to expand its activities in immigration and integration. Because of irregularities, Manitoba stopped participating in the federal immigrant investor program in 1993 (Deloitte & Touche 1992); at the same time, it developed a provincial immigrant recruitment strategy. It held public consultations on immigration and set up an interdepartmental working group on promotion and recruitment, in order to ensure that its strategy would be implemented (Manitoba 1995).

In the area of integration, the province changed its approach, expanding its anti-racism activities and working to pluralize its services for citizens. In collaboration with the federal government, Manitoba also developed a new approach to language training for newcomers.

As well, in 1992 the province established an administrative division devoted to labour market integration. In addition to its well-established programs, the provincial administration began offering individual support to immigrants while keeping to a strict division of responsibilities with the federal government (Manitoba 1993).

New Demands

In 1990 the Manitoba government expressed its intention to undertake immigration negotiations with the federal government; in 1992 it announced that it was "aggressively pursuing the agreement" (L.A., AMN, 9 December 1992, 1410). Accordingly, the government invested in its policy development capacity and acquired knowledge about its needs and its options with respect to a future agreement with the federal government.[15]

Earlier in 1992, the immigration minister, Bonnie Mitchelson, had clearly expressed the importance of an agreement that would allow Manitoba to take control of its immigration destiny:

> [E]ver since Citizenship was moved over and our department was renamed to Culture, Heritage and Citizenship, we have had a more major focus on immigration. One of the first announcements that we made was the desire to negotiate expeditiously with the federal government an immigration agreement not dissimilar to what Quebec has in place so that we would have more control over immigration, the numbers of immigrants, and the classes of immigrants that might come to Manitoba ... We are actively pursuing an immigration agreement that will put in place the ability of Manitoba to receive 4 percent of the immigrants that come to Canada and many other components, of course, to that Immigration Act. We are concerned, yes. Our numbers are down. I think an immigration agreement might resolve some of that problem. (L.A., MN, 16 June 1992, 1700)

The province also tried repeatedly to influence federal policy (Manitoba 1994). These attempts were largely unsuccessful, but this only increased Manitoba's desire for an agreement. In May 1993, Premier Filmon summed up his government's position:

> No, Madam Chairperson, in fact we still think that the rationale for us having a greater influence is strong. In fact, the member opposite talked earlier in the preamble to our discussions about our population not growing as

rapidly as it did in the early '80s, and one of the major differences of course is in the proportionate share that we have gotten of Canadian immigrants coming to Manitoba which has dropped to a third of what it was in the early '80s. We are not going to have an opportunity to get a greater share of immigrants. We are not going to have an opportunity to get a greater share of independent immigrants who may have the skills that we need for particular growth and development areas in our economy or entrepreneurial immigrants who come here with business skills and the capital with which to start a business, if we do not have this agreement. With all of the work that has been done to try and influence the federal system, we are absolutely convinced that we need to have that direct influence by way of a federal provincial agreement. We continue to work towards it and, I dare say, are making some progress. (L.A., MN, 25 May 1993, 2020)

In 1993 the provincial ministry stated that despite resistance from the federal government, negotiations towards a memorandum of understanding for cooperation in immigration had begun. The province signed that memorandum on 28 October 1994; even so, it continued to apply significant pressure on Ottawa in hopes of attaining a greater role in the selection of immigrants.

In both Quebec and Manitoba, the province-building mechanism centred on immigration was activated by the political elite. This activation in the 1990s involved implementing new interventions, supported by an emerging consensus about the role of immigration in provincial society. In Quebec, immigration went from being an element to be controlled to a resource for provincial development. In Manitoba, the legitimating of a strengthened role for the provincial government in immigration marked a break from the past expectations about the divisions of responsibilities, in which the federal government was responsible for immigration. In both provinces, the activation of province-building implied a break with past government practices concerning immigration and was accompanied by increased demands that the federal government assign more power to the provinces.

The Interaction of the Mechanisms of Building and Decentralization

In the 1990s the decentralization mechanism key to the federalization process would be activated, as a result of both federal decisions and provincial demands based on province-building. For Quebec and Manitoba, the interaction of the two mechanisms would have a double impact: it would crystallize the consensus central to province-building and at the same time increase the intensity of provincial activities. Across Canada, this interaction would impact the distributive and ideational dimensions of the immigration and integration governance regime.

The Meech Lake Accord, Quebec, and Immigration

While Quebec was undergoing this turn towards province-building in immigration, the federal government, now led by the Progressive Conservatives under Brian Mulroney, attempted to resolve constitutional tensions related, among other things, to the patriation of the Constitution without the agreement of Quebec by the Liberal government of Pierre Elliott Trudeau in 1982. Both Bourassa and Mulroney wanted to regularize the constitutional status of Quebec, and the premier began the negotiations armed with an approach that was distinct from the one advocated by his predecessor, René Lévesque. A constitutional conference was held on 29–30 April 1987, which culminated in the draft Meech Lake Accord.

Recognition of the provincial role in immigration and the consolidation of provincial gains in that area were among the Bourassa government's demands (McRoberts 1999). One section of the draft accord (section 2, additions to section 95 of the Constitution) gave constitutional status to bilateral agreements on immigration and, therefore, to the powers Quebec had acquired through the Cullen–Couture Agreement of 1978 (Canada 1987). In addition, the draft included a commitment by the federal government to withdraw from the delivery of settlement and integration services, with Ottawa providing "reasonable compensation" to the province (Becklumb 2008). Furthermore, Quebec would be guaranteed a proportional share of immigrants each year. The Quebec government viewed these sections as crucial and made their inclusion a precondition for its acceptance of the draft Meech Lake Accord.[16]

The failure of the Meech Lake Accord in 1990, after Manitoba and Newfoundland refused to ratify it, threw the country into an unprecedented political crisis. Following a spark of hope for the equal participation of Quebec in the federation, relations between the Quebec and federal governments reached a new low. Even before the failure of Meech Lake, support for sovereignty had been growing among Quebecers in response to the tenor of the debates on ratification. That tension would grow even stronger after 1990. The Bourassa government's reaction to the failure of the draft accord was immediate. In 1990, Quebec officially withdrew from constitutional discussions, Robert Bourassa declared Quebec a "distinct society" in the National Assembly, the government set up the Bélanger–Campeau Commission on the political and constitutional future of Quebec, and the Liberal Party adopted the Allaire Report on the future of Quebec after Meech's Failure. Finally, following the recommendations of the Bélanger–Campeau report, in June 1991 the Quebec government passed Law 150, providing for a referendum on Quebec sovereignty in 1992 (McRoberts 1999).

It was in this context of political crisis that the decentralization mechanism for immigration was activated. The Mulroney government – and to a lesser extent the Bourassa government – made efforts to neutralize this crisis and to demonstrate the federal government's capacity for accommodation and good-faith deal-making.[17] Because the province-building mechanism had already been activated, a bilateral agreement on immigration seemed a simple, effective first step towards easing the crisis.

On Bourassa's initative, long before the negotiations on the draft Meech Lake Accord, the two levels of government had begun negotiations on a new immigration agreement (*La Presse* 1990). As noted by a civil servant active in Quebec's immigration ministry at the time, the provisions related to immigration contained in the draft constitutional agreement reflected significant progress in discussions between the governments: "[There] was a political will to reach an agreement, but the negotiations on immigration had taken a much more concrete and much more operational turn, let's say than those on spending power. And so, in a sense … Soon after Meech … it would have been possible to sign an agreement on immigration … Everything was settled."[18]

A signed agreement would not automatically follow the end of discussions about a constitutional agreement. Two elements need to be pointed out here. First of all, the political tensions generated by the announcement of the negotiations dampened the federal will to reach an agreement. The reactions of the other provinces, especially Ontario and Manitoba, to the bilateral immigration negotiations with the Quebec government had the effect of temporarily impeding the talks.[19]

When negotiations were resumed, the key sticking point was funding. Under the Meech Lake Accord, the federal government would have had to compensate the province adequately for its withdrawal from the delivery of integration and settlement services. According to a federal negotiator responsible for the file, it was in the end the decision to increase the funding offer to Quebec that would make an agreement possible.[20] That agreement therefore included reference to the sums that would be transferred to the province for the first four years as part of the devolution of immigration and integration services. The agreement also included a formula for calculating these transfers in subsequent years. This formula was ascending and relatively independent of the number of immigrants received by the province (Québec 1991a, B2–B5).

The Gagnon–Tremblay–McDougall Accord on immigration, concluded in 1991, would have a powerful impact on Quebec. It would enable the province to keep developing its holistic mode of intervention; it would also institutionalize the consensus at the centre of the province-building mechanism centred on immigration. The conclusion of this agreement would have structuring effects on future relations among all Canadian governments in the area of immigration. It stabilized relationships between the federal government and Quebec in the area of immigration and reconfigured part of the institutional regime of governance. Perhaps more importantly, the agreement completely severed the links between immigration and competitive nation-building in Quebec that had already been frayed since Bourassa's election to a second term.

These structuring effects also arose from the fact that the agreement provided ongoing impetus to the decentralization mechanism, related to the federal government's desire to avoid asymmetry. Thus, after signing the accord with Quebec, the federal government began negotiations with other provinces so as not to single out Quebec in the context of the constitutional tensions of the time.[21] For political and especially financial reasons, these negotiations would fail.[22] The sums transferred to Quebec as part of the 1991 agreement would not leave much financial manoeuvring room to the federal government. Nevertheless, the conclusion of this agreement would impact the mobilization of the other provinces and how they defined their interests in the area of intergovernmental relationships related to immigration.

Manitoba: The PNP and Settlement Renewal

In the 1990s the Manitoba cabinet began issuing clear directives for the development of policies supporting an increase in the number of immigrants, their integration, and their retention in the province. Reflecting the activation of province-building centred on immigration in the province, the government's strategy was to demand more powers from the federal government with regard to attracting and selecting immigrants. As related by a senior Manitoba civil servant of the time:

> It was a fight. And the relationship between Manitoba and Canada was not good at the time and … they weren't afraid of the fight – that was just one thing we didn't agree on with the federal government. This was clearly that the province understood its demographics better than the feds did. Clearly the province had the economic [interests] of its population at heart, more than the feds. Clearly, we should be able to be in control of our own destiny.[23]

These demands would spur the federal government to establish the Provincial Nominee Program (PNP) for Manitoba and to sign the first agreements on immigration and settlement services.

Manitoba had concluded a memorandum of agreement in 1994, opening the way for a more substantial agreement on immigration. Even so, the province continued to step up its demands. After Canadians elected a Liberal government in 1993, under Jean Chrétien, these demands had two main targets. First of all, Manitoba criticized the federal government's changes to immigration policy (e.g., Abu-Laban 2004) – among other things, the introduction of higher costs for immigration applications and permanent residency, the creation of new procedures for hearings and for setting immigration levels, and potential changes to the number of family reunifications authorized annually for Manitoba. Political actors in the province viewed these new policies as generally detrimental to Manitoba, given their possible negative impact on migration flows to the province (L.A., MN, 19 June 1995, 1700).

Second, the economic recovery spurred the province to represent the interests of its growing industries. A civil servant active at the time noted that the clothing industry was then among those most regularly making representations to the provincial government, after the activation of the province-building mechanism:

> The province of Manitoba had a … fairly strong garment industry … the province was essentially representing the interests of manufacturing … And they felt that … they needed to have the attraction of permanent residents to attract the numbers that they needed at that time. So … they asked the government to use powers … which were already there in the legislation, but had not been used, in my experience anyway …

to support the permanent residency of foreign nationals who ... did not have the profile to qualify under the point system for the skilled worker selection but had been named by a province under an agreement saying: "The province would like to have them [in order] to give them permanent residency."[24]

The needs of the clothing industry were specifically mentioned in the 1995 Speech from the Throne (L.A., MN, 5 December 1995, 3). And the demand for immigrants was hardly confined to that industry – it was found in other sectors as well, to say nothing of concerns about the province's demographic needs.[25] The previous activation of province-building caused the province's economic and social actors to turn to the Manitoba government, much more than to the federal government, to find solutions to these problems.

Tensions with the Federal Government

According to federal negotiators, Manitoba's demands were not taken seriously – at least not at first – by the Chrétien government.[26] In 1995, representatives of the province were complaining about the lack of openness of the federal employment and immigration minister, Sergio Marchi, to Manitoba's desire to resume negotiations over a new agreement following the memorandum of agreement of 1994. Manitoba's premier summed up the position of his government and its relationship with the federal government in 1995:

> Clearly, we want to do everything ... We are requesting an agreement, and we have an entire proposal that has been worked on for four years now. I mean, it goes back to dealing with the Mulroney government, with the Campbell government. The member may recall that it was one of the issues in the one meeting that I had here with Prime Minister Campbell in her visit as Prime Minister to Manitoba. I raised that particular issue as one of the foremost issues, and it has carried on. So there has been plenty of staff work done by senior staff. The question is when the federal government is going to be willing to enter into such an agreement. (L.A., MN, 1 June 1996, 1750)

Federal resistance continued until the end of 1995 while provincial pressure intensified. According to stakeholders, the resistance of the federal Liberal government can be explained by a number of factors – first of all, by differing views and partisan conflicts between Ottawa and the provincial government. This was very certainly the case for Manitoba, and these tensions were only heightened by the austerity policies implemented during Chrétien's first term. Also, the federal government did not want to exacerbate the asymmetry already present within the regime of immigration governance in Canada. As pointed out by a federal civil servant active in the negotiation of the agreements and the establishment of the program:

> [W]e had originally attempted to do it on a multilateral basis. So we got provincial representatives all into a room and said, "What do you guys think about this? [Is this] something you would like? And there was essentially a three-way split. There were provinces that said, "Fantastic! We love this! This is really something we want to do!" There are others who said, "No way! Immigration is a hot button topic … There is more of a negative sense than positive in our jurisdiction because of the employment rate …" and stuff like that … And then there were those you just said, "We really don't care one way or another. We're not totally opposed to it but we don't see ourselves being able to use it and take advantage of it." Anyway I mean we tried that and after that it became clear we wouldn't get a … consensus. We wouldn't get twelve jurisdictions signing an alliance. So someone … said, "Well, if we can't do it … what about bilaterally?" And so [we visited] the country one by one. Talked to the different provincial representatives. "What do you think? Is there a potential for this or …?" We wouldn't have any money, we couldn't put any money on the table. But it could be as big or as small as you want it to be. You can tailor it specifically. You can make it broad … Our wish is that you're accountable for your decision, you know, in a public sense, in a political sense … And that you use your authority as, you know, like any responsible government."[27]

Finally, federal resistance can be explained by the administrative challenge created by the establishment of new policy instruments in response to Manitoba's demands.

As part of those demands, Manitoba proposed pilot projects to the federal government, including the recruitment of workers for the clothing industry, targeted recruitment in Ukraine, direct contacts through federal immigration offices, and the delivery of English-as-second-language services by the province. Rejected at first, these proposals would finally form the basis of a beneficial working relationship between the federal public service and the province. With the federal government's approval, Manitoba put in place a series of experiments in the area of recruitment starting at the end of 1995; these would be intensified in 1996 following the signing of the pilot PNP. Among the experiments were attempts to recruit temporary foreign workers without a Labour Market Opinion. [28] In theory, this exemption should have permitted the province to recruit workers who were particularly in demand there but who did not qualify for the federal government's skilled worker programs (e.g., L.A., MN, 20 September 1995, 1355–1410).

All stakeholders point to two initiatives as having contributed strongly to the creation of Manitoba's mode of intervention. The first of these was the pilot project carried out in the city of Winkler in 1996, through which the province recruited immigrants from Germany. The other, the same year, was a project to recruit sewing machine operators from the Philippines (L.A., MN, 16 May 1996, 1600–50).[29] The federal and provincial actors who created the program note that by setting up these pilot projects, the province played a significant role in developing Manitoba's PNP – an innovation at the time (Lewis 2010).[30]

The previous activation of province-building would make these experiments a success. Prior provincial investments in the capacity of the public service in immigration as well as in programs for new arrivals were important foundations of that success. The spread of the consensus on the role of immigration for Manitoba society beyond the elite was also a significant contributor. This success partly allievated the federal government's fears regarding the capacity of a province without contemporary experience in managing large migration flows – such as Manitoba – to manage an immigrant selection program. The province would go on sign an agreement permitting it to establish its own PNP, appended to a broader agreement on immigration described below. This agreement would be finalized in 1998.

Administrative Decentralization

Coming out of the program review implemented by the federal government of Jean Chrétien starting in 1995, Settlement Renewal was an episode of administrative and fiscal decentralization directed by Citizenship and Immigration Canada that mainly involved hearings with citizens and service delivery organizations (Canada 1994; Bourgon 2009). The provinces were invited to take part, but there was not much enthusiasm or support from the federal government for their involvement. Manitoba was one of the few provinces that participated very actively, and of its own volition, in the consultations and hearings.[31]

At the end of process, as a cost-cutting measure, the federal government offered to let the provinces administer and implement settlement services. A federal civil servant then working with Citizenship and Immigration Canada in the Prairie region recalled that this offer received various responses from the different provinces:

> Of all the provinces in the country, I think that the four Western provinces were the most interested. At that time Ontario was still maintaining its long held view that immigration was a federal responsibility and they didn't really want to be involved. The Atlantic Provinces may have had interests but ... they felt that if they were to take over the program with that level of funding, they wouldn't be capable of delivering the equivalent programs ... In the West, Alberta gave some indications of interest but decided not to conclude an agreement. Saskatchewan had some initial interest but again, found out at that time that maybe its focus should be on the provincial nominee agreement. Manitoba and BC were interested. All other provinces indicated that there was not enough money for the services they needed to provide. CIC, as a result, went back to the center, to Treasury Board, and explained the situation and was able to obtain another 62 million dollars, which increased the national settlement budget, excluding Quebec, from 108 million I think to about 179. So they increased benefits for everyone across the country, not just the provinces [with whom] negotiations on settlement devolution were taking place.[32]

Following the federal offer, Manitoba signed an addendum to its agreement on immigration in 1998. Thus in 1999, the province became responsible for delivering integration and settlement services on its territory. Accordingly, the federal government withdrew from this policy area in Manitoba. The agreement included an annual financial transfer for settlement services ($3.75 million in 1999) and the relocation of federal employees to the provincial public service (Manitoba 1999, 38).

The funding increase was a major factor in the positive reception of the decentralization offer made to the provinces. This was the case in Manitoba, where political elites expressed fears of a reduction in federal funding for immigrant services. These fears were reinforced by the fact that the Filmon government was then working to get the provinces' finances back on solid ground and feared the budgetary impact of across-the-board cuts in transfer payments from the federal government.

But financial considerations do not entirely explain Manitoba's decision to accept the federal offer. This choice was above all a reflection of previous province-building centred on immigration. In fact, the possibility of being responsible for integration services was in line with the consensus that the province should take charge of its own fate in the area of immigration. The offer was therefore not seen (as was the case in other provinces) as a risky transfer of the costs related to integrating immigrants in the provinces.[33]

As pointed out by a federal analyst who was a member of the team responsible for intergovernmental consultations regarding Settlement Renewal, in the case of Manitoba "their interest predated any offer from us."[34] Elite activation bolstered the view that immigration was a resource for developing Manitoba's economy and for growing its population. At that stage, "for Manitoba it was very much about building their population and seeing this as an important part of making Manitoba a more attractive destination."[35] The implementation of integration services more adapted to the needs and realities of the province – a "Made in Manitoba" approach – thus became realistic through the acquisition of autonomy and additional resources.

What is more, because of province-building, Manitoba already had substantial capacity to deliver integration services. To that capacity was added independent provincial investments. Because of increasing activities and institutional development, the idea of being responsible for settlement services did not represent a key innovation, and those services could be provided at a lower cost. In other provinces the province-building mechanism had not been activated or had barely been initiated, thus the financial, cognitive, and institutional investments required by provincial involvement in a new policy area represented a significant obstacle to acceptance of the federal offer.

The transfer of responsibilities in the area of immigrant settlement in Manitoba, like the implementation of the Provincial Nominee Program, can thus only be understood by recognizing the province's previous involvement in the field of immigration, the result of province-building. The interaction of the two mechanisms would give Manitoba the autonomy and resources to strengthen its mobilization towards immigration and to further develop its holistic mode of intervention. This episode would also have consequences for *all* the institutional actors (federal and provincial governments) involved in the regime of governance of immigration and integration, mainly through the creation of new avenues of intervention for the provinces, namely the PNP.

Consensualization and Institutionalization

After both Quebec and Manitoba obtained powers and resources in immigration and integration, the province-building mechanism continued to operate. The crystallization of the consensus around immigration as a resource was confirmed through the maintenance of key policy principles, despite significant events and changes in the two provinces. Quebec and Manitoba both saw an institutionalization of the holistic approach and a development of interventions independent of federal policies.

Quebec

In 1991 the Canada–Quebec accord on immigration established a trajectory for autonomous development for Quebec. Immigration and integration policies expanded substantially and in keeping with the principles of the 1990 policy statement, which had been issued before Canada and Quebec signed the bilateral accord. That accord would limit the tenor of relationships between Quebec and federal government to primarily administrative and operational issues. In this sense, after 1991, provincial demands for autonomy or resources in immigration and integration as they related to linguistic or cultural questions were neutralized in intergovernmental relationships.

After 1991, following the transfer of funds and responsibilities from the federal government, Quebec's public administration in immigration expanded. The Ministry of Citizen Relations and Immigration (MRCI) increased in size and budget. The province made many proposals to implement new objectives and strategies with the goal of increasing annual levels of immigration. These efforts were accompanied by growth in the capacity for research, analysis, and planning; in the human resources available to produce Quebec's nomination certificates; and in the infrastructure for recruitment abroad (Québec 1992; 1997).

Now that it was solely responsible for selecting new potential immigrants, the province expanded its actions in the field. In 1991, Quebec refined its actions for selection (as it would periodically over the coming years) and increased its interventions with regard to the reception and sponsorship of refugees. It also began to develop – autonomously, but sometimes in collaboration with the federal government – experiments in targeted economic selection. Shortly after signing the 1991 accord, the province revised its selection criteria for immigrant entrepreneurs, and in the years that followed it put in place a series of actions aimed at perfecting its selection methods, making them more targeted while increasing the volume of immigrants welcomed annually.[36] These actions reflected intensive, comprehensive efforts, typical of the holistic mode of intervention in recruitment and selection. Within this framework, the language dimension remained central to the province's interventions, but it was no longer the sole criterion guiding selection.

At the same time, Quebec increased its activities with regard to the settlement and integration of immigrants, beyond linguistic integration. It expanded its reception and integration services – in particular, front-line services, for which it was now responsible. Successive governments would increase the supply of French-language courses and provide more varied formats for linguistic integration services, strengthening the emphasis on employability through the acquisition of French. Also, services in economic integration were extensively developed. In addition, starting in the mid-1990s, the province was very active in the geographic dispersion of newcomers throughout its territory, a policy once again closely linked to the economic aspect of integration (Québec 1992; 1997).

This expansion, in keeping with the consensus that immigration was a resource, also institutionalized new procedures for the joint development of immigration and integration policies. The province put in place instruments for the medium- and long-term planning of immigration. First of all, in 1992 a decision was made to plan immigration levels on a three-year basis – a method of planning that would be refined over the following decades. The province also established a series of procedures for public hearings and deliberations on immigration and integration (Québec 1991b). These planning and consultation efforts provided important links – however imperfect – between the selection policies of the province and the integration policies established as part of the holistic mode of intervention.[37]

The expansion of provincial intervention after 1991 thus was carried out according to the central themes of the province-building mechanism centred on immigration, so as to consolidate the characteristics of the holistic mode of intervention: the dominant logic of a societal project, intensive recruitment based on other criteria besides economic ones, and a continuum approach in the areas of integration and settlement. This institutionalization was confirmed, beyond the implementation of public policies and institutions, by the maintenance of Quebec orientations in the course of a series of tense policy debates and critical junctures between 1990 and 2010. Despite their potential to call into question the principles of the holistic mode of intervention or to halt the activity of the province-building mechanism centred on immigration, these events unfolded with a surprisingly stable immigration and integration policy background in Quebec.

The return of the Parti Québécois to power in 1994, led by Jacques Parizeau, and the subsequent PQ governments of Lucien Bouchard and Bernard Landry would not impede the mechanism, which would continue to move forward in spite of the referendum campaign of 1995 and in spite of Bouchard's "zero deficit" austerity policies. The changes made during this period included a restructuring of the ministry responsible for immigration, which became, in 1996, the Ministry of Citizen Relations and Immigration (MRCI). This revamped ministry had a broader mandate than its predecessor, although immigration and integration continued to receive the biggest share of the budget.[38] During this period, more weight was given to economic indicators and, to a lesser extent, linguistic factors in the selection of new arrivals (Bélanger 2006).

The return to power of the Liberals in 2003 did not halt province-building centred on immigration. Many observers, including Vincent Lemieux, observed that the Charest government's policy "was a continuation of that of the previous governments" (Lemieux 2012, 266). The QLP returned to power with an agenda aimed at increasing the number of immigrants, refining the mechanisms for economic selection, and further expanding the role of community organizations in the integration process for newcomers.[39] In spite of the Liberals' austerity plans and restrictions on public spending – dubbed "state reengineering" (Rouillard et al. 2008) – and in spite of the crisis around "reasonable accommodations" that emerged in 2006 (Labelle and Icart 2007), the consensus around the role of immigration as a tool for societal development was maintained from 2003 to 2010. The government's inability or unwillingness to limit state intervention in immigration and integration showed the strength of the societal consensus on the provincial role in immigration and on the holistic nature of Quebec's mode of intervention.

Thus, despite changes of government and critical events, the province-building mechanism remained active in Quebec from 1991 to 2010. Throughout this period, there would be no challenge to the principles established in 1990 in the policy statement on immigration and integration (*Let's Build Québec Together*). Between 1990 and 2010, quite unambiguously, the province viewed immigration as a resource for developing Quebec's society.

Manitoba

After the 1996 and 1998 agreements were signed, the province-building mechanism centred on immigration continued to drive Manitoba's efforts. The consensus over immigration became more and more general; the principles of Manitoba's mode of intervention became institutionalized.

Over time, the province established more sophisticated units to deal with cases related to immigration, until a ministry devoted to it was created in 2001: the Department of Labour and Immigration. The number of employees assigned to files increased, as did the budget allocated to public administration. Then in 1995, working groups were set up to coordinate the actions of all departments in the area of immigration and integration (Manitoba 1997; Manitoba Labour 2000). Meanwhile, the province participated actively in federal–provincial–territorial meetings on immigration, which Ottawa was just beginning to organize.[40]

Starting in 1997, much of the development of the provincial government's capacity in immigration focused on efforts to select immigrants and on efforts overseas to promote Manitoba as a destination. These efforts stemmed from the implementation in 1996 – even before the signing of the agreement with the federal government – of a provincial strategy to promote immigration and recruitment, the aim of which was to "reverse the decline in immigration to the province that began in the early 1990s" (Manitoba 1997). The practice was then established to target potential immigrants from specific countries – those deemed most likely to contribute substantially to the provincial economy and also to adapt to life in Manitoba. The goal of this policy was to retain newcomers (Manitoba 1997). This approach would continue for some time and culminate in bilateral agreements with third parties (including the Philippines and Iceland) (Manitoba Labour and Immigration 2009; 2008). Manitoba also launched promotion efforts focused on certain major industries in the province, efforts that were sometimes managed by the industries themselves.

The growth and increasing sophistication of the PNP was part of the same movement. In 1998, after it signed the agreement with the federal government, Manitoba was given a quota of two hundred nominees to select per year (Manitoba 1999). In absolute numbers, this quota would increase constantly until the federal government decided, in 2011, to limit the number of provincial nominations under the PNP to about 70 per cent of all immigrants selected by the provinces (Canada 2011a).

Over time, the program shifted from a logic related primarily to the short-term needs of the labour market to a logic of human capital investment. Until 2003–4 the selection of provincial nominees was conducted according to a list of occupations in demand. Then, starting in 2004, the province established a selection model based on applicants' human capital, from the perspective of optimizing the retention and integration of candidates. A senior civil servant of the province explained this evolution:

So it was clear to us early on that the model that worked for Manitoba was … a human capital model. [Around] 2003, we started to dispose of those [occupations] lists because they are rarely accurate because of what real labour market needs [were] … So, we started to look more at the package of skills that the workers … the applicant presented to us and the adaptability indicators that tell us, "they have reasons to come to Manitoba and they have the skills to succeed here and they have the social support that will help them stay here." And that's kind of where we built this hybrid [of] the "skilled workers with social connections."[41]

This new selection method still included language criteria as an important factor. The province also established a series of selection categories that made it possible to favour both targeted occupations (e.g., through direct selection by employers) and immigration based on social ties. In this sense, Manitoba's PNP strengthened the principles of the holistic mode of intervention in immigration and brought the actions of the province closer to those of Quebec.

In accordance with the 1999 agreement on settlement programs, federal employees and monies for the delivery of services were transferred to the province (Lewis 2010). Besides supporting the development of the provincial government's capacities, this transfer gave Manitoba the ability to institutionalize a vigorous approach to integration and to combine increased recruitment activities with more efforts towards the integration of immigrants.

The concrete result of these initiatives was the Manitoba Immigration Integration Program (MIIP), developed starting in 1998 and implemented the following year. Through this program, the province funded settlement services, organizational capacity-building, integration to employment, and other front-line services as well as significant interventions in linguistic integration, in the course of which the types and formats of courses were expanded (Manitoba 1999; Manitoba Labour 2000). Then starting in 2000, the province adopted a "continuum" approach aimed at directing provincial efforts at selecting and integrating immigrants to favour inclusion and retention. Throughout the period studied, Manitoba invested its own resources, in addition to federal funding, to implement programs and policies aimed at the settlement and integration of new arrivals. These investments pointed to the maintenance of the province-building mechanism centred on immigration, reinforced by its combination with the decentralization mechanism. They also illustrate the key characteristics of the holistic mode of intervention in Manitoba.

The Manitoba government also established important links with economic actors in the province – representatives of industries and business associations – to develop joint actions in recruitment and integration.[42] At the same time, it developed close links with organizations delivering services in the province and made significant efforts to coordinate the services offered by these groups, in part to avoid duplication of services.[43]

An Institutionalized Mode of Intervention

The consensus central to the province-building mechanism is still in place today in Manitoba. The principles of holistic intervention that have emerged from this have been remarkably enduring. Also, this intervention was refined even while being institutionalized. The province would continue to select a broad range of new arrivals while taking into account their general contribution to Manitoba society and providing integration services.

The subsequent NDP governments, led by Gary Doer (1999–2009) and then by Greg Selinger (2009–16), would not question these policies and practices. The constant acceleration of the mechanism – surprising, given the traditional position of Manitoba's NDP towards provincial involvement in immigration – showed the depth of provincial commitment to immigration as a resource for developing Manitoba society.

Between 1999 and 2009 the province increased its interventions. The PNP continued to be a key element of this, increasing the number and categories of candidates selected. Manitoba maintained its aim of making interventions on all dimensions of integration, as well as its efforts to strengthen collaboration with community groups when formulating and implementing policies (Manitoba Labour 2000; Manitoba Labour and Immigration 2010a).

Throughout the decade, immigration found its way into other important policy areas. In 2003 the province proposed a new economic development strategy, with increased immigration as one of its seven key objectives (Manitoba Finance 2003). This strategy has been renewed since 2003 without immigration being dislodged as an engine of growth (Manitoba Labour and Immigration 2010b). Finally, during this period, the province maintained important strategic monitoring of the federal public service and the federal government. The province's grievances were related to the numbers of nominees to be selected annually, which it considered to be too low, as well as to the management of the Temporary Foreign Worker Program and federal immigration policy in general (Manitoba 2009). Another indication of the maintenance of provincial mobilization and the continuing support of economic actors is that Manitoba established more services for temporary foreign workers (Manitoba 2007; 2010a). The NDP, which formed the government of Manitoba from 1999 to 2016, did not question the principles behind province-building. Immigration remained a key resource for societal development, and over time a consensus developed among all political, economic, and community actors, given the successes achieved.[44]

The emphasis placed by the NDP government on the social and community dimensions of intervention in immigration and integration would further align Manitoba's approach with that of Quebec, although at least initially, the economic dimension tended to play a greater role in Manitoba. Over time, the provincial government came to be seen as a productive partner and even a spokesperson for immigration and integration stakeholders. These elements are clear evidence of the dissemination and institutionalization of the consensus central to the province-building mechanism centred on immigration in Manitoba until 2010.

Despite significant differences, Quebec and Manitoba have the most similar immigration and integration policies in Canada. This unexpected resemblance is the result of similar trajectories, beginning in 1990, of elite mobilization in the area of immigration. That mobilization was launched by the activation of the province-building mechanism centred on immigration in the two provinces. In late-1970s Quebec, this mechanism was distinguishable from a previous dynamic of competitive nation-building based on identity and language. In Manitoba, the mechanism was activated for the first time in the 1990s, although the province showed some interest in a role in immigration as far back as the 1960s. In both cases, the mechanism was not spurred by mobilization in civil society or by immigrants themselves; rather, it was the result of the mobilization of the political and bureaucratic elite. Elite actors, including the provincial premiers, expressed new visions of the state and tabled economic development plans that would colour the emerging consensus – namely, that immigration can be harnessed as a resource for societal development. The province-building mechanism centred on immigration would prompt Quebec and Manitoba to increase their interventions in immigration and integration and to ask for more powers and resources from the federal government. The spread of a contemporary consensus around the role of immigration and the institutionalization of policies in this domain have ensured the continuation of the holistic mode of intervention in Quebec and Manitoba despite significant political changes in both provinces.

The operation of the province-building mechanism in Quebec and Manitoba was interdependent with decentralization. At the outset, it was the demands of these two provinces that activated the decentralization mechanism. In this sense, these two provinces were the first movers in the process of federalization; by rejecting the status quo, which had been characterized by the dominance of the federal government, they forced a reconfiguration of the regime of governance of immigration and integration in Canada. These cases show the importance of tracing the evolution of provincial interests and provincial political lives to understand change in the federation. In this regard, the example of Manitoba and Settlement Renewal and, to a lesser extent, that of Quebec and the failure of the draft Meech Lake Accord are important. It was only to the extent that the provinces – in particular, the provincial elites – identified immigration as a resource for provincial society that a revision of the sharing of responsibilities between levels of government came to be viewed not just as acceptable but as an opportunity to exploit. The trajectories of the other provinces will show that in the absence of an active province-building mechanism, decentralization will have little or no impact.

This first interaction of province-building and decentralization would have consequences for the entire federalization process. Quebec's mobilization and Manitoba's, and the holistic modes of intervention that they developed, would show the other provinces that a provincial role in immigration was possible and potentially desirable. These two cases demonstrated that a provincial role in immigration could be based on many principles, first and foremost on economic development, and not just on identity-building or protection of language. Witnessing the emergence of alternative models of intervention in immigration and integration, the eight other provinces would use these two provinces' gains as a baseline in their requests to Ottawa.

The interaction between the province-building mechanism centred on immigration and decentralization would also have significant distributive consequences for the regime of governance of immigration and integration. Quebec's accord would isolate that province from intergovernmental dealings, thus opening the door to new dynamics based on the changing interests of other provincial actors. With respect to the federal government, the recurrent and increasing monies transferred to Quebec have set a benchmark for some provinces, besides limiting Ottawa's willingness and capacity to respond to financial demands as part of the negotiation of other bilateral immigration agreements. In addition, the creation of the PNP would give the provinces a tool to gain a measure of autonomy in this policy sector. Manitoba would provide a template for the other provinces, especially those that did not have substantial policy capacities in the area of immigration. Some provinces went so far as to copy procedures from that province's PNP. In the medium and long term, the spread and growth of this program would have important impacts on Ottawa's management of the economic stream of its immigration program. These consequences would trigger different responses by all the actors at various times during the federalization process, which had been set in motion by Quebec and Manitoba.

Chapter 3

Ontario and British Columbia: Expansion and Contraction

Since the 1990s, Ontario and British Columbia have developed a reactive mode of intervention in the area of immigration and integration. The two provinces carry out limited, targeted immigration activities while practising dualist intervention in the area of integration. On the one hand, they have general integration programs aimed at meeting the needs of the unskilled immigrant population; on the other, they are creating a series of programs aimed at the economic integration of skilled immigrants. This chapter shows that besides being a response to the on-the-ground realities of immigration in these two provinces, these characteristics are partly the result of the activity of the province-building mechanism centred on immigration.

After the federalization process had already been set in motion by Quebec and Manitoba (see the previous chapter), the province-building mechanism in Ontario and BC was activated by the election of two Liberal governments – Dalton McGuinty's in Ontario in 2003 and Gordon Campbell's in BC in 2001. Although immigration was not a campaign issue in either province, both new governments launched policy reorientations that affected their relationship with Ottawa and changed the orientation of their programs.

The processes in Ontario and BC illustrate the distributive consequences of changes to the institutional regime of governance of immigration. The interaction of the decentralization mechanism and the province-building mechanism in Quebec and Manitoba changed the interests of other provinces along with Ottawa's will to accommodate them. In a general context of diminishing fiscal resources, Ontario and BC's relation to immigration would evolve, with Quebec and

Manitoba serving as positive and negative references. However, this evolution occurred at a time when the federal government was entering a period of relative resistance to decentralization, given the increasing costs associated with transfers of responsibilities and resources to the provinces, which it had witnessed in Quebec and Manitoba.

The Federal Context

Ontario and BC are distinguished from the other provinces by a particularly rich history of provincial public interventions in immigration and especially in integration. Yet the activation of the province-building mechanism in the 2000s represented a substantial break with past policy. This break unfolded in a context where the combined consequences of changes in fiscal federalism and federal labour market policies were felt strongly by provincial governments. These general changes modified the interests and capacity to act of provinces and, in particular, reinforced the importance of immigration as a source of capital for provincial societies. This context affected all the provinces during this period, but especially Ontario and BC.

The first of these changes was the establishment of the Canada Health and Social Transfer (CHST) in 1995. This new system of block funding changed the logic of federal contributions in the areas of social and health policy and substantially decreased in the sums transferred (by more than one third over two years). It also led to changes in equalization among the provinces.[1] The decrease in transfers in 1995 was only one more step in a series of measures taken since the 1980s that limited the monies transferred to the provinces. These changes led to a disparity between the financial situation of the provinces and territories, and that of the federal government. In addition, the absence of an indexing formula resulted in considerable uncertainty for provincial governments regarding the amount of the transfers to be received. The unilateral nature of these changes would become a bone of contention for the provinces; so would the issue of the vertical fiscal imbalance (Ruggeri 1998; McIntosh 2004; Pelletier 2002).

For Ontario and BC, these changes were of great importance. In the early 1990s the two governments began using rhetoric suggesting that their capacity to act in their areas of jurisdiction was limited by decreases in the monies transferred by the federal government. In practice, these changes in transfers substantially increased the fiscal pressures on the two provincial governments, which in turn had qualitative and quantitative effects on their social policies (Graefe 2006; Battle 1998).

This consequence was all the more dramatic in Ontario, where the financial situation was affected by a recession and by structural changes in its economy (Battle 1998). The legacy of this change was a certain resistance to becoming involved in what they saw as new areas of social policy – which would have required the intervention of the two levels of government – and, in the case of Ontario, a substantial hardening of positions on intergovernmental relations.

A second change, related to the first, affected all the provinces in the 1990s but had a particularly significant impact in Ontario and BC: the federal decision to transfer to the provinces the administration of labour market policy. Faced with deficits in the 1990s, the federal government made drastic cuts to its own programs and withdrew from cost-sharing agreements with the provinces. These federal policy changes spurred provincial demands for a more decentralized management of programs and even for devolution to the provinces.

The situation created by the Charlottetown Accord (which contained provisions for recognizing jurisdictions in labour market training), the second Quebec sovereignty referendum of 1995, and the sweeping overhaul of the unemployment insurance program (which became Employment Insurance [EI]) would prompt the federal government to respond to provincial demands. Thus in 1995, the federal government began negotiations with the provinces and territories to establish partnerships for the provision of employment services and programs beyond the delivery of benefits. Alberta would conclude the first agreement in 1996; in the coming years, beginning in 1998, all the provinces except Ontario would conclude agreements on labour market development. This would be followed, in 2005, by new partnerships with Ontario, Manitoba, and Saskatchewan to facilitate the delivery of services covered in the agreements on labour market development (Wood and Klassen 2008; 2009).

This change in the division of responsibilities had significant repercussions for the development of the reactive mode of intervention. In Ontario, which declined to take on this responsibility at a time when its employment sector was in serious difficulty, changes in federal policy would further harden intergovernmental relationships. Changes to EI and cuts in funding, for example, seemed to be reflections of the fiscal imbalance Ontario was complaining about (Courchene 2005). In conjunction with changes in federal transfers, these changes partly explain the development of Ontario's discourse on the "fair share" in fiscal federalism. As this chapter documents, as part of this discourse integration policies were presented primarily as social policies.

In BC, the situation was different. The province would accept the federal offer, which was in keeping with the desire of the NDP provincial government to maintain a significant social policy presence despite a difficult financial situation. At that time, BC accepted responsibilities in exchange for funding it viewed as adequate. The transfer of these responsibilities to the province would expand its administrative and analytical capacity and satisfy its demands for the redistribution of resources between levels of government, especially with respect to social policy. This reconfiguration having succeeded, the province would harbour similar reservations about getting involved in the integration of immigrants, even though this intervention was conceived until the 2000s as largely a matter of social justice and inclusion.

A third change is relevant for situating the context of the activation of province-building. In 1986 an "immigrant entrepreneurs" category was added to the economic category of skilled immigrants and investors, replacing the business immigration category established by the Immigration Act of 1976 (Walsh 2008; Harrison 1996). This new selection category was related to a broader reform of the Canadian immigration regime, in which immigration levels were increased despite difficult economic conditions (Veugelers 2000). The reform established a category that permitted passive investment while maintaining the possibility of entering the country for immigrants wishing to start a business in Canada. Under the new program, the provinces played a double role. First, they evaluated investment plans submitted to the federal government. Second, they were responsible for administering the sums received from investors, through the establishment of investor funds. This program would send a steady stream of business and entrepreneur immigrants to the provinces until the end of the 1990s, when the global economic context changed and Canadian regulation of these investments was reinforced.

This program was of key importance for Ontario and BC, for the two provinces were in an ideal position to benefit from it in terms of economic development. Business immigration was recognized early on as a tool that would help provincial governments boost revenues and stimulate the local economy. The subsequent decrease in these migration flows and the limits placed on the program by the federal government in the early 2000s would contribute the activation of the province-building mechanism centred on immigration.

Besides increasing fiscal and social pressures on Ontario and BC, these three changes had two other important consequences. First, they consolidated a new discourse on the redistribution of resources within the federation. This discourse would colour discussions on the renewal of the distribution of responsibilities between the governments with respect to questions broadly related to immigration. Second, these changes would lead to a dualization of public policies on immigration in those provinces, continuing until the 2000s. On the one hand, given the large population of immigrants, the integration of immigrants would be configured as social policy whose objectives were equality, social justice, and recognition. As social policy, integration of immigrants therefore remained a shared responsibility for these governments. On the other hand, immigration was understood as the targeted recruitment of investors or newcomers bringing in capital. This conception maintained the predominance of the federal government in the management of immigration in Canada – Ontario and BC refusing to get involved in the area – while recognizing the potential benefits of highly targeted intervention in the promotion of the provinces as markets and living environments. This dualization would continue until the activation of the province-building mechanism in Ontario and BC.

Ontario: Genesis and Turmoil

As Canada's industrial heartland and the primary beneficiary of national economic-development policies, Ontario has always been the primary destination for immigrants. Before the 1950s, Ontario was generally not very active in immigration, beyond a few projects to recruit specialized workers and initiatives to attract foreign capital. Between 1950 and 1970 the government slowly developed programs and structures focused on integration. In 1971 the province inaugurated a reception service for immigrants in airports, and in 1973 it opened the Welcome Houses, a centralized service for reception, orientation, and language instruction for new arrivals (Amin 1987). These efforts continued throughout the 1980s despite significant economic changes; at the same time, the public administration responsible for integration was consolidated (Fine-Meyer 2002). The Liberal government of David Peterson (1985–90) continued along the same path as the previous Progressive Conservative government, maintaining Ontario's involvement in integration and settlement and creating new programs to support civil society organizations active in that domain (Biles et al. 2011).

The election of an NDP government in 1990 coincided with the beginning of a severe recession in Ontario, aggravated by a structural transformation of its economy. The new government, led by Bob Rae, inherited a difficult fiscal situation. In its 1991 budget it adopted a largely Keynesian approach, relying on government intervention to counteract the recession. This strategy was short-lived, however, and would be replaced by the *Social Contract* aimed at reducing the provincial budget by $4 billion through cuts in the public service and a reform of social assistance policies (McBride 1996). In spite of all this, the government maintained relatively stable integration policies. Throughout the term of the NDP government, the idea that immigration is above all social policy would thus persist.

Without completely reversing the province's traditional passivity with regard to intergovernmental collaboration, Rae atttempted to negotiate an immigration agreement with the federal government, spurred by a general perception that Ontario had been adversely affected by federal cuts in the 1990s. A discourse emerged that combined federal responsibility in immigration with the fiscal inequalities among the provinces in the area of integration. The Ontario government's representatives maintained that the province was not receiving enough money compared to the other provinces, particularly when the number of immigrants received was taken into account (L.A., ON, 1 November 1995, 1450–1500). For example, in 1994 the citizenship minister, Elaine Ziemba, explained to the opposition that the province was not receiving its fair share of federal funding:

> [I]f you take a look at the average amount of dollars that is spent per immigrant by the federal government in the various provinces across Canada, you would find that most provinces get $1,500. The average payment per immigrant in Quebec is $1,900. Ontario receives $780 per immigrant … That is why we are entering into an agreement with the federal government to make sure, not just that we are getting our fair share, although that's important, but that people who choose to live in Ontario are treated equally and fairly as all people are treated across Canada. (L.A., ON, 29 March 1994, 1440–60)

Thus, starting in 1993, the Ontario discourse on the fair share of intergovernmental funding, coupled with an ideal of social justice, played an important role in discussions about immigration and integration. Ontario's complaints had three targets: the federal government's general lack of generosity, the unilateral nature of its cuts to transfer payments, and the sums received by Quebec under the bilateral immigration agreement signed in 1991 (L.A., ON, 18 April 1994, 1340–50). The following declaration, made by Premier Rae to the Legislative Assembly, reflected the tone and content typical of Ontario's demands: "The Canada–Quebec immigration agreement guarantees Quebec a certain amount of money. Quebec now gets about 35% of federal funding for immigration, yet Quebec only receives 18% of the immigrants. For each new immigrant in Quebec, the federal government spends $1,900; for each new immigrant in Ontario it spends only $764" (L.A., ON, 20 April 1994, 1350–400).

During the five years the NDP was in power, it continued the policies of its predecessors, even in a context of austerity and economic slowdown. The crushing defeat of the NDP government in 1995 put an end to many of the actions undertaken by the Rae government and its predecessors. The "fair share" argument, however, lingered as a political legacy around which subsequent governments would continue to mobilize.

The victory of the Progressive Conservative Party in 1995, under Mike Harris, marked the beginning of an era of state withdrawal from intervention in immigration and integration. Armed with a clear electoral mandate – the "Common Sense Revolution" – Harris broke with established practices in these policy areas while maintaining the discourse and general demands of Ontario regarding the "fair share."[2] Until its defeat in the 2003 election, the province's Conservative government would maintain the same orientation.

At odds with the social justice objectives of preceding governments, the Conservatives saw immigrants in terms of "special interests"[3] and were acutely aware of the costs associated with social policies. Immigrants were also now seen as people who could commit fraud, threaten public security, or abuse the system. As such, there was a noticeable shift and partial withdrawal from activities associated with immigration – activities that conflicted with the Conservative government's desire to limit the state's role in integration and equality policies, which they viewed as private sector responsibilities.

The Harris government restructured the provincial public service responsible for integration and created the Ministry of Citizenship, Culture and Recreation, while making draconian cuts to the number of civil servants working on these files.[4] The government sharply cut settlement and integration programs. The Welcome Houses were closed. The province's general settlement program was restructured and had its funding cut by almost 50 per cent at the beginning of the

first Conservative term, and programs to combat racism were elimi-
nated (Biles et al. 2011). The government justified these changes both
by a desire to limit costs (Ontario 1996) and by a conviction that civil
society was capable of delivering such services on its own (L.A., ON 5
October, 1995, 1500–10). These cuts would foster long-lasting divisions
and a lack of trust between the provincial government and the organizations responsible for delivering immigrant services.[5]

From 1995 to 2003, the Ontario government did not view intervention in immigration and integration as a priority.[6] Nevertheless, it
maintained a minimal level of services in settlement and economic
integration, putting in place measures to favour access to professions,
and it continued to support the search for immigrant investors and entrepreneurs to boost the economy and create jobs.

Upon its election, the Harris government announced that it would be
pursuing an accord with the federal government, and in 1996 it reached
an agreement with Ottawa to increase funding for settlement and integration services over three years. Despite an administrative agreement
(Ontario 1997), demands for a fair share of resources would continue to
be heard throughout Harris's term. In 2000 the Minister of Citizenship,
Culture and Recreation, Helen Johns, presented the province's position:

> Let me tell you that even though the province is putting $4 million into
> nearly 100 newcomer settlement programs that work with immigrants
> to ensure that they settle quickly in this province, the province only re-
> ceives 40% of the dollars that are spent on immigration across this country,
> when we receive 55% of the immigrants that come. Yes, of course, we need
> to work with the federal government because we need more dollars …
> We continue to lobby the federal government to make sure that Ontario
> receives its fair share of the dollars. (L.A., ON, 8 June, 2000, 1500–10)

As was the case under the Ontario NDP government, the province
limited its demands to the funding of integration services. It did not
seek to become more active in the selection and recruitment of immigrants. In fact, there was a certain resistance to federal overtures in the
area, which were perceived as attempts by Ottawa to unload its responsibilities onto the province (e.g., L.A., ON, 26 June 2002, 1500–15).

British Columbia: Immigration as a Social Issue

Although this province has always been one of the two natural poles of
attraction for new arrivals to Canada, it was especially after the Second

World War that immigration to BC began to increase substantially, stimulated by labour needs and the government's desire to increase the population. The migration flows reflected a major change in source countries, with European immigration decreasing after the 1930s in favour of immigration from Asian countries. Marked in its beginnings by exclusionary practices – in particular with respect to Asian populations (Roy 1990; Ward 2002) – provincial activity in the area of immigration and integration was liberalized and modernized in the late 1960s. Like other provinces, BC signed administrative and collaboration agreements with the federal government after the Second World War. In the 1960s the province left to private and charitable organizations the task of welcoming immigrants and facilitating their integration.

BC finally established settlement and integration services in the 1970s. After a slow beginning, the 1980s saw an increase in immigration and integration activities under Social Credit governments led by William Richard Bennett (1975–86), then by Bill Vander Zalm (1986–91). In particular, the political situation in Hong Kong was viewed as an opportunity to attract foreign capital and immigrant entrepreneurs to the region (Mitchell 2001). The Social Credit governments tended to view immigration as a tool for economic development, and integration services as part of social policy, especially by the end of Vander Zalm's term.

At the beginning of the 1980s the province took steps to reach an immigration agreement with the federal government. According to a federal civil servant active in the negotiations at the time, the government was attracted by the possibilities related to the new federal program on immigrant investors, seeing it as a source of capital (L.A., B.C., 21 June 1989, 7721–3). Without asking for direct powers of selection, the province took steps throughout the 1980s to establish mechanisms that would allow it to involve itself more in immigration planning. Thus, at the end of the decade, as part of the negotiations around the Meech Lake Accord, the province made overtures to the federal government regarding a possible agreement, even though it did not issue specific demands in writing.[7]

In addition to demands related to business immigration, a discourse on the limits of federal funding emerged with respect to settlement and integration services. These demands, similar to those of the Ontario government, were based on the idea that it was important to properly divide the costs of immigrant integration between the two orders of government (L.A., B.C., 25 April 1989, 6364–5). At the time, the provincial demands in the area of funding were related to a discourse according to which the province was the victim of changes in federal immigration policy. Faced with large flows of immigrants, the province felt significant fiscal pressure with respect to the delivery of integration services, as stated by the education minister, Anthony Julius Brummet:

> We are negotiating with the federal government regarding the rapid increase. The immigration policy of the federal government affects the amount of demand on our system, at what time and at what sudden rate ... We are negotiating with the federal government, and we think that the immigration policy affects the funding that we have to come up with and that therefore they should contribute to it. I don't like the impression the member was trying to leave that we are trying to foist it all onto the federal government. That is not true, it is not correct, and I think I've given some of the facts. When you put in $60 million for ESL plus a lot of effort and work towards that, and when the districts and other people in this province are putting in a lot more to make that happen, then let's not try and leave the impression that we are trying to absolve ourselves of the responsibility by putting it all on the federal government. (L.A., B.C., 15 June 1989, 7518–19)

In the 1980s, BC's discourse around integration was similar to Ontario's. However, under the Social Credit government, business immigration was given priority. According to a provincial civil servant active in integration during this period, "initially, when I started working at the branch, [integration] was fairly low on the radar."[8]

The election of an NDP government, led by Michael Harcourt (1991–96), heralded a change in the general orientation in BC. Buoyed by a resounding election victory in 1991, this government was characterized by a desire to embody social democracy both from the point of view of practices (consultation, inclusion, etc.) and in terms of public policy (Ruff 1996). This orientation would change somewhat during the NDP's second term, starting in 1995. Under the leadership of Glen Clark (1995–2000) and Ujjal Dosanjh (2000–1), the NDP adopted an approach of "brokerage pragmatism" and diluted its social democratic agenda (Carroll and Ratner 2005). Faced with economic headwinds and a substantial decline in federal transfers, the government made large budget cuts and simultaneous tax cuts (Howlett and Brownsey 2001).

For the NDP of the time, immigration was primarily a social issue (Kataoka and Magnusson 2011). The new government's concerns were in keeping with the values of social inclusion, participation of immigrants in society, human rights, and social justice. It thus became important for the province to make interventions to favour the inclusion of newcomers, especially refugees, as well as to take measures that would permit their participation in the labour market, in order to fight against social and economic exclusion. This new orientation, which did not imply a withdrawal of provincial activity from business immigration, was in line with the ideas promoted by the province when it came to sharing responsibilities between the levels of government (British Columbia 1999; 1998).

The first sign of this new orientation was the transfer of responsibilities for immigration and integration from an economic ministry to the education ministry in 1991. The latter department was renamed the Ministry of Education, Multiculturalism, and Human Rights, with one branch responsible for integrated services in immigration and integration – an orientation that was consolidated in 2001 (British Columbia 2001a, 2001b).

At the same time, the provincial government began providing substantial funding for settlement services. In 1992 the province established an independent settlement program to provide for the needs of immigrants at risk of criminality, social exclusion, and poverty (L.A., B.C., 31 March 1992, 351–6). The program was expanded considerably over time in terms of both budgets and activities supported (British Columbia 1998). Throughout the 1990s, immigrants were presented as making a positive economic contribution to the province – a feeling that prevailed in the discourse. At the same time, the government knew this contribution depended on the effective integration of newcomers (British Columbia 1999; 2001a).

The province became more active in the integration of immigrants, yet it retained a strict concept of the division of responsibilities with Ottawa. As the minister explained, provincial efforts complemented the federal actions (L.A., B.C., 31 March 1992, 352). This discourse was reinforced by changes to policies and federal transfers made in the 1990s.[9]

The NDP's focus on the social dimension of immigration had a significant impact on BC's demands in intergovernmental relations. The province's grievances now took two directions. First of all, there was a focus on the general inadequacy of federal transfers (L.A., B.C., 27 April 1995, 1375), reinforced by the 1995 federal budget. Lacking adequate funds, the NDP reduced social spending and focused more and more on employability (McBride and McNutt 2007). It must be said, however, that BC's reaction was less intense than that of Ontario.

Second, the province denounced cuts and the reorientation made specifically to federal immigration and integration programs. These decisions were seen as a burden for the province, which had to step in and provide additional funding for service delivery. More broadly, the BC government viewed the federal government as making unilateral attempts to unload its responsibilities on the province (L.A., B.C., 17 April 2002, 2703). While BC remained tied to a strict idea of the social nature of immigration and to the sharing of responsibilities between the two levels of government, its demands were somewhat different from those of Ontario during the same period. In BC, these fears of federal withdrawal and a transfer of costs were not expressed in a "fair share" discourse.

In Ontario and BC, activities related to integration implemented in the 1960s and 1970s were motivated by an important logic of social intervention. During this period there also emerged a concern regarding the equitable division of costs related to integration between governments. Both Ontario and BC had large immigrant populations and came to see themselves as disadvantaged with respect to sums received from Ottawa. In both provinces, changes in government had a profound impact on modes of intervention. The Ontario Conservative government, elected in 1995 and in power until 2003, limited Ontario's intervention in immigration and integration. Conversely, in BC, the presence of an NDP government from 1991 to 2001 resulted in the maintenance of provincial activity in immigration, as well as a strengthening of an orientation related to objectives of social justice.

Decentralization and Settlement Renewal

In Ontario and BC, Settlement Renewal preceded the activation of the province-building mechanism centred on immigration. The federal decentralization offer happened against a backdrop of changes to fiscal federalism and restructuring of labour market policy and at a time when both provinces were struggling to respond to social problems that were perceived as arising from the presence of a large immigrant population. In the absence of a functioning province-building mechanism, the federal offer was turned down by Ontario but accepted by the BC government.

The Ontario government categorically refused the Chrétien government's 1995 offer to transfer responsibilities for settlement services. During hearings on Settlement Renewal the province took a very passive attitude – it simply did not take a position. It would instead be societal actors – especially groups active in immigration and service delivery – that participated in consultation activities.[10] Having been subjected to cuts by the Harris government, these actors fiercely opposed the transfer of responsibilities to the province.[11] This pointed to the distance and lack of trust between the political elite and social actors since the Harris team came to power. In 1996 the Ontario cabinet unanimously refused the federal offer.[12]

This refusal can be explained by the confluence of various dynamics. Ontario had demanded an immigration agreement in the preceding decades, but those demands were never contingent on assuming greater responsibility for integrating immigrants. The federal offer was understood as entirely Ottawa's idea and as coinciding more broadly with Ottawa's desire to shed its responsibilities to the detriment of the provinces. Also, the offer coincided with the election of the provincial Conservatives and the launching of the "Common Sense Revolution," a program in which, as we have seen, integration was not a priority.

Also, the Ontario government maintained a strict conception of the division of responsibilities in these sectors. The Harris government viewed immigration as a federal responsibility and integration as a shared one.[13] Civil servants active at the time point out that long before the Harris government was elected, and even more so starting in 1995, the province had formulated substantial grievances regarding the indirect costs of immigration for Ontario.[14] That the federal offer did not address those long-standing demands only strengthened the Harris government's opposition to the federal project.

This administrative and fiscal decentralization coincided with what was probably the high point of tensions in the area of intergovernmental transfers as they related to Ontario. In the early 1990s, Queen's Park had adopted a "fair share" discourse to demand substantial financial transfers for immigration and integration. After 1995 that discourse grew more strident in the context of massive cuts to federal transfers and a difficult economic situation. More generally, Ontario was unable to agree with the federal government in several other areas affected by fiscal federalism, in particular with respect to the labour market.[15]

By contrast, BC responded positively to the federal offer based on Settlement Renewal, and in 1997 that province signed an agreement for the transfer of responsibilities for the administration of settlement services. That agreement was for five years and came into effect in 1998. It also systematized financial transfers for integration and gave the province some power over selection, power that would later be increased under the PNP. Finally, under the agreement, opportunities for the province to influence the planning and development of federal policies were increased (Hiebert and Sherell 2011).

The BC government's decision to accept this transfer was strongly supported by organizations delivering services, community organizations, and ethnic associations in the province.[16] This decision emerged from the alignment with the objectives of the NDP government of the time, which was trying to revitalize its intervention in a difficult fiscal environment. The federal offer also coincided with the province's desire to intervene more robustly in integration, in line with principles of social justice. In particular, the NDP government sought to offer programs that could be adapted to regional disparities instead of being "caught up in that national structure."[17] Similarly, many thought that the federal offer might allow the province to forge important links between settlement services and its other programs (education, health). As pointed out by a senior analyst active at the time:

> We got to a place where we said, "The province provides education, health care, social services … We provide all of those services and then the federal government has this whole program where they provide money to organizations to provide which are really community services for immigrants …" So, what we were saying was, in order to provide a better set of integrated community services to immigrants, we would be in a better position to link the settlement programs to all the other areas of programs that we have. It would be a better integration of services.[18]

Given the provincial objectives of social justice, many considered the province to be the appropriate level for formulating and delivering settlement and integration services:

> The term that we used back then was "made in BC." We wanted a made in BC approach to settlement services. The thinking was … that the provinces were better positioned [to deliver] education services, settlement services … and that … it made sense for the provinces to be doing it. So there was a sense that there [was a need to develop] a BC approach to all of this.[19]

This comparative advantage was coupled with the fact that the provincial government had by then been active for many years in the delivery of programs that mitigated the shortcomings of federal policies.

Ujjal Dosanjh, the minister responsible for immigration at that time, explained: "We believe that we can provide those services better, and the federal government seems to agree" (L.A., BC, 29 April 1997, 2907).

In this sense, the federal offer was in line with the objectives and political ideology of the province when it came to social policies. It would allow the political elite and public service actors to consolidate their relationship with the immigrant service sector and thereby preserve their central position in the province. At the same time, the province took the view that in order to meet these social objectives, it was important for it to have substantial authority over migration flows (L.A., BC, 27 June 1996, 62–3). This led it to demand better planning of national selection policy. But unlike in Manitoba or Quebec, the idea was not for the province to have access to immigrant selection tools. Commenting on the implementation in 1998 of the immigration agreement signed in 1997, the minister declared in the House: "I think there's a consensus that British Columbians don't want us to have a duplicate system of selecting immigrants for British Columbia. What we do want, however, is more consultation and more input into policy and planning for the national immigration policy" (L.A., BC, 19 May 1998, 7876).

Although the agreement laid the foundations for provincial selection powers, it wasn't until the province-building mechanism centred on immigration was activated in BC that that province would become involved in immigrant selection.

The federal offer to transfer settlement services also addressed BC's financial needs at a time when it wanted to revitalize its relations with the federal government. BC – and several other provinces at the time – took the position that any intergovernmental agreement could only be considered if it came with a minimum level of funding. Faced with these reservations, Ottawa improved the financial package it was offering as part of Settlement Renewal and increased funding for its own settlement program. This allowed BC to move beyond "fair share" rhetoric in the area of the integration of immigrants. A provincial civil servant explained:

> That was certainly a key milestone in terms of engagement between the federal and the provincial governments ... The big issue was that we were basically saying ... was "If that's the kind of money that you are going to put on the table, we're not interested." We were very interested in principle, we understood the arguments. We believed that settlement services

were seriously [underfunded]. And when we compared this to the province of Quebec, we thought it was unjust ... It was so unbalanced across the country in terms of resources that were available to do the settlement for the immigrants that we didn't want to take on the responsibility that had so little money attached to it and so little resources.[20]

To this satisfactory offer was added the conclusion of other agreements, including an agreement on labour and another that made it possible to implement services for immigrants from Asia (L.A., BC, 16 June 1997, 4494).

This funding increase allowed the province both to meet its social objectives in a difficult fiscal context and to launch new interventions. Even so, probably because of the absence of a province-building mechanism centred on immigration in this period, the province continued to emphasize that there was a federal responsibility in the area of integration. As pointed out by Ujjal Dosanjh, in a context of devolution, this responsibility was seen as primarily financial: "If the federal government ever decides not to fund us for the devolution of services, which is about $24 million at this time, at that point I think we have the room to walk away from providing those services if there's no money. And the federal government knows that" (L.A., BC, 19 May 1998, 1635). Not until province-building centred on immigration was activated was BC able to move away from this strict conception of the division of responsibilities.

The immigrant integration experience acquired by the province since 1992 also made the federal offer more attractive. Unlike Ontario, BC maintained and even expanded its public service personnel for these services. Thus at the time of the offer, the province had a more substantial administrative and political capacity and was able to carry out more responsibilities.

This provincial experience generated societal support for the decentralization of responsibilities in integration – for example, among organizations delivering services – as indicated during interviews with representatives of community organizations in the province.[21] And as pointed out by a former BC civil servant, now active at the federal level: "We thought that we did a better job with the funding that we had, for the settlement activities. We provided core funding for settlement services. We provided funding for people that were ineligible for federal settlement programs[,] asylum seekers[,] and we got encouragement from stakeholders. Settlement agencies [said that] we were [and] we would be … a better administrator for settlement services."[22]

This combination of capacities, experience, and societal support made the federal offer to transfer responsibilities for the settlement program attractive, but also profitable, for BC. Although this decision was made before the province activated the province-building mechanism, the changes brought about through these agreements would be crucial to its activation.

The Activation of the Province-Building Mechanism Centred on Immigration

The different responses of Ontario and BC to the decentralization mechanism indicate that federalization was not simply the result of federal decisions – it was also depended greatly on the evolution of provincial interests and actions. The activation coincided with the election of new governments: in Ontario, Dalton McGuinty's Liberal Party (2003–2013), and in BC, Gordon Campbell's Liberal Party (2001–2011). These changes in government, though they were not decisive, created favourable conditions for placing immigration on the agenda. Activation created a break with the government positions that had made immigration essentially a domain of social policy; immigration was now viewed as a resource to be developed for the benefit of the provincial economy and society. As these cases demonstrate, this new consensus emerged and was conveyed by elite actors in both provinces, in relative autonomy from society.

Ontario

The McGuinty government, elected in Ontario in 2003, accelerated the activation of the province-building mechanism centred on immigration. That election was the first in Ontario in which the immigration issue received a high level of attention from the leading parties. The NDP continued to view immigration as a social justice issue, while the Conservatives pushed a "law and order" approach that aimed at limiting fraudulent claims by immigrants and that targeted integration policies as too costly (Maddren 2003; Pedwell 2003). These questions were not placed on the agenda through social mobilization. Community actors' influence on the federal government and the strong relationships that resulted, as well as the fact that the provincial public service responsible for immigration had been sharply cut, reinforced the idea that immigration was outside provincial jurisdiction. Instead, political elites became the primary champions of questions relating to immigration.

The Ontario Liberals' election platform praised immigrants and highlighted the contributions they made in Ontario. It also emphasized the importance of reinforcing settlement and integration services (Liberal Party of Ontario 2003). During the campaign, the party leader expressed a desire to forge an agreement with the federal government to fund integration services (Oliver and Ibbitson 2003). Yet it was clear that the integration of immigrants in Ontario had the objective of maximizing their economic contribution: "We will put our brain gain to work. No workforce benefits more from immigration than ours. Sixty percent of new Ontarians have post-secondary education and yet thousands face barriers to employment at their skill level. The Harris-Eves government has failed to capitalize on this brain gain. We will harness the skills and expertise of new Ontarians" (Liberal Party of Ontario 2003, 13). McGuinty also made a strong commitment to implementing measures for access to regulated professions (McCarten 2003).

McGuinty's victory brought to power a government whose agenda focused on social investment and democratic renewal (Perrella et al. 2007) and that viewed immigration as a key asset for the province. In its first Speech from the Throne, the government reiterated the position it had defended throughout the campaign: "Your new government believes our province's diversity is a tremendous source of strength. It will work with the federal government to finalize immigration and labour market development agreements that build on this strength. It will keep its commitment to ensure that highly qualified, internationally trained tradespeople and professionals can work in their chosen field, here in their chosen province" (L.A., ON, 20 November 2003, 8).

The Liberals had not won the election because of McGuinty's discourse or his party's approach to immigration. The primary reasons, rather, were the unpopularity of the Conservative Party after close to eight years in government and memories of the failed NDP government that had preceded it. Nevertheless, the Liberal victory activated the province-building mechanism centred on immigration. According to a principal analyst active on the immigration file, the change of government enabled the diffusion of new ideas and interests in the public service.[23] The commitment of certain members of the Liberal Party and the Liberal cabinet to immigration as a tool for development made it possible to place the issue on the agenda. This movement came primarily from the political elite, in large part because of the absence of links between the provincial government and traditional immigration social actors, a consequence of policy restructuring under the Harris government. In this sense, although it coincided with an election, the activation of province-building centred on immigration in Ontario was initiated by the elite, even while provincial society continued to view immigration as the government's responsibility.

The Foundations of a Consensus

These interests were reflected in the rise of a vision that advocated an economic reading of immigration and that saw the presence of immigrants as a resource for Ontario. A large immigrant population was no longer seen as a burden on the government – in terms of social costs and public security – but rather as an asset. This shift in vision was clear in a statement McGuinty made to the Legislative Assembly in 2005:

> We understand who creates our wealth: the people of this province. You've often heard me say this, but it bears repeating: Our strength is our people. We understand that our wealth is created by the skills and hard work of our people. That is our competitive advantage … We understand that immigration strengthens our society and our economy. (L.A., ON, 24 February 2005, 1345)

However, the vision that emerged in Ontario did not highlight the importance of an increase in migration flows. The desired mode of intervention was based instead on the idea of making the best use of the presence of immigrants, to "maximize the Social and Economic Benefit of Immigration," with the objective of "increas[ing] the percentage of internationally trained people becoming qualified to work in Ontario" (Ontario 2004b, 37).

In this conception, the role of the Ontario government was to ensure the rapid economic integration of newcomers (L.A., ON, 14 June 2004, 1455). In its 2004 budget the Ontario government highlighted the government's responsibility towards immigrants. Its vision was no longer linked to social justice but rather to economic justice:

> Every year about 125,000 people arrive from around the world to make Ontario their home. They enrich our province both culturally and

> economically. Indeed, Ontario was built on immigration; and you know, sir, that without it, our economy would grind to a halt. We owe it to new Ontarians and we owe it to ourselves to speed up their integration into our workforce. As I mentioned earlier, we are more than doubling the number of assessment and training positions for international medical school graduates. But we will also start to tear down the barriers that immigrants face trying to enter their trades and their professions. We are going to introduce close to $10 million this year, and it will grow to $12.5 million in 2005-2006, to improve foreign-trained workers' access to the jobs they are trained to perform. (L.A., ON, 18 May 2004, 1655)

Thus the provincial government's role was to ensure the integration of immigrants into the labour market. This objective was important for the development of the Ontario economy and society as well as for the newcomers themselves.

This novel concept was accompanied by a new version of the traditional "fair share" argument. Still seeking more funding for integration, the Liberal government presented its demands from the perspective of the impact of precarious economic integration of new Ontarians on the economy and society (L.A. ON, 13 June 2004, 1510). In 2005, despite the increase in resources transferred to the province, the premier condemned the ongoing fiscal inequality in the area of integration:

> We understand that immigration strengthens our society and our economy, but yesterday's [federal] budget did nothing to correct the unfairness that sees $3,800 invested in immigrants who land in Montreal and just $800 in those who land in Toronto. Some have argued that we should not be complaining, that we are receiving our per capita share of the new immigration money. But that, too, is unfair: When we receive over half of the country's immigrants, it is unfair that we receive only 40% of the new federal immigration funding and 34% of the old federal immigration funding. (L.A., ON, 24 May 2005, 1350)

The Foundations of Institutionalization

With a new consensus on the value of immigration as an economic resource, it seemed justifiable to reorient and improve provincial activities in this area. In 2004 the provincial government established the Ministry of Citizenship and Immigration, replacing the Ministry of

Citizenship established in 1985. This was the first time since the end of the Second World War that Ontario had clearly identified a public body as responsible for immigration, giving it significant visibility. This centralization strengthened the province's analytical capacity in the area of immigration policy[24] and shifted the emphasis of public action from social justice to the economic dimension of immigration (Biles et al. 2011). Thus, while remaining involved in immigrant settlement, the province began to reorient its interventions in integration. An interdepartmental group on the integration of economic immigrants was created in 2003, and efforts to recognize competencies and diplomas increased (Ontario 2004a). The province also continued its activities in business and investment immigration.

The province's demands on the federal government increased accordingly. During the 2003 election campaign the Liberal Party tried to distinguish itself from its adversaries as being the only party prepared to settle a series of contentious issues with the federal government (Oliver and Ibbitson 2003). Immigration was on this list, as were taxation and labour market policy. To put this new agenda into practice, the government began negotiations and gave the ministry responsible for immigration an explicit mandate to lay the foundations for a framework agreement (Ontario 2004a; 2004b).

Given the new consensus on the potential value of immigration, the province began to focus on improved distribution of financial resources, according to the new version of the idea of the "fair share," previously mentioned. The province explicitly demanded more powers with regard to selection, although it continued to prefer to influence the direction of federal policy.[25] The province also tried to influence federal policy with regard to the economic integration of skilled workers (L.A., ON, 14 April 2005, 1450–500).

At the beginning of the government's term, the province's representatives were relatively optimistic that they would be able to negotiate an agreement with the federal government (L.A., ON, 11 May 2004, 1450). Quickly, however, the province's hopes faded in the face of federal resistance. This only heightened the intensity of the provincial demands. Those demands would highlight more and more explicitly the imbalance between the proportion of immigrants received by the province and the percentage of national funding it received. Those same demands would be adopted by the opposition; clearly, a consensus was emerging regarding the province's new role in immigration (L.A., ON, 4 April 2005, 1330).

British Columbia

In 1997, after BC signed an agreement that transferred responsibility for administering and delivering settlement services, but before the Liberals were elected in 2001, the province went through a period of enthusiasm and growth with respect to immigration and integration. In 2000 the Ministry of Multiculturalism and Immigration was created and many services were centralized within it. This reflected the growth of the province's administrative and policy capacities with regard to settlement and integration, a consequence of the monies and civil servants transferred by the federal government. Moreover, after the agreement on the transfer of settlement services was implemented in 1998, the province created the BC Settlement and Immigration Program (BCSIP) to oversee the funding of organizations providing settlement services for the province. The province also began to experiment with selecting immigrants, with the creation of the British Columbia Nominee Program. This program remained very small and was designed to complement the federal Temporary Foreign Worker Program (British Columbia 2001b). Despite this progress in the area of selection, the government continued to have a strict conception of the sharing of responsibilities between the levels of government: immigration was still presented as a federal responsibility (L.A., BC, 29 June 2000, 16960–16965).

The province-building mechanism centred on immigration was set in motion after the 2001 election of a Liberal government led by Gordon Campbell and, in particular, after the re-election of that government in 2005. By now, following the activation of the decentralization mechanism in the late 1990s, more resources were available to the province. Despite Settlement Renewal, it was not until after Campbell was elected that real links were forged between immigration and economic development, replacing the social conception of immigration that had prevailed until then in BC. This link was facilitated by the presence of policy entrepreneurs within the province's administrative elite (Paquet 2015); for them, renewed provincial action in immigration seemed a possible bulwark against challenges to their power.

The election of the Liberals coincided with the launch of a restructuring project by the provincial government. Spending cuts and reorganizations affected both the form of the public service and its implementation strategies. The Campbell government also instituted measures to reposition the province within the Canadian, regional, and global economy (McBride and McNutt 2007; Leo and Enns 2009). In this context, immigration emerged as a resource for the province's political elite and, in particular, for the provincial Liberal Party. During its first term, the Campbell government promoted a new discourse on immigration. In 2001 the party platform had openly criticized the inaction of the NDP government with regard to selecting skilled immigrants. That document declared that a government "[has] to attract and retain more foreign-trained doctors and nurses. Inexplicably, the NDP chose not to use the federal-provincial immigration program that Ujjal Dosanjh signed two years ago" (Liberal Party of British Columbia 2001, 24). Immigration and integration were absent, however, from the NDP's election platform in 2001, as well as from the platforms of the other provincial parties.

During the 2005 campaign, immigration took on even greater importance for the Liberals – without, however, being taken up by concrete societal forces (public opinion, social movements, interest groups). In economic integration programs, clear commitments were made with regard to recruiting doctors and professionals for which there were shortages, as well as with respect to increased funding for linguistic integration (Liberal Party of British Columbia 2006). Also, the Liberal Party presented its government as a leader in Canada when it came to attracting immigrant investors. For its part, the NDP continued to view immigration as a social issue, presenting immigrants as a population that was often poor and disadvantaged – even more so since the Liberals' rise to power (New Democratic Party of British Columbia 2006). The NDP would maintain this position until 2005.

A New Consensus

Starting in 2001, in accordance with the interests of the elite, perceptions of immigration began to shift: it was no longer primarily a social issue; now it was seen as a resource for the provincial economy and society. BC's new official objective was to maximize the benefits of immigration. This vision – much like the discourse that emerged in Ontario a few years later – was distinguished by a double emphasis that combined the importance of provincial intervention to ensure the economic integration of immigrants already in the province with more vigorous efforts to attract immigrants who were skilled or who possessed economic capital. This led to public actions that would eventually institutionalize the reactive mode of intervention.

In this new vision, immigrants brought skills the provincial economy needed as well as capital, and they could inject the province with more entrepreneurial spirit. The government's role was to ensure their integration so that society would benefit: "Enabling and expediting immigrant settlement helps to ensure that the social and economic benefits of immigration are maximized" (British Columbia 2004, 46). This recognition of the crucial role immigrants played in the provincial economy[26] was expressed as follows by the Minister of State for Immigration and Multicultural Services, Gulzar Singh Cheema, in 2004:

> British Columbians benefit greatly from the economic engine of immigration. Immigration is an important part of our history. The diversity of our population translates directly into economic advantage and opportunity for all British Columbians. British Columbia's diversity is increasingly recognized as an asset in the domestic and international markets, and is a major contributor to Canadian economic prosperity. New immigrants to British Columbia can count on our government's commitment to provide the means to become full participants in all aspects of our society. (L.A., BC, 12 February 2004, 8515)

Within this consensus, the provincial government was presented as having two major roles. First, it was the government's responsibility to ensure that immigrants in BC could participate fully in the province's growth; this was to come about primarily through economic integration. Second, the province needed to ensure that its economy would benefit from the contributions of immigrants. To that end, it needed to position itself as a prime economic destination for qualified individuals (British Columbia 2005). The ministry therefore proposed that "to maximize the benefits of immigration, BC work[] to attract and retain immigrants who are best able to contribute to British Columbia's economy" (British Columbia 2005, 60).

New Institutions

This emerging consensus began to be consolidated in the policies and institutions established by the province. This consolidation did not mean immediate growth. Since the province had a well-developed structure as well as a strong capacity to provide integration services even before the province-building mechanism was activated, the principal aim was to transform the province's approach. The government decided to restrict its spending and to revise its method for awarding contracts to community organizations for the delivery of social services (including integration and settlement services) (British Columbia 2005). As a civil servant active at the time recalled:

> [T]he government changed in 2001 – we got a Liberal, much more conservative government … And a key priority of the government at the time was introducing competitive bidding … [T]hat was a cold bucket of water poured over the sector … Not a lot of focus in programming at the time … A lot of service providers at that time got very disillusioned. I remember, when I started, seeing letters to the federal government asking to take it back.[27]

These cuts reflected the budgetary approach taken by the Liberals throughout the provincial government. As pointed out by this civil servant, they were also the result of a decrease in the number of new immigrants to the province.

But this decrease in funding for organizations providing services did not mean that the province was prepared to withdraw from the delivery of settlement and integration services. At this point, a key characteristic of the reactive mode of intervention was established: the dualization of provincial intervention, which combined services to meet the needs created by the presence of a large immigrant population with services aimed at maximizing the economic benefits that could be gained from their presence. However, starting in 2001, these two sets of services were increasingly presented as focused on maximizing immigration as a resource.

The Liberal government also dismantled the ministry responsible for immigration, which the NDP government had created in 2000. From now on, immigration and integration would be parcelled out among several ministries.[28] The decision to restructure the public service no doubt suggests that the government wanted to distance itself from the approach advocated by its predecessors. In the end, the government's economic inclinations with regard to integration gained ascendency in the ministries.[29] These changes, which were highly unpopular with service providers and with organizations representing immigrants, reflected the relative autonomy of the interests of the elite with respect to society within the province-building mechanism.

During the same period, the province sought to strengthen its intervention in immigrant attraction and selection. The province resorted more to its Nominee Program, improving its administrative capacity and seeking more recruits, whose number, though, would remain relatively small (for example, only two hundred in 2002–3). The province emphasized the recruitment of highly qualified people, such as aerospace engineers, biotechnology workers, and others with highly sought-after skills, such as health and education professionals (British Columbia 2004). Despite some growth, BC's Nominee Program was still a niche effort, and this limited use reflected the will of the government of the time.[30]

The province also took serious interest in the recruitment and retention of foreign students, who were viewed as an economic resource. It also undertook activities in international promotion aimed specifically at health professionals (doctors and nurses), for which the province had a great need (L.A., BC, 3 April 2002, 2404–5). These efforts were combined with general activities in marketing and attraction aimed at immigrant entrepreneurs and investors (British Columbia 2005).

The Liberal government also invested in economic integration and remained active in immigrant settlement. It continued to develop programs for the recognition of skills and for access to employment established in 2001, investing further funds in this in 2004 (British Columbia 2005). The province innovated by creating a bridge program in employment for qualified immigrants – the BC Skills Connect – in 2004, and began to offer language courses in the workplace aimed at immigrants who were already employed (British Columbia 2004). In addition, the new government reformed the funding program for settlement services by renaming it the BC Settlement and Adaptation Program (BCSAP). This affected the program's administration and the funding allocated to it. The government began to present the objectives of this program as being related to imperatives of economic integration (L.A., BC, 9 March 2004, 9322).

The activation of the province-building mechanism in BC spurred new demands on the federal government. The province issued grievances regarding the formula for calculating transfers for settlement and integration and demanded more fiscal transfers.[31] It also began to show interest in expanding its capacity to select economic immigrants, while maintaining a relatively strict concept of the federal role in that field.[32] But unlike in other provinces, the presence of an operating immigration agreement with financing gave those demands an incremental nature. During this period, relations between the province and the federal government were characterized by collaboration.

A Second Encounter: Decentralization in the 2000s

After province-building centred on immigration was activated in Ontario and in BC, the demands of the two provinces generated further pressure to activate the decentralization mechanism. The unique evolution of these two provinces' interests and their distinct positions in the federalization process did not, however, create similar interactions between province-building and decentralization.

Ontario

After the province-building mechanism was activated, Ontario increased its interventions, mainly in integration, but growth was still limited by the perception of a general fiscal imbalance affecting Ontario. With a broader will to rectify Ontario's position in Canadian fiscal federalism and a certain openness on the part of the federal government, the province committed itself to concluding an agreement that would permit it to benefit from immigration.

The two governments came to a provisional agreement in 2004. That protocol set forth the foundations for a possible final agreement (Seidle 2010a). The ministry responsible for immigration and integration was given a clear mandate to negotiate. Discussions lasted a little more than a year and were marked by strong federal resistance.[33]

According to many observers, the provincial government's main objective at the beginning of negotiations was the complete devolution of powers with regard to integrating new arrivals.[34] The negotiators pointed out that the agreement on immigration with Quebec had codified the financial relations between the levels of government and given the province full independence in the administration of the monies transferred for settlement and integration. According to a senior federal civil servant, "Ontario wanted very much the Quebec model and then, that was not possible."[35] The federal immigration minister, Joe Volpe, rejected the idea of an agreement like Quebec's, contending that that accord had been an error by the Conservative government of Brian Mulroney when faced with a particular situation (*La Presse canadienne* 2005b).

Faced with this refusal, the Ontario government changed its strategy. It tried to get the federal government to recognize the existence of an imbalance in funding for integration, pointing to a "gap" that made it almost impossible to achieve growth objectives. At the same time, it became much more energetic in expressing its grievances in the intergovernmental arena, criticizing the federal government for its financial decisions and for signing more generous agreements with other provinces (Cornellier 2005). In light of the distributive consequences of the institutional regime as it evolved, the federal government resisted Ontario's demands. In particular, with regard to Quebec's immigration agreement, Ottawa continued to insist there were not enough funds available to meet provincial demands (L.A., ON, 18 April 2005, 6314).

In the spring of 2005, tensions between Ottawa and Queen's Park finally began to dissipate, in large part because of the electoral strategy of Prime Minister Paul Martin.[36] In February 2005, Volpe finally recognized the existence of a fiscal imbalance for Ontario, particularly with respect to immigration (Leslie 2005). In May 2005, an agreement between Dalton McGuinty and Paul Martin was announced; in November of that year, it was signed. In announcing the agreement, the Ontario premier declared to the Legislative Assembly:

> With respect to the immigration agreement, for example, new Canadians arriving in Ontario, instead of benefiting from $800 worth of supports, will now get $3,400 worth of supports. I think that is a significant increase. By the way, that funding does not flow to the Ontario government; it flows to our settlement services, ESL services and the like. With respect to the labour market agreement, funding will go from about $1,100 per worker to $1,800 per worker. Again, that money does not flow to the Ontario government; it flows to our training agencies. This is an agreement that benefits the people of Ontario. (L.A., ON, 9 May 2005, 6888–9)

It is important, however, to point out that the additional resources and powers desired by Ontario were earmarked by the province for its intervention in the integration of immigrants. This reflected the very limited role for the province in immigrant selection under the reactive mode of intervention. In reality, even after the province-building mechanism was activated in Ontario, it did not demand immigrant selection powers. During the negotiations, the province resisted the inclusion of an appendix on the creation of a PNP. This resistance can be explained by fear of the costs related to implementing and administering a provincial immigration program, which could have been particularly high because of Ontario's strong pull for immigrants. The province would claim that such a program would not be necessary if the federal government adequately administered its immigration program and, in particular, the selection of skilled workers. Once a financial commitment from the federal government was obtained, such an appendix would, however, be included in the final agreement – a formal condition of the federal government for the conclusion of an agreement.

The five-year Canada–Ontario agreement on immigration had three principal elements, the first being a federal commitment to fund settlement and integration services. These services were now presented as co-managed, which would prove to be difficult in practice.[37] In exchange for additional resources, the province committed itself to investing more in the integration of immigrants. Second, the agreement recognized a significant role for cities and provided tools to take into account their needs for program and policy development. Third, the agreement established the guidelines for an Ontario PNP. According to a senior federal civil servant, this agreement had as a direct effect "a huge injection of cash in Ontario."[38] It even created problems related to the province's capacity to spend the monies allocated (Vineberg 2012).

British Columbia

Given the impact of the decentralization mechanism in BC in the 1990s, the demands of the Gordon Campbell government were consistent with the powers the province then held. In this regard, BC's experience illustrates the incremental and self-reinforcing nature of the two mechanisms over time.

The province's demands were related in large part to the renewal of an agreement on the transfer of settlement services, planned for 2003. The two parties agreed to a one-year extension to allow time to negotiate the details of a deal. A new agreement would be signed in April 2004. This five-year agreement was presented by the Campbell government as including "further mechanisms to increase the benefits of immigration to BC" (British Columbia 2005, 7–8). The new measures included additional funding for advanced second-language courses, new projects to attract foreign students and business immigrants, and initiatives to regionalize immigration. The agreement also gave the province additional means to influence federal policy and made possible new developments for BC's PNP.

In these negotiations, the provincial government's primary aim was to counteract the reduction in funds transferred and to preserve its gains. But after the province-building mechanism centred on immigration was activated, provincial concerns expanded.

The experience of having delivered settlement services since 1998 had a certain effect. According to a senior civil servant active at the time, this finally dissipated fears within BC's public service and society:

> I remember when we first started to do the program, it took considerable efforts and lots of discussions with our decision makers on whether we wanted to do it or not and why would we need to do it and was it worthwhile ... there was a mindset around ... concerns about federal offloading [...] We were concerned that it would cost us money, that they would download the services and then pull money out ... You know, that kind of stuff. There was a lot of suspicion if you will and that probably speaks to the general relationship of the federal and the provincial governments as much as anything. Not just about integration but rather about the bigger picture. And there was considerable suspicion so whenever ... The mindset certainly around the ministry of Finance at that time was ... and probably for good reasons ... that they were "Oh, this is another offloading-downloading experience here and so let's be careful." But then I think ... the big shift was "That's not happening, it didn't happen in fact" ... The settlement transfers were significant for the province. They were considered to be adequate, they increased ... They were healthy transfers with good reporting and good accountability, but not accountability that was over the top. So, everybody started to look at it and say "Ok, we're getting good resources here to do this. We're to be accountable but we want to be accountable anyway. Now, this is working."[39]

This evaluation of past experience led the province to conclude that an even more substantial agreement could be reached without too great an impact on its public finances.[40]

Second, in line with its past experience in economic selection and with its new interest in the contributions of immigrants, we can glean BC's desire to get involved in selection. According to an analyst active at the time, the idea of more robust and coordinated intervention in international immigration developed.[41] This trend would strengthen over the years, while decentralization reinforced the province-building mechanism.

On 16 February 2005, the minister responsible for immigration, Patrick Wong, described the new bilateral agreement and concluded enthusiastically that all its provisions "will help create wealth for all

British Columbians and increase the long-term growth of the GDP of our province" (L.A., BC, 16 November 2005, 11929). So it is possible to observe that the province perceived a new agreement, facilitated by good working relationships between the governments, as a means to continue the growth in immigration that had begun with the election of the Liberals in 2001. The signing of a new intergovernmental agreement to transfer integration services in 2004 stabilized and increased transfers to BC while giving the province increased capacity in selection. This agreement thus reinforced trends already present and established a relationship of interdependence between the two mechanisms, since province-building increased pressure on the decentralization mechanism and the latter, in turn, increased the intensity of province-building centred on immigration. In BC, this would maintain pressure on the federal government to increase funding for settlement services and for greater provincial capacities in selection (British Columbia 2007).

Consensualization and Institutionalization

After the province-building mechanism was activated in Ontario and BC, new interests and demands activated the decentralization mechanism. The experience of these two provinces shows, however, two types of interaction between mechanisms. Ontario illustrated a more traditional, situational, and conflictual type of interaction, in which provincial pressures ended up limiting the federal government's capacity to act or increased the costs associated with its resistance. The case of BC, by contrast, illustrates incremental, self-reinforcing interactions.

In both provinces, the interaction of the two mechanisms would foster a consensus on a new role for the provincial government in the area of immigration and would encourage its institutionalization. In this way, the principles of the reactive mode of intervention were established beyond any doubt in the policies and programs of the two provinces. During this period, new intergovernmental dynamics in immigration were also set in motion, dynamics that continue to this day.

In Ontario, the immigration agreement of 2005 greatly strengthened the province-building mechanism centred on immigration. The positions put forward by the McGuinty government regarding the province's role in immigration and the role of immigration as a resource for provincial society would be firmly established as a consensus after 2005. This consensualization was observable in the changes of discourses and in the behaviour of the opposition parties. All actors, in fact, came to support a new role for the provincial government and to conceive of immigration as a resource. A particularly striking example was the place given to intervention in immigration and integration in the platform of John Tory's Conservative Party in the 2007 election. Having been viewed during the previous election as a "law and order" issue and, in general, as a costly element to control, by 2007 immigration had become a resource to be exploited. The Conservatives promised to increase the supply of ESL classes as well as the number of employment internship programs (Conservative Party of Ontario 2007). In addition, their platform devoted an entire section to the reception of skilled immigrants, proposing economic integration measures and committing the party to negotiate a more substantial immigration agreement.[42]

Implicit in this shift in discourse was a fading of partisan divisions around immigration in Ontario. The political consensus extended to society as a whole. More precisely, at the centre of this consensus was growing recognition of the province's role as an important partner in the area of immigration. Many actors, including representatives of community organizations, remarked that the agreement rebuilt links between the public service and the settlement and integration sector. The same thing happened with the municipalities, which, besides being parties to the agreement, were the target of government policies.[43] Starting in 2005 we can observe a more substantial mobilization of economic actors – for example, the Toronto Region Immigrant Employment Council (TRIEC) – and of hybrid organizations in immigration and integration – for example, the Maytree Foundation, which forged direct relations with the government.[44]

Following this consensualization, the principles central to the reactive mode of intervention became institutionalized in government polices and programs. The province-building mechanism resulted in a reinforcement of key characteristics – namely, limited and targeted intervention in immigration as well as dualist integration policies that met the needs created by immigration and were aimed at improving access to the labour market for highly qualified immigrants.

The province maintained its autonomous intervention and collaborated with the federal government in the area of settlement and the general teaching of languages. At the same time, Ontario created many programs to meet the needs of specific clients – for example, an interpreters program – and anti-racism and multiculturalism policies. Finally, in addition to policies on community development in the regions,

Ontario strengthened its relationships with the municipalities after 2005. In collaboration with the federal government, it signed a memorandum of understanding on immigration with the city of Toronto in 2006 and took part in the development of the Local Immigration Partnerships program. The province also established an e-portal in 2006 to provide information on services available to newcomers.

Provincial intervention targeting integration into the job market for skilled immigrants was reinforced after 2005. The Ontario Ministry of Citizenship and Immigration created important working relationships with the ministries responsible for implementing an agreement on the labour market to ensure the implementation of policies and programs serving immigrant clients. In 2007 the province developed a bridge program on employment, including a loan program to cover training costs and internships for highly qualified individuals, which would be continued and expanded beyond 2010 (Ontario 2007; 2010). In terms of legislation, the province innovated with a law on access to regulated professions in 2006 and worked to develop transparent, equitable procedures within the professional orders. It also collaborated with the federal government in the area; meanwhile, a pan-Canadian framework to recognize competencies was being established (Ontario 2011).

Compared to the explosion of initiatives in integration that followed the 2005 agreement, the province was very slow to develop its own PNP owing to the limited capacity of the public service, but also because it was able to maintain its capacity to attract skilled immigrants without such a tool.[45] Only in 2008 did the province begin to use the PNP, albeit in a very limited way, focusing on candidates previously selected by employers and on graduate students who had previously studied in Ontario.

Institutionalization maintained the pressure on the decentralization mechanism, through demands regarding the acquisition of resources and powers that would allow the provincial government to play its role in maximizing immigration as a resource. Within the framework of the 2005 agreement, political actors and the Ontario public service from the outset accused the federal government of paternalism. The federal government repeatedly resisted provincial initiatives and was slow to transfer promised funds to the province (L.A., ON, 30 October 2006, 5848). These dissatisfactions and frustrations were exacerbated by the agreement's time constraints, which made it hard to spend all the money on time. Federal funding cuts to settlement service providers also created frictions, as did the announcement of a numerical limit on

PNP annual intake. These changes affected Ontario in particular, where many organizations were directly hit by the cuts just as the province was finally attempting to expand its immigrant selection program.

In this context, new provincial demands arose for more resources, more powers, and greater consideration of Ontario's circumstances. Regarding negotiations on a new immigration agreement, the "fair share" argument resurfaced:

> While the first immigration agreement produced highly positive results for Ontario and for Ontario's newcomers, we must nonetheless remember that other federal–provincial immigration agreements have disproportionately benefited other provinces. For example, in 2009–10, federal government funding for newcomers was approximately 50% more on a per capita basis in Quebec than it was in Ontario. We don't think that's fair. It's not fair to Ontario and it's certainly not fair to our newcomers. (L.A., ON, 28 September 2010, 2342)

In December 2010, as an indicator of consensualization and institutionalization, the Legislative Assembly passed a motion to renegotiate its immigration agreement with the federal government. During the debates leading up to the vote, the opposition criticized the McGuinty government's management of the agreement as well as how it allocated the funds. But at no time during that debate was a step backward (i.e., towards greater passivity in immigration and integration) ever discussed. All of the actors supported extending the agreement, and many opposition MPPs even wondered what prevented Ontario from signing a devolution agreement similar to Quebec's (L.A., ON, 30 November 2010, 3803–4). After 2010, the province mobilized strongly on immigration in the public and intergovernmental arenas. This mobilization intensified after negotiations to renew the agreement failed. By 2010 the province's aggressive actions in this policy sector were reminiscent of its past behaviour in province-building.

In BC, the renewal of the agreement to transfer integration services to the province in 2004 strengthened the province-building mechanism. Until 2010 the Campbell government defended the discourse that immigration was a resource the government should maximize by intervening in economic integration and by attracting and selecting skilled immigrants and immigrants with capital they were prepared to invest (British Columbia 2009). This objective applied to interventions both in integration and in selection (British Columbia 2006), while the province's PNP was presented as a means to "increase the economic benefits of immigration to the province" (L.A., BC, 26 November 2007, 9453). The impact of these ideas would be reinforced by a growing concern about labour shortages in the province (British Columbia 2008).

One sign of consensualization was that other political parties accepted the ideas the Liberals had started promoting in 2001. In the 2009 election the NDP included in its platform elements related to immigrants as resources. The NDP's election platform remained aligned with an ideal of social justice, but now it also included measures relating specifically to the economic integration of immigrants (New Democratic Party of British Columbia 2009). However, the Conservative Party – a marginal party in the province – still did not mention immigration in its platform (Conservative Party of British Columbia 2009). Finally, in large part because of the growth of the PNP, economic actors were beginning to openly support and disseminate the provincial consensus. They favoured a provincial role in selection as a means to address labour shortages, especially outside the Vancouver region.[46]

After the 2004 agreement was signed, provincial intervention was institutionalized according to the characteristics typical of the reactive mode of intervention. The province still has an important settlement program as well as an economic integration program specifically for skilled immigrants. Relative to Ontario, however, BC was injecting substantially more resources in the area of immigrant selection, especially after 2008. Also, the public service was by now aligned more closely with the new consensus. In 2006, responsibilities for immigration and integration were transferred to the Ministry of Economic Development; then in 2008, they were passed on to the Ministry of Advanced Education and Labour Market Development.

In the area of settlement and integration, the province maintained services under the Welcome BC program and the province's adaptation and settlement program. It funded language courses for adults, orientation services, and development in the settlement sector. Funding for these programs remained stable, and the province expanded its activities over time to include, among other things, an online portal, measures to respond to critical situations, anti-racism programs, and a settlement program in schools (British Columbia 2007; 2009). In accordance with the dualization characteristic of the reactive mode of intervention, these services were meant mainly to meet the needs of new unskilled immigrants not selected by the province.

This period also saw an increase in economic integration activities. The province maintained its BC Skills Connect program and all the initiatives established when the province-building mechanism was activated. As labour market management measures were being planned, immigration grew more and more important in the government as a whole, and the executive communicated this strongly to the public service.[47] Similarly, the province developed, autonomously or in collaboration with the federal government, policies to recognize prior learning and experience. It set up intermediary and advanced language courses aimed at improving employment access for skilled immigrants. Finally, the province worked to involve economic actors more closely in plans to recruit and integrate skilled immigrants by creating the Immigrant Employment Council of BC (British Columbia 2006; 2009).

During this period, BC's interventions in the selection of skilled immigrants saw explosive growth. The province increased its administrative capacity and enhanced its policies in the areas of recruitment and business immigration (British Columbia 2008). In particular, the province's PNP was constantly expanding, supported by discourses on interprovincial competition for skilled immigrants and on labour shortages in BC (British Columbia 2005). The program focused on candidates with job offers, whether these were highly qualified workers or people in in-demand professions, as well as on immigrants who wanted to start businesses or invest in the province (British Columbia 2009). A senior civil servant pointed out that the cabinet supported this expansion.[48]

Following this institutionalization, the province continued to demand that the federal government provide increased resources and powers. Unlike Ontario, however, the province remained active within a dynamic of self-reinforcement of the mechanisms of province-building and decentralization. As province-building centred on immigration became consolidated, decentralization continued incrementally, without political crises or substantial tensions between the levels of government.

In this context, the province demanded an increase in its funding, which it would receive for the period 2006 to 2008 (British Columbia 2007). Similarly, without much fanfare, the 2010 agreement to transfer settlement responsibilities was renewed, with an increase in transfers to the province. BC also demanded more powers in selection, especially an increase in the number of candidates it could select and an increased capacity to support employers who wanted to use the federal

Temporary Foreign Worker Program.[49] These demands would in large part be reflected in the appendices to the 2010 agreement. Similarly, during this period the province became very active with other governments in the development of coordinating institutions and in the establishment of regional or interprovincial strategies.[50]

Conclusion

In the provinces implementing reactive modes of intervention – Ontario and BC – activation of the province-building mechanism centred on immigration occurred in the 2000s, after two Liberal governments took power, and called into question the traditional approaches favoured until then. With these changes came the establishment of new consensuses that presented immigration as a resource to be exploited for the benefit of the provincial economy and society. These new conceptions of the role of the provincial government in relation to integration and immigration brought about a reorientation of provincial interventions and an increase in demands on the federal government in these policy areas. The interaction of the mechanisms of province-building and decentralization occurred in a tense intergovernmental context, due to the evolution of fiscal federalism and the restructuring of labour market management policy. This interaction, which would give the provinces resources and powers that would permit them to institutionalize their modes of intervention, was also strongly coloured by the distributive consequences created by past encounters between the two mechanisms when Quebec and Manitoba were activating the federalization process.

Ontario's trajectory demonstrates the relevance of conceptualizing political institutions, such as federalism, as institutional regimes. Augmenting the classical understanding of institutions as constraining action, the concept of regimes draws our attention to the distributional consequences of the formal and informal arrangements associated with federalism. The highlighting by Ontario's political elites of an injustice in the distribution of fiscal resources in the area of immigration, with reference to the 1991 agreement between Quebec and the federal government, shows how much the evolution of that province's interests within the institutional regime of governance of immigration was contingent on past practices and their consequences within that regime. A more subtle effect was also at stake in BC. The possibilities for a substantial provincial role in selection, created by the invention of the PNP in line with Manitoba's demands, were crucial to achieving less conflictual relationships between BC and the federal government. In fact, once the mechanism was activated in the province, the government was able to take over these new areas of influence and action within the regime of immigration governance in order to serve its interests. In both provinces, immigration was identified by the elite independent of social dynamics. Despite the presence of a sizeable immigrant population and of social networks representing that population's interests, it was only when the political actors and provincial administrators had identified public action in immigration as an appropriate response to their needs that province-building was activated.

Setting aside similarities, the emergence of the Ontario and BC provincial governments as key actors focusing on immigration as a resource illustrates two different sequences in the interaction of the mechanisms of province-building and decentralization. Ontario went through a traditional sequence in which the activation of the province-building mechanism moved the activation of the decentralization mechanism forward by increasing pressure on the federal government, pressures amplified by related political crises. This interaction can be viewed as a policy punctuation in a long period of stability (Jones and Baumgartner 2012). Conversely, in BC the decentralization mechanism was activated *before* the province-building mechanism. This pre-existing activation provided actors with additional resources during the activation of the province-building mechanism. What's more, once the second mechanism was triggered, it set in motion a self-reinforcing, interactive trajectory that led to constant incremental changes. These dynamics continued after 2010 and, given the political, demographic, and economic weight of these two provinces, had considerable impact on the federalization process.

Chapter 4

Alberta and Saskatchewan: Immigrants as "Natural Resources"

The 1991 immigration agreement between Quebec and the federal government and Settlement Renewal in 1995 had substantial impacts on demands related to immigration made by the provinces of Alberta and Saskatchewan. Those two provinces would sign agreements on provincial nominee programs (PNPs), but in the absence of a real mobilization on immigration, both would be slow to implement them extensively. For many years they observed the decentralization mechanism at work in other jurisdictions without experiencing its consequences.

Not until the end of Ralph Klein's Conservative government in Alberta (1992–2006) and of Roy Romanow's NDP government in Saskatchewan (1991–2001) – both political dynasties characterized by a push for austerity – did these provinces finally back away from an approach directed at immigration as a tool for attracting foreign capital. Their successors – Ed Stelmach in Alberta (CP, 2006–11) and Lorne Calvert in Saskatchewan (NDP, 2001–7) – declaring themselves more interventionist, and possessing sufficient fiscal resources, established a new type of relationship between immigration and the economic fate of their respective provinces. In doing so, they initiated the province-building mechanism centred on immigration. This did not come about through citizen mobilization or electoral debates; rather, it was the product of a long-term mobilization of the administrative elite, which had finally come into alignment with the changing interests of the political elite. In a context of economic recovery and labour shortages, the governments of Alberta and Saskatchewan made immigration a resource for their respective provinces.

Province-building in immigration in Alberta and Saskatchewan entailed a shift in perceptions and a renewed vision of immigration as a resource for expanding the provincial economy. Central to this vision was the image of immigrants as workers who settled in the province to fill labour shortages. Thus the government's role was to support the recruitment of workers by employers and to ensure the quick integration of immigrants into the provincial labour market. This vision would guide provincial interventions from 2005 to 2010, institutionalized in the form of the bridging mode of intervention. Over time it would become established as a consensus in these two provincial societies.

The activation of province-building centred on immigration in Alberta and Saskatchewan was initially carried out more slowly than in other provinces since the political elite did not share the interest of the public service in developing a provincial role in immigration. Over time, however, the mechanism accelerated in an unprecedented way, overcoming the concerns of the political elite. Coinciding with exceptional economic prosperity, provincial intervention became a target of mobilization for economic actors (employers, chambers of commerce, large factories, and industry representatives), and this propelled province-building. The mechanism thus created growing pressure on the federal government, and this strengthened the operation of the decentralization mechanism.

Early Interventions

Immigration had, of course, played a key role in the early days of settlement in Western Canada. In the 1970s, Alberta and Saskatchewan began focusing their actions on business and investment immigration.[1] However, economic instability and a succession of governments intent on reducing the size of the state slowed down interventions throughout the 1990s.

In Alberta, signs of increased interest in immigration were noticeable during the Conservative government of Peter Lougheed in the 1970s, a time of economic expansion in the province. This interest coincided with a classical moment of province-building centred on the growth of the provincial government as an actor in economic development with a focus on the exploitation of natural resources (Smith 2001). In 1975 the government set up an interdepartmental committee on immigration and began bilateral negotiations for an immigration agreement with the federal government (Garcea 1994, 376–402). In the 1980s, under Lougheed and then his successor, Don Getty (CP, 1986–89), the province began to show a more significant interest in immigration, in particular business and investment immigration (Frideres 2011). Immigration thus came to be seen as a source of capital at a time when the economy was declining.

It was in this context that Alberta signed a first five-year immigration agreement in 1985. The province undertook the negotiations with great ambitions, but in the end it accepted a limited federal offer, motivated by its desire to gain more control over business immigration. The provincial government saw this agreement as a preliminary step towards more substantive negotiations on collaboration on immigration (Garcea 1994, 438). In spite of this enthusiasm, when the agreement expired in 1990 it would not be renegotiated by the province. This can be explained by the constitutional context of the time as well as by substantial changes to Alberta's economic and political situation. Nevertheless, the practices of collaboration established by this agreement would remain in place among the administrative actors until agreements were signed in the 2000s.[2]

In the 1990s, with Ralph Klein as premier, the province accumulated a substantial debt and went through a period of significant economic decline (Gazso and Krahn 2008). Klein's government proposed a new definition of the division of responsibilities between the provincial government and society. Government was conceived as having to limit its interventions to basic services and as being responsible in the area of fiscal policy (Wesley 2011). After another election victory in 1993, the Klein government implemented a series of measures aimed at eliminating the provincial deficit and debt, while aligning government intervention with new ideas of governance (Denis 1995). Klein's reforms would have the effect of limiting total government spending and returning the province to balanced budgets in 1996 (Smith 2001).

Despite reductions in spending and services, the province remained active in integration, supporting many organizations delivering services as well as initiatives in language teaching (L.A., AL, 10 April 1991, 422; 13 April 1993, 178–280). However, these interventions remained limited. Priority was given to business immigration, which was viewed as bringing capital to the province. The program would be overseen by the Alberta Department of Advanced Education and Career Development from 1994 to 1999.

Before the 1990s, Saskatchewan's interest in immigration and integration was limited to questions of business immigration. As in Alberta, these interests were contingent on the province's political context and economic cycles. In the context of a certain level of economic growth in the 1970s, provincial interest in business immigration was maintained (Phillips 1998). This coincided – under the governments of Allan Blakeney (NDP, 1970–82) and Grant Devine (CP, 1982–91) – with the development efforts of the provincial government and a form of province-building characterized by an interventionist role in economic development, often financed with deficits (de Clercy 2005). Attracting foreign investment, in collaboration with the federal government, was thus integral to the province's economic development strategies. It was in these circumstances that the province attempted, between 1985 and 1990 – without much success – to negotiate a new agreement with the federal government.[3] The election of Roy Romanow in 1991 brought an end to the province's negotiations on immigration.

The 1991 election signalled an important change for the province. Faced with a growing deficit and a sluggish provincial economy, the Romanow government broke with the interventionist approach of the previous government in favour of market-oriented policies with a view to putting provincial finances in order (Pitsula and Rasmussen 1990, 286; Rasmussen 2001). During this period, the government implemented an austerity program called "Common Sense Financial Management" and maintained the primacy of economic development sustained by the private sector (Wesley 2011). As a result of Romanow's policies, Saskatchewan saw a budget surplus in 1995 (de Clercy 2005). However, interventionism did not return to Saskatchewan after provincial finances were solved.

Despite the cuts, the Romanow government continued the business immigration activities implemented under the Devine government, though immigration was not a flagship activity.[4] From 1991 to 1997, immigration was overseen by various iterations of the ministry responsible for economic development. Its key interventions included management of the business immigration program with the federal government, provision of advisory services for business immigrants (e.g., how to create a business in the province), and promotion of the province as an investment destination (Saskatchewan 1992; 1995). The government also funded a few integration initiatives, but that activity remained minimal (Bodhan 2011).

Decentralization without Much Impact

The activation and operation of the decentralization mechanism in the 1990s – through the 1991 accord between Quebec and Ottawa and following the period of Settlement Renewal that began in 1995 – had limited impact on Alberta and Saskatchewan. The signing of PNP agreements in the late 1990s and early 2000s also had little impact on these provinces. It would take many years, with the decentralization mechanism operating, for province-building to finally be set in motion in Alberta and Saskatchewan.

After the 1985 bilateral agreement expired, the Alberta government did not attempt to negotiate an agreement with the federal government. Nevertheless, starting in the late 1980s, Alberta's interests in immigration became more closely linked to broader demands with respect to the Canadian Constitution – demands that concerned, among other things, Senate reform, the management of natural resource revenues, and the status of Quebec. The 1990 Speech from the Throne expressed the place of immigration on the Alberta government's constitutional agenda:

> My government will continue to support constitutional change on the principle that change must make Confederation whole, with all provinces as full participants. Recognizing that change must provide for the constitutional equality of the provinces and that Albertans will not accept second-class status, that change must not grant any special powers or status to any one province, that change must provide the provinces with a greater role in immigration and appointments to the Supreme Court of Canada, that change must strengthen the provinces' ability to carry out their responsibilities without interference from the federal government and their fiscal powers, and finally recognizing that change must provide a process through which Senate reform will be achieved, my government wishes to see these changes to our Constitution succeed. (L.A., AL, 9 March 1990, 2)

The Alberta government saw the bilateral agreement between Ottawa and Quebec as symbolic of a broader imbalance of power and responsibility, especially given that Alberta was attempting to finalize an agreement to increase its business immigration (L.A., AL, 20 March 1990, 108). That same year, Alberta tried to mobilize the Western premiers to increase regional pressures for a greater provincial role in immigration, emphasizing the fact that control of immigration was as important for Alberta as it was for Quebec (L.A., AL, 15 May 1991, 1246):

> In spite of significant frustrations with respect to constitutional questions, Alberta would not maintain a discourse on fiscal or demographic equity following the signature of the Quebec agreement. This is notable, given

that during most of the decade, the government tried to sign a new agreement on immigration with the federal government, with little success. (e.g., L.A., AL, 16 March 1996, 569)

During the period of Settlement Renewal, Alberta at first reacted positively to the federal offer and got involved in negotiations to transfer responsibilities in the area of settlement to the province. However, it concluded no agreement. According to a provincial civil servant active in those negotiations, this failure can be attributed to two factors:

If you go back before that, there was an interest on the settlement side ... We participated in the negotiation for devolved settlement services when this came up ... The climate though changed while these negotiations where happening. Two things happened: one, the economy in Alberta took a downward trend, which made it a more difficult thing to agree to ... The second thing that happened there was, after they secured Manitoba and BC's agreement, they lost interest in negotiating with us.[5]

Even in the absence of an agreement, the collaborative practices in the area of funding implemented after the bilateral agreement of 1985 was signed would be maintained. According to a senior federal civil servant, relationships remained positive and functional between the federal government and the province during the 1990s.[6] This can in large part be attributed to the relatively stable level of funding of the province's integration programs, in spite of economic and political uncertainties.[7] This collaborative relationship would be systematized at the administrative level in 2001 via a memorandum of understanding, and finally by a formal agreement on integration services signed in 2007. More broadly, during the 1980s the public service developed an interest in maintaining and expanding provincial intervention in the area of immigration.

In 2001 the province signed an agreement to establish a pilot PNP project. As explained by a federal civil servant active in the negotiation of that agreement, the provincial government's decision was not motivated by a clear desire to take a hand in selection: "Well, they just didn't see the role for it. At the time they didn't have the labor market pressure that they do now. And if you look at ... And I mean I think that probably they entered into this agreement because the rest of the West had an agreement and they were getting pressure ... 'Why shouldn't we? Clearly, our neighbors get benefits and we want to have the benefits.'"[8]

Notably, this agreement was concluded without great fanfare by the province and was, in large part, a result of the desire of the federal public service to extend these agreements to all the provinces in the early 2000s.[9] This desire was, to some extent, a result of the federalization process. It also matched the interests of Alberta's public service, which worked in the background with this new policy instrument. However, the program would not become a key element of Alberta's intervention until the province-building mechanism was activated.

In Saskatchewan, the limited place of immigration on the government agenda in the 1990s and the economic slowdown the province was facing partly explain the limited impact of the decentralization mechanism there. Saskatchewan remained interested in selection but showed little interest in acquiring powers and resources in settlement and integration. Even so, Saskatchewan would be the first province to sign a PNP agreement.

When the Quebec–federal bilateral agreement was signed in 1991 and then during Settlement Renewal, Saskatchewan showed no clear interest in acquiring increased powers. In fact, it resisted decentralization; mainly, it wanted to remain active in business immigration. The limited sums invested in integration, and the more general tendency to focus on domestic matters – a characteristic of the Romanow government – also weakened interest in immigration during this period.[10] As pointed out by many stakeholders, the province only began to take an interest in settlement and integration policies when these came to be seen as instruments to ensure the retention of immigrants in the province, and this interest would emerge much later, in the 2000s.[11]

However, largely for logistical reasons, Saskatchewan signed a PNP agreement before Manitoba. According to a provincial civil servant who helped negotiate that agreement, it was the public service of Saskatchewan that took the lead in this (Paquet 2015). At the time, the absence of pressure from the business community[12] for a provincial role in selection, the limited capacity of the provincial public service, and the novelty of the program also explain the lukewarm response of the provincial actors:

> I wouldn't say there was a lot of political interest at that point; this was seen as a good thing to do, it was very small, [our] initial agreement allowed for about 75 [nominations], it was kind of an intriguing program idea that nobody thought of before or had been involved in before, the idea that provinces could have a role in selection, but I wouldn't say that

it was pushed at the political level … It was mostly evolving … out of officials' work.[13]

In spite of this agreement, the province would not invest substantial resources in the program. The agreement would nevertheless be renewed in 2003, and in the following years, collaboration between the levels of government would expand (Newswire 2004).

The activation of the federalization process had only a limited, short-term impact in Alberta and Saskatchewan. The two provinces showed little interest in decentralization before the 2000s, preferring to stick to a relatively limited role in immigration. They would begin negotiating agreements on the PNP but remain primarily discreet actors. Setting aside this minimal response, the period was crucial in laying the groundwork for the two provinces, for it provided them with instruments and resources that would favour mobilization once the province-building mechanism centred on immigration was activated. A structuring legacy of that time is a certain level of mobilization in the public service in favour of creating institutions and interventions in immigration.

A Changing Federal Context

Changes in the federal and provincial context created the conditions for activating the province-building mechanism centred on immigration in Alberta and Saskatchewan. That context was marked by the decentralization of responsibilities in the labour market (see previous chapter). For the two provinces, this transfer increased administrative capacities and resources in this policy area. In the same vein, the activity of the decentralization mechanism fostered a new ideational context in which the provinces had a responsibility and an advantage in the area of labour market management. Given the important links between immigration and the human resource needs of provincial economies in the bridging mode of intervention, this related decentralization was therefore an important contributor to province-building.

The return of economic growth in the region starting in the 2000s, stimulated by higher petroleum prices and the development of the Alberta tar sands, and by the spillover effects in Saskatchewan, were also highly significant elements of the context (Hiller 2009; Barnetson and Foster 2013). This growth was not, however, sufficient to initiate province-building centred on immigration in Alberta and Saskatchewan.

However, the bases of the mechanism were established before the boom times in these economies, and moreover, province-building centred on immigration remained operative despite the economic slowdown that began in 2008.

At the federal level, two other elements shaped this context of activation. The first of these was the changes of government in Ottawa from 2003 to 2006. The second was the growing importance of a new agenda in the area of federalism and immigration brought forward by Stephen Harper's Conservative government in 2006. These two elements fostered a climate conducive to the expression of provincial demands and an increased willingness by the federal government to meet those demands. As this chapter will demonstrate, these demands were the result of the internal political dynamics in the provinces.

The years 2003 to 2006 saw a change in government – the end of Prime Minister Jean Chrétien's tenure and the coming to power of Paul Martin, leading a minority government – followed by a change in the governing party. With the sponsorship scandal and the Gomery report as background, the Martin government placed many ambitious policies on the agenda. Besides a project to reform democratic institutions, Martin's tenure saw an increase in transfers to the provinces and the implementation of the "Agenda for Cities," as well as interventions in early childhood services (Bickerton 2010; Aucoin and Turnbull 2003).

Regarding the governance of immigration in this period, two elements are particularly important. First, there was the Martin government's sensitivity to the demands of municipalities (Sancton and Young 2003), which was accompanied by a greater openness than under the Chrétien government to decentralization and deconcentration.[14] This tendency was legally embodied in the bilateral agreement on immigration signed with Ontario in 2005, but it can also be seen in the general behaviour of the federal government beginning that same year. Second, under the Martin government, there were substantial efforts made to curb the geographic concentration of immigrants by promoting their distribution outside the three major centres (Toronto, Montreal, and Vancouver) (Abu-Laban and Garber 2005). Those efforts, set in motion by the publication of the results of the 2001 census, would take many forms. For example, the federal government began to promote the involvement of cities, regions, and community actors in the development of "welcoming communities." This promotion was done through training, the creation of resources, and financial support. In addition to these efforts, the federal government began working to extend the PNP to all Canadian provinces (Canada 2003a; 2002).

These concerns would be combined, starting in 2006, with the emergence of a new approach to federalism, one that coincided with the election of the Conservative Party led by Stephen Harper. In power for the first time, this party – the result of a merger between the Progressive Conservatives and the Canadian Alliance – promoted a new doctrine on intergovernmental relationships: "open federalism" (Montpetit 2007). As presented in the party's 2006 election platform and in the 2007 Speech from the Throne, "open federalism" entailed the following: respect for provincial jurisdictions (especially in the area of social and economic policies); support for a more decentralized federalism in which strong provinces could exist and express themselves through institutions such as the Council of the Federation; a limitation on federal spending power in areas of provincial jurisdiction; the search for common ground that would lead to harmonious intergovernmental relationships; and official recognition of the specific characteristics of Quebec (Caron and Laforest 2009; Bickerton 2010; Harmes 2007; Cody 2008). With some notable exceptions, this approach would not be substantially implemented by the Harper government during its first two terms (2008–11). Nevertheless, the era of open federalism created a context in which provincial demands – especially those related to the economy and not requiring the financial participation of the federal government – were better received by the federal government.

In addition to this concept of open federalism, there were new ambitions in the area of immigration. The new Conservative philosophy gave considerable room to the provinces, at least until 2012. The Harper era was characterized by a substantial increase in the federal government's activities in the area of public security as it related to immigrants and by the development of new policies on Canadian identity and citizenship (Dufour and Forcier 2015; Paquet 2012). In addition to these new interventions, the tendency, begun under Paul Martin, was to support a certain level of decentralization with regard to attracting, retaining, and integrating immigrants, as well as an increase in the role given to employers with respect to selecting immigrants, be they temporary or permanent (Andrew and Bradford 2011). These new ambitions were compatible with a substantial provincial role, all the more so given that the federal government focused much of its attention to immigration on questions outside areas of provincial jurisdiction (e.g., security and naturalization).

Alberta

These changes created pressures and opportunities for a repositioning of the provincial government in Alberta. The province-building
mechanism centred on immigration began operating in 2005. Province-
building was the outcome of a political and societal reflection on the
role of immigration in the provincial economy and society, stimulated
by changes to Alberta's economic situation. This reflection continued
while responsibilities in labour market development were being devolved to the province starting in 1996, which made the provincial
elites those most concerned with these questions (Wood and Klassen
2009). The political elites needed to reposition themselves in order to
ensure their central place in the management of the province's new
economic destiny. The transition from relative passivity to substantial
activity in immigration in Alberta would bolster the establishment of
a bridging mode of intervention, one that expressed the needs of the
province as well as the economic, political, and social forces supporting
the province-building mechanism centred on immigration.

Activation

The activation of province-building unfolded through a process of reflection among Alberta's political and bureaucratic elite with respect to the
relationship between economic growth and immigration. This process
began in 2001 as part of the economic development strategy outlined in
Prepared for Growth: Building Alberta's Labour Supply, which was aimed
at ensuring the maintenance of adequate human resources in Alberta
(Alberta 2001). In this strategy, immigration was identified for the first
time as an element of great importance for the development of the province's workforce. It mentioned a PNP, not yet implemented, and it proposed a partnership with the federal government to achieve the objective
of increasing the number of immigrants to Alberta by 2005. These objectives would be repeated in similar documents over the coming years.

In 2004 the strategic plan for Alberta, at that time led by Ralph Klein,
called for the creation of an immigration strategy as a pillar for developing the province's human resources. This plan, titled *Today's Advantage, Tomorrow's Promise: Alberta's Vision for the Future*, stated:

> The Alberta government will take steps to attract skilled workers from
> outside the province, which could include a made-in-Alberta immigration

policy that focuses on skilled immigrants. Government also needs to be sure that immigrants to Alberta get full recognition for the professional qualifications they bring with them so that they can make the greatest possible contribution to the province. These new strategies will help position Alberta more competitively in the global market, supplement the province's future supply of skilled workers, and ensure full participation in Alberta's communities. (Alberta 2004b, 8)

Following consultations, the government published a document titled *Integrating Skilled Immigrants into the Alberta Economy*, the aim of which was to foster economic integration, and which made the general diagnosis that the skills of new arrivals already in the province were being underutilized (Alberta 2004a; 2005a).

While the government was looking for ways to intervene in immigration, economic recovery increased employers' demands on the provincial government. An Alberta civil servant recounted: "Employers had been increasingly knocking at the government door as labour shortages were building up to get the government to help get the right workers ... and so immigration was seen by employers as a key tool to address these shortages ... The government really has answered to these demands."[15]

Another civil servant identified these growing pressures as a factor prompting the implementation of a PNP, but also as a force behind the implementation of an integrated immigration strategy for the province.[16] The same pressures were beginning to be felt in the Legislative Assembly from 2001 to 2005. The theme of labour shortages, appeals for actions to facilitate the mobility of workers, and calls for increased recruitment became more current (e.g., L.A., AL, 25 February 2004, 174). Over the same period, the province's civil servants and elected officials tried to acquire better knowledge on immigration in Canada and the potential policies to be implemented. With respect to other provinces, this research focused on the PNPs already in place (*Whitehorse Star* 2007).

Thus, from 2001 to 2005, following this internal reflection started by the political and bureaucratic elite, immigration came to be viewed as a resource for a rapidly growing economy. The previous role of the province in human resources, following the devolution of powers of 1996, and the acquisition of new powers in the selection of newcomers following the 2001 immigration agreement, made the provincial government the venue to which economic actors addressed their demands. Alberta now began to assign a role to immigration in its development strategy and to position itself as a partner in the support and maintenance of economic growth.

Consensualization

Following this period of reflection, the Alberta government implemented its very first immigration strategy and all existing immigration programs expanded, thus establishing the bridging mode of intervention. Beginning in 2005, the provincial government's discourse on the role of immigration in Alberta society shifted in favour of dissemination of a clear consensus: newcomers were necessary for the province's economic growth. According to this consensus, the provincial government had to ensure a constant flow of immigrants through attraction efforts, selection programs, and collaboration with the federal government. Moreover, the government was presented more and more as needing to act in order to provide immigrants with quick access to the Alberta labour market. This would be accomplished through bridging programs to employment and through selection processes adapted to the needs of specific employers.

That consensus would become obvious during the last years of Klein's government. The preamble to the 2005 provincial immigration strategy, *Supporting Immigrants and Immigration in Alberta*, included this observation, very representative of the government discourse of the time:

> Over the past 20 years, Alberta's economy has grown at an average annual rate of 3.7% … Alberta may face a shortage of 100,000 workers over the next ten years … Small-and large-scale projects are at risk if we do not find enough people to fill this shortage … There are over $100 billion worth of capital projects planned or underway in this province. If Alberta does not attract enough people with the knowledge and skills to fill our labour shortages, many of these projects will have to be delayed or abandoned. This would damage Alberta's international reputation and hurt future efforts to promote further investment. (Alberta 2005b, 4–5)

The government also emphasized the importance of sharing responsibilities among communities, employers, and the government to ensure the integration of new arrivals.

The consensus continued to spread after the departure of Ralph Klein as leader of the Progressive Conservative Party of Alberta. During his campaign for the party's leadership, Ed Stelmach announced that increased powers in immigration, obtained through an agreement similar to that of Quebec and through an expansion of powers in the selection of immigrants, were necessary for sustainable growth in the province (CBC Edmonton 2006; Canadian Press 2006a). The same year, addressing the legislature, Stelmach made an evocative parallel between immigration and natural resources: "Another important area, Mr. Speaker, is gaining control of the tools to manage immigration policy. It could be as fundamental to Alberta's future prosperity as the affirmation in 1929 of constitutional jurisdiction over natural resources has been to our present prosperity" (L.A., AL, 27 February 2006, 72).

Immigration was given a full role in the second strategy for managing and developing human resources, titled *Building and Educating Tomorrow's Workforce* (2006). Written following public hearings, the document named the attraction and retention of new immigrants as two of the four themes of the provincial strategy to meet human resource needs. The document identified clear targets: the reception of 24,000 newcomers in 2009 and the reception of 10 per cent of Canada's total immigration until 2016. These targets were seen as serving the general objective of increasing the "supply of appropriately skilled, knowledgeable workers in the province" (Alberta 2006b, 21). In 2007, in the Speech from the Throne, the government identified intervention in immigration as a tool to address the pressures created by an increased rate of growth. In this context, the government committed itself to supporting recruitment and to helping immigrants to integrate into provincial society:

> Despite so many people moving to Alberta each year, our economy is in dire need of people to answer the calls for "help wanted" across the province. To help meet this demand, your government will focus on better co-ordination of economic development, immigration, and labour force planning. It will craft a made-in-Alberta solution to labour needs. Like the early settlers who helped build our province, immigrants today come here with hopes of creating a better life for themselves and a better future for their children. The Alberta government will help new Albertans realize their dreams. It will encourage them to put down roots, raise their families here, and contribute to and share in Alberta's prosperity. (L.A., AL, 7 March 2007, 2)

This consensus spread beyond the government and was taken up by most political actors in the province. During the 2008 election, the role of immigration in economic development was mentioned in election platforms, and that issue was not subjected to debate among the parties. The Progressive Conservatives reiterated their achievements in the area of immigration, linking them to jobs policy (Progressive Conservative Party of Alberta 2008, 5). Social Credit also mentioned immigration in its 2006 platform, and again in 2008 (Alberta Social Credit Party 2006). For its part, the Liberal Party of Alberta promised to expand the PNP and proposed a more active role in the recruiting and processing of temporary foreign workers (Alberta Liberals 2007).

Upon re-election, the Stelmach government expressed the same principles in its Speech from the Throne, indicating beyond any doubt that a consensus had been established:

> With an anticipated shortage of workers and slowing interprovincial migration Alberta is looking abroad to help meet future labour needs. As part of Alberta's immigration strategy a foreign qualification recognition plan will be implemented this year. It will put in place mechanisms to ensure that newcomers with foreign credentials and work experience are able to make the most of their skills in Alberta's economy. Your government will expand the provincial nominee program. This program allows Alberta to better target immigration towards our specific labour needs. The number of people nominated will double, to 5,000 next year. Alberta will also continue to work with the federal government to ensure that the temporary foreign worker program meets Alberta's needs and protects temporary foreign workers. Your government will provide support to workers through new advisory offices opened in December and through stepped-up inspection of workplaces. (L.A., AL, 4 February 2008, 2)

Thus starting in 2005, immigration was seen as a crucial resource for Alberta, as reflected in the discourse of both the government and the other parties. This consensus would be strengthened even more by institutions and public policies in immigration and integration.

Institutionalization

By 2005 the Alberta government had greatly expanded its areas of intervention in immigration, as well as many of its programs, and had increased its financial investments in the area (Alberta 2010). This growth institutionalized the consensus central to the province-building mechanism in Alberta. The province directed its efforts in particular towards the recruitment of needed workers and their integration into the job market. Alberta's bridging mode of intervention was developed primarily from an economic perspective, which was seen as an extension of provincial policies on economic development and labour market management.

The activation of the province-building mechanism strengthened the importance of immigration in the public administration. Beginning in 2005, the government augmented its capacities for analysis and administration and allocated more resources to the coordination of government activities (Alberta 2006c). As pointed out by one analyst, "prior to that, it was a low profile program that the province invested in but [not a] priority ... Starting in 2005, that really changed ... We became much more active on the policy side, on the programming side, we started to want more involvement from our federal partners on that."[17]

This expansion of activities was expressed, in 2006, through the shift of responsibilities for immigration to a new ministry, the Ministry of Employment, Immigration and Industry, whose mandate was to "attract ... and welcome ... newcomers into Alberta to primarily offset our labour and skills shortages" (Alberta 2007). A clear link between responsibilities in immigration and those in employment and industry is typical of the bridging mode of intervention. In 2008 this ministry was renamed the Ministry of Employment and Immigration, thus reinforcing the link between employment policy and interventions in immigration (Alberta 2009).

To achieve its objectives the Alberta government also made targeted interventions in the area of immigrant recruitment. With respect to promotion, the province carried out specialized recruitment missions starting in 2006 with the objective of recruiting skilled workers, or less skilled but much-needed workers. Employers were invited to participate in these missions (Alberta 2006a; 2009). In 2007 the government, with partial financial support from the federal government, reinforced its efforts by building a website for immigrants and setting up a telephone assistance service for prospective migrants (Alberta 2009). These initiatives were complimented the same year with a marketing strategy to sell Alberta as an immigration destination. The following year, an agreement on labour mobility was signed with the government of the Philippines (Alberta 2008).

With similar objectives, the province implemented its PNP, initially with the help of employers and economic actors; until 2008, a job offer in Alberta was a condition for nomination. Linked to the development of the public administration in immigration, the budget allocated to the program was gradually increased to permit the quick processing of a growing number of applications (Progressive Conservative Party of Alberta 2008, 5). The program rapidly expanded, both qualitatively and quantitatively, having basically lain dormant since its creation in 2001. The selection channels were gradually expanded starting in 2008 to include semi-skilled workers, and for certain categories of much-needed workers, the selection of nominees in the absence of job offers was permitted (Alberta 2009; 2006c). These efforts brought results. From 2005 to 2010, the number of nomination certificates issued by the province went from 392 to close to 5,000.[18]

Alongside this exponential increase in selection activities, the activation of the province-building mechanism centred on immigration favoured an increase in provincial interventions in integration. In keeping with the consensus, this intervention institutionalized economic integration as a priority. Many of these efforts – including support for immigrant settlement organizations, basic language courses, and certain services for temporary foreign workers (TFWPs) – were funded in collaboration with the federal government. Co-financing, a practice approved administratively in 2001, would become official in 2007 when an agreement on immigration was signed, following the complete institutionalization of the consensus.

The services the province provided included language training programs in the workplace or focusing on employability as well as a range of programs – ranging from information to direct financial support – aimed at facilitating direct access to employment for skilled immigrants (Alberta 2007; 2008). To facilitate access to employment, Alberta was also very active in the recognition of prior learning, training, and professional experience. For example, in 2005 the province established a public service division for the recognition of training that provided certificates of equivalency as well as information to employers. It also signed a memorandum of understanding with the federal government in 2005 to fund projects for the recognition of training and experience acquired abroad. Similarly, in 2008 the province published a plan that would recognize foreign credentials in which the participation of employers was presented as crucial (Alberta 2009).

The activation of the province-building mechanism centred on immigration in Alberta coincided with the return of prosperity to the province and with the advent of a more interventionist provincial government after the Klein years. Responding to pressure from employers, the provincial government repositioned itself starting in 2005 as a partner in economic growth and added immigration to the list of its key activities. Immigration was now identified as essential to maintaining the province's economic prosperity. This was facilitated by the previous mobilization of Alberta's senior public administration. Reflecting the emerging consensus, provincial intervention in immigration was institutionalized along the lines of the bridging mode of intervention. That intervention included increased activities in selection for economic purposes as well as activities aimed primarily at access to the labour market.

Province-building made Alberta an active player in the federalization of the governance of immigration, especially as its contribution to the national economy increased. In 2005 the province increased its pressure on the federal government. After the Canada–Ontario agreement on immigration was signed, Alberta asked for an increase in the funds transferred for the integration of immigrants (Canadian Press 2005a). These demands would intensify after Ed Stelmach came to power as Alberta's premier. In 2006 the government armed itself with an official mandate to negotiate a new immigration agreement for the province – a clear indicator that the mechanism had been activated. This agreement was presented as crucial "to resolv[ing] the province's critical labour shortage" (Canadian Press 2007a) and to facilitating quick integration of new arrivals into the provincial labour market (CBC Calgary 2007). The province demanded an increase in the quotas for the selection of immigrants as well as an increase in funding. Also, it was very active in the intergovernmental arena both at the regional level and in terms of relations with the federal government. Thus Alberta, starting in 2005, after the province-building mechanism was activated, played a leadership role in the area of the recognition of prior learning and tried to mobilize other provinces to increase provincial powers in immigration.

The Province-Building Mechanism in Saskatchewan

After signing its first agreement on immigration in 1998, Saskatchewan began a long period of reflection during which immigration was ever-present but never a major part of the government's agenda. As a result of economic growth – brought about in part by a spillover effect of the Alberta economy – and the rise of a new political elite that was open to suggestions from the public service, the province-building mechanism centred on immigration was finally activated in Saskatchewan. That mechanism was based on and disseminated a consensus that presented immigration as a demographic resource that would enable the province to meet its labour market needs. This was the core of Saskatchewan's bridging mode of intervention.

Activation

Despite a persistent interest in investment immigration and the renewal of the PNP agreement, it was a long time before the province-building mechanism centred on immigration was activated in Saskatchewan. Before 2005, the province's civil servants worked on creating the foundations for a mobilization of the elite in the area of immigration. Unlike in Alberta, the elite's interest was not related to labour market management, nor was it based on a recognized period of growth in the provincial economy. Instead, it should be viewed as the outcome of a general desire to revitalize the province's economy and demography.

Still led by Roy Romanow, the Saskatchewan government opened public hearings in 2000 about the "kind of role Saskatchewan should play, if any, in immigration" (*Daily Herald* 2000; Saskatchewan 2001, 26). The first observation to arise from these discussions was that attraction and retention were challenges for the province; efforts to strengthen economic immigration were proposed (Laflamme 2002). This priority was welcomed enthusiastically among those sections of the public service involved in immigration, which had been trying for some time to attract the cabinet's attention about the issue.[19] The government then decided to create an autonomous immigration division, but also to hold additional public hearings regarding needs in settlement and integration. In 2002 the province published the report *Meeting Needs, Making Connections*, which was intended to present the views of societal actors with respect to needs in the area of integration (Saskatchewan 2002b).

Public hearings continued under the Calvert government (NDP, 2001–7). In 2002 the premier appointed MLA Pat Lorjé legislative secretary responsible for immigration. Her mandate was to conduct a study of the province's needs as they related to immigration and integration. Her report was based on the experiences of other provinces (Lorjé 2003). Even though it had sponsored the report, the Calvert government did not implement all of its recommendations.[20] According to Kordan Bodhan, this was because of the province's limited administrative capacity as well as fears that Aboriginal leaders would raise opposition (Bodhan 2011). Nevertheless, the government continued to hold consultations in the years that followed in order to better understand the needs on the ground and especially to rally economic actors (Saskatchewan 2004).

According to a provincial civil servant, the province also grew concerned about demographic issues. The results of the 2001 census were seen as demonstrating the need for a proactive approach to recruitment. In the absence of clear political direction, the public service played a crucial role in the development of the provincial intervention:

> We did the immigration branch in 2001 ... The idea at the time was to [unite] together the two or three pieces of responsibility over immigration in one branch and give power to one branch that was recognized within government ... At that point, it was still a ... bureaucratic project ... The bureaucracy was pushing it ... Let me tell you that the push for an immigration branch did not come from the political side, from elected officials, it came from the public service. Myself and my supervisor specifically.[21]

The existence of an administrative unit responsible for immigration services and a mobilized bureaucratic elite drew the attention of societal and political actors to immigration issues. Also, other provincial actors had begun to notice Manitoba's success and to grasp the PNP's potential. As related by a Saskatchewan civil servant:

> First of all ... the 2001 census ... the linkages between "gee, we have a lot of employers who aren't successfully filling jobs" and the demographic problems ... and the other thing that happened that really accentuated the interest at the political level was the success that Manitoba was having with its program. A neighbouring province was seen as having developed a program that was successful in bringing/attracting a number of people, that had the support of the business community and was seen as having a real impact ... So we had a branch, we had the vehicle, the provincial nominee program, we had begun broadening out from the very very narrow scope that we began with ... and we were gradually adding a number of new categories and broadening the existing categories. During that time, the provincial interest was growing.[22]

During this period the Saskatchewan government began to see immigration as a potential area for intervention. The province-building mechanism was finally activated when the province started to experience economic growth, at which point immigration was seen as an economic rather than a demographic resource. This activation was confirmed beyond any doubt by the establishment of a new development strategy by the Calvert government.

Consensualization

The emergence of a new vision of immigration's role in provincial society was fundamental to the activation of the province-building mechanism centred on immigration. In Saskatchewan this repositioning began among political actors during the 2003 election and was consolidated in government actions starting in 2005. Immigration was now being presented as a resource to support the province's economic growth, but also as a human capital resource that could enrich the province.

The first version of this vision emerged during the 2003 election campaign. The province's Liberal Party referred to immigration largely from the perspective of diversity and social justice; however, its platform also noted that provincial intervention in immigration could be a means to "address the increasing dependency ratio and lack of enterprise in the province" (Saskatchewan Liberal Party, 2003, 37). In that document, immigrants were presented as workers bringing ideas and capital that could "create exciting opportunities for the people of Saskatchewan" (Saskatchewan Liberal Party, 2003, 37). The NDP, the outgoing government, presented immigration as a means to build a skilled labour force in the province (Saskatchewan New Democratic Party 2003). After 2003, immigration would be included in the platforms of all the Saskatchewan parties, in every election. During the 2007 election the NDP promised to intensify the efforts already begun, while the Saskatchewan Party – in power since then – called for growth in targeted economic recruitment. This same orientation would be maintained during the 2011 election (Saskatchewan New Democratic Party 2007; Saskatchewan Party 2011).

After the NDP, led by Calvert, came to power in 2003, the provincial government's discourse confirmed the emerging consensus. The new government established a ministry responsible for immigration and assigned an especially activist minister to that file.[23] In 2004 the department responsible for immigration (Saskatchewan Government Relations and Aboriginal Affairs) formally presented the decrease in the number of immigrants in Saskatchewan as a problem for the provincial economy (Saskatchewan 2004, 19–20). This diagnosis would be repeated the following year in the general *Action Plan* published by the Calvert government. The outcome of public hearings, that plan for the first time directly identified immigration as a possible means to act on the province's economy and labour market (Saskatchewan 2005). In the years that followed, the link between immigration and the provincial economy would be reasserted in official discourses. The 2005 Speech from the Throne presented general targets for migration flows to the province and consolidated the idea of a provincial role in immigration:

> Just as we did 100 years ago, Saskatchewan is turning again to the world and opening our doors to new immigrants. In partnership with communities, businesses, and immigrant families, the Saskatchewan Immigrant Nominee Program will identify and attract thousands of new immigrants to our workplaces, farms, and businesses. When the program is fully operational by 2008, my government expects approximately 5,000 new immigrants a year will make Saskatchewan their home. Government will work with our settlement agencies, postsecondary institutions, occupational bodies, and other partners to connect newcomers to jobs, communities and cultural groups – to ease their transition and create a more welcoming atmosphere in which they will prosper and thrive. (L.A., SK, 7 November 2005, 7)

Within that consensus, the economic aspects of immigration took precedence over demographic concerns, which nevertheless remained present. Acting in immigration was presented as a way of "bolstering the workforce and economy of [the] province" and addressing labour shortages (Saskatchewan 2007a; 18).

When it launched a new immigration strategy in 2009, the government declared that its goal was to create the best immigration program in the country. This program was meant to promote Saskatchewan's economic growth, increase business and investment opportunities, expand the labour force, and boost innovation (Saskatchewan 2009b). Similarly, the province's reports presented immigration as a resource that could ensure prosperity in the province: "Immigration is an important factor in building and sustaining dynamic communities and economic growth in Saskatchewan ... Immigration is vital to Saskatchewan's future as a high growth, diverse, dynamic and vital society" (Saskatchewan 2009a, 20).

This portrayal of immigration was maintained in the following years, while provincial programs expanded and attracted growing societal support.

Institutionalization

Besides consolidating a discourse on the importance of immigration for the province's future, the activation of the province-building mechanism centred on immigration directly increased the provincial government's interventions. Their institutionalization would make efforts at targeted recruitment and policies favouring quick movement into the labour market crucial elements of the province's activities in immigration. In this way, the bridging mode of intervention would be institutionalized with the support of economic and social actors.

After 2005, Saskatchewan's public service was gradually modified to embody the new vision of immigration as a resource for the province. After the first branch specifically responsible for immigration was created in 2001 (Saskatchewan 2001), responsibilities in this domain were transferred to the Ministry of Industry and Resources in 2006. Then in 2007, immigration became the responsibility of the Ministry of Post-Secondary Education, Training and Labour. Finally – a sign of the speed of the mechanism – the province created in 2010 a Ministry of Advanced Education, Employment and Immigration.

As immigration took on importance in the public service, the province increased its investments in administrative capacities (Legislative Assembly of Saskatchewan 2008). The government gradually increased the funds for managing the PNP and created new administrative services aimed at meeting the societal needs created by immigration (Saskatchewan 2007b).

Saskatchewan significantly increased its actions in the area of immigrant recruitment. From the outset, the province substantially enhanced its efforts in that area by developing promotional materials, participating in employment and immigration fairs, and launching targeted recruitment drives (for farmers and health professionals, as well as for skilled workers and Asian and European entrepreneurs) (Saskatchewan 2002a; 2008). In 2006 the province signed an agreement with the Philippine government to facilitate the recruitment of workers; in 2010 it concluded a similar agreement with the government of Vietnam (Saskatchewan 2007b; 2010b).

Province-building supported the expansion of the PNP. In 2005 the government increased the number of professions that could be accepted under the category of skilled workers and created new selection categories (e.g., agricultural workers, health professionals, truck drivers). The program also expanded quantitatively. Finally, in 2010, the province began using the program to recruit entrepreneurs by creating and promoting new selection channels.

Saskatchewan also began interventions in the area of temporary foreign workers (TFWs). Besides collaborating with specific industries to meet their labour needs, the province opened a support office in

Saskatoon for employers wanting to hire TFWs. In 2010 it created an administrative unit on program integrity and made efforts to ensure the protection of TFWs on its territory.

From 2005 to 2010 the funds allocated to integration in the province steadily increased. In the early 2000s the province provided limited funding to integration services in collaboration with the umbrella association of Saskatchewan organizations providing services (SAISA) and maintained a coordinating council on integration (Saskatchewan 2002a; Lorjé 2003). In 2005 the government substantially increased its funding of integration services, while making it clear that the services thereby created were to focus primarily on access to employment. The services funded included language teaching programs (the costs of which were shared with employers), support programs for entry into the labour market, mentorship programs for economic integration, internship programs, language training programs, and bridge-to-employment programs. The province also became active in the recognition of training and experience acquired abroad (Saskatchewan 2006; 2008).

The province also began developing services directly related to the settlement of immigrants on its territory. This was a new kind of intervention for Saskatchewan.[24] In 2009 and 2010 the province established a model for managing settlement services and increased the availability of those services throughout its territory (Saskatchewan 2009a) by opening regional service centres for new arrivals; it also began to fund beginners' language courses in the province's major centres (Saskatchewan 2010a).

The activation of the province-building mechanism centred on immigration in Saskatchewan would make immigration a strongly present and highly visible area of intervention for the province starting in 2005. That mechanism, bolstered by the consensus that immigration was a provincial economic resource, propelled growth in provincial intervention in immigration and integration. This growth consolidated the characteristics of the bridging mode of intervention in Saskatchewan at a time when the provincial government was repositioning itself regarding the management of the economy in a changing political and ideational context.

The activation of the province-building mechanism increased the province's demands on the federal government; the focus here was on increasing the number of people the province could select through the PNP. But because of the lower intensity of province-building, the province maintained a kind of "apprenticeship" relationship with the federal government over the period studied.[25] Indeed, the province invested heavily in multilateral bodies in order to acquire information about how to increase its involvement in selection (L.A., SK, 9 May 2005, 2918). As the mechanism picked up speed, the actors in Saskatchewan began demanding greater autonomy from the federal government regarding program administration.

The Interaction of the Mechanisms

After 2005, province-building centred on immigration in Alberta and Saskatchewan spurred the incremental activation of the decentralization mechanism. The provincial governments emerged as the jurisdiction through which societal actors – especially economic actors – could express their grievances and their interests. As economic growth and labour needs increased in the two provinces, these societal pressures intensified.[26] In line with their desire to reposition themselves as central partners in economic development, the governments of Alberta and Saskatchewan responded to these pressures by positioning themselves as representatives of the interests of the economic actors with the federal government, and called for changes to national policies. At the same time, the provinces demanded additional powers so that they could respond directly to societal needs and thereby support provincial growth. The two mechanisms ultimately interacted in a process that fuelled federalization.

The demand for an increase in the number of immigrants that could be selected under the PNP was crucial to this interaction. According to a federal civil servant, these pressures were constant and ever-increasing: "If it was up to the provinces, they would get half a million a year."[27] These pressures were expressed within the framework of bilateral relations between the governments and in the multilateral forums that brought together the provinces, the territories, and the federal government.[28]

For Alberta, activation of the province-building mechanism had two key consequences with respect to relations with the federal government. First of all, the province signed a formal agreement for the joint management of settlement services in 2007; this codified the collaborative relations already in place and increased funding transfers to the province (Mailhot 2007). That agreement was evidence of the province's desire to formalize its role in administering settlement programs and to increase its power with regard to selection. It is also possible to see this as a direct consequence of demands in the area of immigration expressed by the Alberta government and intensified by Ed Stelmach after 2006.

This agreement would strengthen the links between the Alberta government and the settlement sector, besides permitting a more collaborative approach in the province.[29] A federal civil servant noted that "Alberta had financial resources to bring to the table as well, and could invest in … a public administration to describe it. [So] they were able to start to play [in] a more serious way. And they wanted to use those as ways of … you know … creative ways of expanding, training and that kind of things."[30]

Alberta later signed an appendix to its immigration agreement that assigned it a substantial role in the selection of temporary foreign workers. This indicated clearly that the province desired to represent the interests of economic actors with the federal government and to directly serve the employers on its territory. Over time, other provinces would sign similar agreements, inspired by Alberta's example.

In general, relations between the federal government and Alberta remained positive over the period studied, despite the province's increasing demands. Faced with the province's rising demands, Ottawa attempted to ensure that there would be no abuse or problematic use of Alberta's selection program. As time passed, the province increasingly saw federal supervision as an intrusion into areas of provincial activity.[31]

In Saskatchewan the mechanism of province-building had the key consequence of maintaining pressure to increase provincial nominations. The provincial demands were coupled with the general growth of the program, which caused some concern in the federal government. A federal civil servant described the typical relationship of Ottawa with the province with respect to the PNP:

All of them seem to want more of a say in selecting [...] All of them I would suggest think that immigration is a silver bullet to all their economic problems … Saskatchewan is pretty aggressive about getting people in as well. We recently had some issues related to … what we thought were fraudulent activities and they were somewhat reluctant to move forward on that … There is always that tension, the provinces trying to push the envelope.[32]

In addition, the province signed an appendix on information-sharing and collaboration in the area of temporary foreign workers in 2008 (Canada 2008). This agreement was not as extensive as that of Alberta;

even so, it pointed to the Saskatchewan government's desire to position itself as a go-between with employers in the province.

When the Saskatchewan Party led by Premier Brad Wall came to power in 2007, there were changes in the relationship with the federal government (McGrane 2008). Because of the effects of the province-building mechanism and Saskatchewan's desire for greater autonomy, the exchanges grew more tense. As time passed, the province attempted more and more to act independently and no longer sought to forge new policy links with the federal government.[33]

In Alberta and Saskatchewan, the interaction of the province-building and decentralization mechanisms had powerful effects. The provinces, having recognized the link between immigration and economic growth, constantly demanded a strengthening of their capacity for selection as well as changes in federal policies. The federal government understood the importance of addressing these matters. To the extent that the region emerged during this period as an engine of national economic growth, it was politically and economically difficult for Ottawa to curb the desire for expanded powers as expressed by Alberta and Saskatchewan. Until 2010, the interaction of the two mechanisms occurred smoothly.

The legacy of this period was therefore to make immigration a key area of intervention for these two provinces. This spoke to the interests of the political elites, who aimed to protect their power by creating new institutions and launching new public actions to address a changing economic context. After 2010 the links between immigration and this provincial mindset were confirmed. The governments of Alberta, Saskatchewan, and British Columbia collaborated significantly as they applied pressure on immigration questions with the federal government and public service.[34] Also, the Saskatchewan government reacted strongly to regulatory changes made to the PNP by the federal government in 2012. The provincial minister responsible for the program, Rob Norris, cast those changes – which in Ottawa's view were aimed at ensuring the integrity of the program – as an obstacle to Saskatchewan's capacity to meet its own needs, and declared his province committed to "continue to ask Ottawa to increase the overall number of immigrants the province can bring in, something business leaders are also urging" (Hall 2012, 2). In Alberta, fluctuations in natural resource prices and the instability of public finances after 2010 did not curb the province's activities in immigration. These examples clearly show the institutionalization in these two provinces of the consensus on immigration as a resource.

Conclusion

In the 2000s the province-building mechanism centred on immigration was activated in Alberta and Saskatchewan. This increased the impact of provincial interventions in immigration and integration, sustained by new ideas linking immigration to the needs of the provincial labour markets. Thus during this period intervention in immigration became a tool to support rapid economic growth, but especially to affirm immigration's central importance to provincial society. This trajectory explains the institutionalization of the bridging mode of intervention in Alberta and Saskatchewan. When it came to immigration, the provinces were at first only weakly influenced by the operations of the decentralization mechanism described earlier in this chapter.

In fact, the growth of interest in these two provinces occurred after those episodes. What ended up affecting the activation of province-building were broader political changes in Ottawa: the evolution of the federal *modus operandi* in intergovernmental relationships, and federal immigration policy changes and labour market management agreements. These generated pressures and opportunities to reposition provincial governments in relation to their economies and societies. Bureaucratic actors, who had developed an interest in immigration even before province-building, were crucial here. These actors, working autonomously from society, facilitated the identification of intervention in immigration as the solution to the challenges of the provincial elites in a changing context.

In general, the trajectories of these two provinces show beyond any doubt that decentralization did not automatically spur the activation of the province-building mechanism centred on immigration. In fact, these examples illustrate a trajectory in which provinces could accept powers emerging from the decentralization mechanism without actually implementing them. This shows that the province-building mechanism was a necessary condition for the emergence of provincial immigration activities from 1990 to 2010.

As time passed, the two provinces increased their pressure on the federal government, and this contributed to maintaining the decentralization mechanism active. Ultimately, and especially after 2010, Alberta and Saskatchewan would continue to put considerable pressure on Ottawa within the institutional regime of governance of immigration and integration. These pressures remain influential, insofar as many characteristics of the bridging mode of intervention – primarily economic selection linked to employers and measures for quick access to the labour market – are now embodied in the reforms of federal immigration programs implemented after 2010.

Chapter 5

Atlantic Canada: Immigration for the Survival of Provincial Societies

After 2005 the governments of the Atlantic provinces broke with their historical passivity in favour of a proactive approach to immigration. Despite significant differences, Prince Edward Island, New Brunswick, Nova Scotia, and Newfoundland and Labrador created similar modes of intervention, labelled here "attraction–retention." These modes of intervention are characterized by strong efforts to recruit immigrants – be they families, skilled workers, or entrepreneurs – and by measures aimed at consolidating their attachment to the provincial territory. The interventions these provinces carried out were less substantial than those of the other provinces and focused less on integration. In 2010 this mode of intervention was still being consolidated, and accordingly, it was also characterized by a particular emphasis on developing the capacities of public administration responsible for immigration and on developing stronger relationships with immigrant serving agencies.

The activation of the province-building mechanism centred on immigration created the conditions for the development of this mode of intervention. Concerned by shifts in demography, the Atlantic provinces came to see immigration as a resource for human rather than financial capital. Elite interest in immigration developed more incrementally than it did in the rest of the country. Political actors, and especially the provincial cabinets, came to view this area of intervention as a lever with which to raise up their central position, through a renewed role as key players in social and economic development. But before provincial governments could openly express such strong discourse, they needed to address certain political dangers associated with a mobilization towards immigration in the region.

Having engaged in the federalization process, each of the Atlantic provinces proposed immigration strategies and established public administrations responsible for immigration. They also increased their interventions in the recruitment of new arrivals and, to a lesser extent, in integration. As this chapter shows, these activities were maintained despite the passage of time and despite the election of new governments with differing political orientations. The trajectory of these provinces demonstrates the establishment of a consensus around the role of immigration in the provincial societies of Atlantic Canada.

To understand how the Atlantic provinces contributed to federalization, it is important to consider timing and sequence. Compared to other provinces, the first stages of decentralization occurred almost imperceptibly in the Atlantic provinces, and when nominee programs were created and agreements signed, it was without much fanfare. The decentralization mechanism did not spur province-building centred on immigration in the region. Moreover, these provinces did not contribute to the pressures that were the source of the activities of the decentralization mechanism before 2010. Not until after the province-building mechanism centred on immigration was activated did these provinces build on the powers acquired through decentralization and finally demand an expansion of their capacity regarding selection.

First Interventions

Despite general fears related to depopulation that took root in the 1960s, Prince Edward Island, New Brunswick, Nova Scotia, and Newfoundland and Labrador had complex relationships with immigration. Economic structures and low migration flows tended to reinforce the ambivalence about immigration among provincial governments (Belkhodja and Traisnel 2011). Their lukewarm attitude to intervention in that area can be explained in part by fear of the possible political costs. In particular, elected officials feared a potential backlash from inviting more immigrants into the region because of the relatively high unemployment of the local population (Marquis 2008). These four provinces therefore focused on attracting immigrant investors, who were seen as a vector for regional economic development. Within this approach, the meagre resources these governments invested went to promoting their provinces as places to invest. These years were also characterized by pressures placed on the federal government with respect to the administration of the immigrant investor program. These demands were primarily administrative and not highly conflictual in nature. These provinces signed agreements on collaboration in immigration with the federal government at the end of the 1970s and remained relatively satisfied with the division of responsibilities in the area until the 2000s (Garcea, 1994, 462–3).

Prince Edward Island

From the end of the Second World War to the 2000s, the PEI government was shy about intervening in immigration policy. Like other provinces in the region, it signed an agreement on collaboration in immigration in 1978 while maintaining a vision according to which immigration was solely the responsibility of the federal government. The only provincial area of intervention in immigration in the 1980s related to investment immigration, which was supported by few financial and administrative resources. The integration of new immigrants was completely absent from the provincial radar and was always presented as a federal responsibility (Arsenault 2000).

In the late 1980s the province set up six immigrant investment funds. Its program was very effective, attracting close to $269.5 million to the province between 1986 and 2000. These funds were reinvested in economic development but also used to support the population. For example, PEI used the private investments to provide interest-free loans to farmers (L.A., PEI, 15 April 1997, 706). Although there was some political support for this form of intervention, the province remained relatively discreet about it. Despite the important role played by the funds raised from immigration for the provincial economy, the government was reluctant to involve itself more deeply in this sector (Morrison 1991).

New Brunswick

Compared to PEI, New Brunswick governments showed greater interest in immigration. But so long as the province's economic situation remained precarious, its intervention in immigration was a sensitive subject.

Demographic concerns were still very present in the province but focused primarily on out-migration (Belkhodja and Traisnel 2011). Despite the climate of modernization created in large part by the "Other Quiet Revolution" brought about by the government of Louis Robichaud (1960–70), government ambivalence towards immigration persisted (Steel 2006). It was against this backdrop that the New Brunswick government signed a collaboration agreement on immigration in 1978.

Political sensitivity related to immigration limited the provincial government's involvement in the pan-Canadian management of questions related to population growth. A high unemployment rate and fears that the francophone population would react poorly to the arrival of large numbers of anglophone immigrants explains this position (Hawkins 1991; Steel 2006). This ambivalence, which lasted into the 1980s and 1990s, did not prevent the province from developing a few formal interventions, mainly with a view to attracting investment (e.g., New Brunswick 1990). Capital raised through immigration was presented as a vehicle for provincial economic development, leaving aside the idea of a substantial increase in the number of immigrants.

In addition to these interventions, New Brunswick created integration-related activities in the late 1990s. These were the result of stronger interest in immigration on the part of the McKenna government (Liberal Party, 1987–97) at the end of its term (New Brunswick 1997; Ouellette 2012). In addition to its multiculturalism policy, the province provided very limited subsidies to organizations delivering services (New Brunswick 1993; 1997).

Nova Scotia

It was not until the late 1980s that a certain level of political concern with immigration emerged in Nova Scotia. At the end of the term of the Buchanan government (Progressive Conservative Party [PC], 1978–90), rising immigration to the province was seen as an objective to pursue. However, that seed of interest was swept away by changes of government. Under the Progressive Conservative government of Donald William Cameron (1991–93) – a government noted for its frugal approach to government funding (Bickerton, 2001 60–4) – the province did not want to play a significant role in the selection of immigrants. The Liberal government of John Savage (1993–97) – which established a program to rationalize government activities and spending – resisted growing pressure from provincial civil society for greater intervention in integration (Morrison 1991; McLeod 2006; McLaughlin 1997).

Like the three other Atlantic provinces, Nova Scotia focused on attracting immigrant investors. In spite of its interest, the province did not invest substantial resources in these activities, and its intervention was not as dynamic as that of other provinces (McLeod 1991). In the early 1990s the provincial government, through its education ministry, began to distribute, on an ad hoc basis, small amounts of funding for integration (Akbari et al. 2007).

Newfoundland and Labrador

Before becoming a province, the Dominion of Newfoundland implemented highly exclusive immigration policies. When the province entered Confederation, it had to align its policies with the federal paradigms of the era, which involved liberalizing selection criteria (Bassler 1994; Chowdhari Tremblay and Bittner 2011).

Because of a difficult economic situation and tense relations with the federal government, Newfoundland paid little attention to immigration from 1945 to 2000 (Marland 2010). Newfoundland and Labrador carried out some activity with regard to recruiting immigrant entrepreneurs, but its efforts were limited compared to those of other provincial governments during the same period. Similarly, although it received a comparatively large number of refugees, the government of Newfoundland and Labrador took very limited actions provide them with support. The province's non-intervention stimulated the creation of an important network of charitable and private organizations to assist immigrants. In the mid-1990s these actors tried, with little success, to raise awareness of the importance of provincial interventions in immigration and integration.[1]

In a difficult economic context, immigration was perceived as a politically sensitive area of intervention for the governments of PEI, New Brunswick, Nova Scotia, and Newfoundland and Labrador from 1945 to the 2000s. Thus the first immigration interventions in the Atlantic provinces focused on efforts to attract capital for economic development. These activities remained low-profile and did not involve substantial investments of human and financial resources from the governments of these provinces.

Decentralization in the Atlantic Provinces

The decentralization mechanism had only slight effects in the Atlantic provinces until the 2000s. This was due to elite ambivalence as well as to the fact that most of these provinces were still very comfortable with the proactive, interventionist role of the federal government in the area of economic development and social service delivery (MacDonald 1998).

No province in the region included immigration among its demands during constitutional negotiations in the 1980s and 1990s. All four faced economic problems and had to deal with a sense of regional alienation. Instead, the Atlantic provinces' demands focused largely on equalization, provincial prerogatives related to natural resources, and reform of federal political institutions, primarily the Senate (Finbow 1994).

The signing of the 1991 immigration agreement between Quebec and Canada did not generate a strong reaction from the Atlantic provinces. Given the absence of immigration on the agendas of these governments, and the lack of need for services for new arrivals on their territories, the agreement was merely another irritant for these provinces. It did not become the basis for making immigration-related demands, as was the case in other parts of the country.[2]

This characteristic lack of provincial interest was also at play during the Settlement Renewal process. The four provinces would not accept the federal offer to take over responsibilities in settlement services. The federal analysts responsible for consulting on the project pointed out that there was little attention paid to integration by the governments of those provinces at the time and that the provincial civil servants responsible for the file – when there were any – were often isolated and overworked. It has been suggested that the consultations were therefore primarily carried out with the associations active in providing immigrant services in the four provinces rather than with the provincial administrations themselves.[3]

These associations would have preferred that the federal government remain responsible for services for new arrivals in the Atlantic provinces. According to a federal analyst responsible for consultations in the region, this opinion arose from the lack of interest in immigration shown by the provincial governments and by the lack of capacity of those governments:

They were for the most part, almost entirely content dealing with the federal government on that file. They felt I think that the provinces weren't equipped or knowledgeable … The knowledge of refugee experience they felt was federal and … the provincial folks would not be able to pick up on that. And just, their own experiences that they had with the provincial government … haven't been that favourable and for the most part, the provincial government representatives were fine with not assuming responsibility for this file and were content with maybe a greater consultation or input … The prevailing mood in every province was that they preferred the federal government to be responsible.[4]

Many analysts responsible for consultations also noted that demonstrations of interest in the matter stemmed from the independent actions of provincial civil servants. But these policy entrepreneurs were not yet able to convince their respective governments of the benefits of a more substantial role in integration (Paquet 2015).

The passive resistance in the Atlantic provinces can be explained in part by stated concerns about the transfer of costs by the federal government. The program review exercise launched in 1995 shook up the region, and Settlement Renewal appeared to be an additional catastrophe. An analyst active in the negotiations maintained that the Atlantic provinces were very perplexed by and not very interested in the federal offer. Their responses can be summed up as a complaint of powerlessness, as one negotiator recalled: "[When we met with the Atlantic provinces], the reaction was 'We don't know anything about immigration!' In the context of program review it was like 'What, are you going to dump another thing on us?' They did not have a single policy officer on these files."[5]

The PNP was therefore the only element of the decentralization mechanism that interested the Atlantic provinces early in the process. Between 1999 and 2004 the four provinces signed agreements permitting them to create their own PNPs. These first agreements were characterized by the presence of important numerical limits on the nominees and by their short duration. PEI signed an agreement in 2002 and established its PNP the following year (Prince Edward Island 2002, 35). New Brunswick, following the limited interest shown by Frank McKenna at the end of his term, signed an agreement in 1999 (New Brunswick 2000, 25). After many years of negotiations, Nova Scotia signed its agreement in 2002, which led to the creation of a nominee program and was seen by the province as a first step towards a more substantial agreement (Nova Scotia 2004). Newfoundland and Labrador signed a first agreement in 2004.

Except in the case of Brunswick, these agreements did not lead to public announcements by the provincial governments of the Atlantic region. Indeed, they went relatively unnoticed and appeared at first to be extensions of those governments' efforts to attract capital through immigration. The agreements did not mobilize elites around immigration in Atlantic Canada. Not until the activation of the province-building mechanism did these programs begin to expand and achieve greater visibility.

Province-Building in Context

Through the decentralization mechanism, the Atlantic provinces acquired limited powers in selection but not the increased financial or symbolic resources they would have needed to support provincial intervention in immigration. After 2005 the gradual activation of the province-building mechanism showed that the provincial governments were overcoming their hesitation about playing an open and active role in immigration. Central to the mechanism being activated in these provinces were new visions that situated immigration as an economic and demographic resource vital for the survival and self-sufficiency of provincial society. In the medium term this vision would be established as the consensus in Atlantic Canada.

Despite the persistence of demographic concerns in the Atlantic region, immigration was not seen as a solution in these societies until the 2000s. The identification of immigration as a demographic and economic resource thus marked a significant change in the Atlantic provinces. This was driven by a repositioning of the provinces in the Canadian and global economies as part of a broader shift towards the knowledge economy (Savoie 2006; 2004). It was also the result of activities and ideas put forward by the federal government and by Atlantic Canada's regional institutions (e.g., by the Atlantic Provinces Economic Council [APEC]). These actors raised awareness of the potential benefits of immigration and, in time, created the motivation needed for meaningful action in this area.

At the federal level, four contextual elements favoured the activation of province-building mechanisms centred on immigration in the Atlantic region. The first was Ottawa's growing interest in the regionalization of immigration (Abu-Laban and Garber 2005). As we saw previously, this interest was accompanied by the promotion of agreements to create PNPs. At the same time, Ottawa was actively promoting capacities to attract and receive new arrivals in less traditional destinations (McLeod 2002; Arthur 2003; Canadian Press 2003; Canada 2003a), first under Paul Martin, then during the first terms of the Harper government (Andrew and Bradford 2011). Second, as part of the work of the Atlantic Canada Opportunities Agency (ACOA),[6] activities for attracting immigrants were cast as among the strategic responses to the region's new economic realities (Lebrun and Rebelo 2006). These first two elements can be seen both as a confirmation of concerns expressed through the results of the 2001 census and as responses to those concerns.

Third, starting in 1996, agreements on labour market management with the Atlantic provinces underscored the importance of immigrants as participants in the provincial labour market. Because they identified underemployed new arrivals as a target group for provincial intervention, these agreements also indirectly increased the immigration-related funds accessible to provinces. Fourth, as was the case in other regions, changes to the federal immigrant investor program reduced the potential to attract capital through immigration in the Atlantic provinces.

At the regional level, many elements created a climate conducive to putting immigration on the agenda. First of all, non-governmental institutions such as the Atlantic Provinces Economic Council, the Atlantic Institute of Market Studies, and the Council of Atlantic Premiers (CAP)[7] began to view immigration as an important area of intervention for the demographic survival and economic development of the provinces (Atlantic Provinces Economic Council 2004). This shift in perceptions was expressed through the production of studies and information documents and the organizing of strategy sessions and was advanced through the creation of the Atlantic Population Table in 2005.[8] This table was both an intergovernmental working group and a space for coordinating provincial activities in the area of recruitment. Federal and provincial civil servants as well as many organizations providing services have emphasized the central role of this platform for social learning and information-sharing about immigration.[9]

Thus, regional-level activities and federal policies favoured a reframing of immigration as an issue of demography. It also supported the identification of immigration and immigrants as resources for the region (attraction, retention, and economic integration of immigrants as means of supporting the provincial society and economy). These favourable circumstances created a stronger base of societal support for the hitherto elite interest in a greater provincial role in immigration. Subsequently, the province-building mechanisms centred on immigration were activated in the four Atlantic provinces.

Province-Building in Prince Edward Island

PEI underwent a gradual shift from a vision of immigration as a source of financial capital to one of immigration as a resource for the survival of provincial society. The activation of province-building occurred in 2006 under Pat Binns (PC, 1996–2007), and provincial interventions were institutionalized under Robert Ghiz, the Liberal premier, starting in 2007.

The election of Pat Binns (PC) in 1996 put an end to a decade of Liberal Party government in PEI. The goals of the new government were to reduce the provincial debt and to restore order to government finances. These objectives would be achieved starting in 1999 thanks to a return of growth and an increase in federal transfers to the province (Dyck 2006, 63). The Binns government, which would remain in power for three consecutive terms (1996–2000, 2000–3, 2003–7), owed its popularity to a low unemployment rate, an increase in provincial exports, and the development of new economic initiatives (MacKinnon 2007, 70–1).

In addition to economic policy, the political elite of the province – in particular the Binns cabinet – showed interest in the demographic question, conceived as an essential factor for progress towards modernization and provincial economic independence. In the 1998 Speech from the Throne the premier announced his government's intentions:

> My Government believes that as we enter the new millennium, it is an important time to engage Islanders in a discussion regarding our population base. The growth encouraged by completion of the Confederation Bridge, a province-wide broadband network, more equitable energy costs, tax changes, targeted job creation initiatives, and the recognition that Prince Edward Island is a very desirable place to live, suggest the need to examine population-related issues. We will ask Islanders to consider the level of growth which could be encouraged by government policy … The results of this discussion will lead to the formation of a population strategy for the new millennium. (L.A., PEI, 12 November 1998, 11)

Having expressed this commitment, the government kicked off a series of consultations and public hearings on demography and organized an expert panel on the subject (PEI Population Strategy '99 Panel 1999). In 2000 a report based on these reflections concluded that the province needed to develop its own immigration strategy in order to compete in attracting immigrants (Institute of Island Studies 2000). The expert panel's recommendations were not implemented; even so, the Binns government continued to present immigration as a challenge for the province (Canadian Press 2001; 2002).

During the PCs' second term (2000–3), PEI signed an agreement for a pilot PNP (Baldacchino 2011). This led to the establishment of a PNP in

2002 as well as measures to promote the program, including a website. These activities were still presented largely as means to attract capital to the province (L.A., PEI, 14 November 2002, 11), an orientation reinforced by the selection categories then used by the province.[10] Although the first version of the program made it possible to nominate skilled workers, two of its three admission categories – immigrant entrepreneurs and immigrant partners – had, as a condition for nomination, investments of $200,000 per principal applicant. At that time, the province did not really invest in the development of expertise for administering the program and tended to delegate its management to private actors (Prince Edward Island 2003, 18–19).

Demographic concerns took on renewed importance after the Binns government was re-elected for a third term in 2003. Although immigration had not been an election issue, the government announced soon afterwards the creation of a unit responsible for the file – a first in the province's history. The Population Secretariat was assigned the task of increasing the population by 1.5 per cent each year through repatriation, immigration, and retention policies. When it was created, however, this secretariat had only one employee and was funded in large part by ACOA. It focused primarily on recruitment policy and international representation.[11] At that stage it conducted no integration activities.[12]

Efforts by the cabinet and the provincial public service to generate political and popular support for a proactive provincial role were signs that the province-building mechanism had been activated. In 2004 the Legislative Assembly office instructed the Standing Committee on Community Affairs and Economic Development to study how immigrants could be attracted to the province (Prince Edward Island 2005b; 2005a). Also in 2004, the secretariat began a new round of consultations and public hearings on demographic growth, led an interdepartmental working group on the issue, and developed analyses intended to provide the basis for a provincial immigration strategy. Finally, in November 2005, the secretariat organized a public forum on immigration and integration with the goal of determining how the island could attract, retain, and integrate immigrants. The forum included actors from the integration sector, economic actors, union representatives, politicians, and citizens.[13] This consultation work helped assuage fears of more forceful provincial intervention in immigration.

By late 2005 the activation of province-building centred on immigration was highly visible in PEI. Central to the mechanism was a new consensus that presented immigration as a solution, besides injecting foreign capital. More precisely, a consensus emerged that immigration was a resource for the province's transition to a knowledge economy. As stated in the 2005 Speech from the Throne:

> Immigration has always contributed to the social and economic development of both Canada and Prince Edward Island. Bringing new people to the province will be an important aspect of future prosperity. The most critical labour market issue facing Prince Edward Island from 2005 onward will not be unemployment, but skill shortages. The knowledge-based economy combined with changes across the traditional sectors has created a demand for a more highly skilled and adaptable workforce. (L.A., PEI, 16 November 2005, 8, 9)

In the years that followed, in documents related to immigration, the link between immigration and the province's survival in a new political and economic context was constantly reiterated. Key to this vision was a proactive role for the provincial government in maintaining a young and employable population. Attracting newcomers possessing skills as well as economic and human capital was considered an ideal means to achieve that objective, in addition to repatriation policies targeting people who already had links to the island.

Thus, by 2005 the PEI government viewed immigration as a legitimate area in which to intervene. To support this consensus, which assigned a central role to the state, the public service responsible for the file was expanded. In 2006 two new analysts were assigned to immigration; the following year the position of manager of immigration, recruitment, promotions, and integration was created (Prince Edward Island 2007a, 11). Also in 2006, the province launched its first immigration strategy, which included a series of measures such as the expansion of the PNP and establishment of new categories, an increase in research, and additional efforts to publicize job opportunities in the province (Prince Edward Island 2006; 2007a; Canadian Press 2005b). This strategy and a reinforced public service supported an increase in the province's activities, both in the area of promotion abroad and within Canada in the area of the retention of new arrivals.[14]

The Binns government's efforts were consolidated after Robert Ghiz, a Liberal, was elected premier in 2007. The fact that these changes were not just carried over but actually institutionalized by the succeeding government indicates that the vision of immigration as an important resource had spread among the elite. Having campaigned on the theme of change (MacKinnon 2007), the newly installed Liberals linked provincial efforts in immigration to a new "2009–2014" strategy for prosperity. Immigration was presented as a pillar of this economic strategy, especially with respect to efforts to recruit skilled immigrants and foreign students (Prince Edward Island 2007b). Although the government wanted to focus its development on a broader and more progressive vision of immigration, the official discourse maintained a vision of immigration as a demographic *and* economic resource for the province (Prince Edward Island 2008, 11). The 2009 Speech from the Throne restated the consensus that had been forming since 2005:

> In our global society, our future success also depends on building a vibrant and diverse population. Immigration is making a vital contribution to this goal. From July 2008 to June 2009, our Island experienced its highest rate of population growth in a quarter century. Our population grew by over 1,500 people or more than one per cent – the highest growth rate of any province east of the Prairies. Immigrant investment has also brought major benefits to Prince Edward Island. Over 1,500 applications under the Immigrant Partner Fund have been approved by the Federal Government, resulting in a net investment of $120 million in Island businesses. (L.A., PEI, 12 November 2009, 11)

The Ghiz government expanded the description of its responsibilities in immigration. Having started as an agent for recruitment and population-building, the province gradually became a key actor in the integration of immigrants.

As part of this development strategy, coloured by the consensus central to the province-building mechanism, provincial funding related to immigration policy, but also to integration, was increased starting in 2008 (Baldacchino 2011; Prince Edward Island 2010b). The government restructured the Population Growth Secretariat in 2008, allocating it more human and financial resources. It was also moved to a new ministry, the Department of Innovation and Advanced Learning.

In the area of immigration, the province continued its efforts in recruitment, with an emphasis on skilled workers from Europe. The province continued to rely on its PNP until 2010 (Prince Edward Island 2008; 2009). Despite scandals related to how the PNP was administered, the province expanded its nomination process, to include options to facilitate the acquisition of permanent residence for temporary foreign workers on its territory (Prince Edward Island 2010a).

To meet the needs of its expanding immigrant population, the PEI government offered supplementary funding for services provided by the federal government starting in 2008. These efforts were carried out largely by educational institutions, but also by the province's central agency for settlement services, the PEI Association of Newcomers to Canada. The services funded mainly involved language training, integration of new arrivals into the job market, and diversity management (Prince Edward Island 2009).

Over the course of five years, PEI transformed its relationship to immigration and established an "attraction–retention" mode of intervention. After a very slow start in the province, immigration became a pillar of efforts at economic and demographic modernization. The political elite, having ascertained that immigration had at least some societal support, viewed intervention in the area as a means of maintaining its influence. Successive governments identified immigration as a resource for provincial society, taking the view that it was the provincial government's responsibility to manage this resource. The relatively recent activation of the province-building mechanism centred on immigration in PEI meant that the attraction–retention mode of intervention of the island was still being consolidated, as evidenced by the publication, in 2010, of the first official provincial strategy on integration (Prince Edward Island 2010b).

Province-Building in New Brunswick

In New Brunswick, province-building centred on immigration was not activated until 2007, the year Shawn Graham, a Liberal, was elected premier. A first immigration agreement had been signed in 1999, but actual activity on the immigration front was curtailed with the election of Bernard Lord, a Progressive Conservative, whose government focused on the province's economic health and closely monitored programs in order to maintain low spending levels in particular sectors (Dyck 2006).

The province nevertheless implemented its PNP, which was still oriented towards attracting capital. Besides maintaining a business immigration component, New Brunswick's PNP had two selection categories between 1999 and 2006: skilled workers, and immigrant entrepreneurs (New Brunswick 1999b; 2005). Though they generally lacked visibility, promotion efforts were launched abroad in the hope of attracting immigrants from Europe.

During its second term (2003–6), the Lord government did not place much emphasis on immigration. The final Speech from the Throne before the election recognized immigration as an important component of the province's strategy of internationalization and economic development, through the direct foreign investment that immigrants could make in New Brunswick (L.A., NB, 19 November 2002, 12). Subsequently, as part of the implementation of its economic plan, *Greater Opportunity: New Brunswick's Prosperity Plan, 2002–2012*, the government identified intervention in immigration as a means to achieve its objective of "investing in people" (New Brunswick 2002) and promised efforts to attract investment immigration. In the end, the measures implemented would be limited to increased recruitment efforts. Despite a general lack of activity (New Brunswick 1999a), this period did see modest moves towards a greater provincial role in immigration, moves that would persist and lead to stronger actions in the future.

The Liberals, under Shawn Graham, returned to power in New Brunswick in 2006 on the heels of an economic slowdown and budget cuts, especially in health, both of which had contributed to the decline in popularity of the Lord government (Desserud 2008, 52–3). The Liberals had campaigned on a theme of provincial self-sufficiency. Graham proposed a societal project based on a change of status for the province. In the preamble to his platform, he declared: "I want New Brunswick to join the ranks of the 'have' provinces and I want the province to accomplish this over the next 20 years" (Liberal Party of New Brunswick 2006, 1). In his platform, and in the campaign, the party promised to promote a demographic strategy for the province and to increase provincial intervention in integration (Canadian Press 2006b; 2006c; White 2006).

Once elected, the Liberal government set about giving shape to its project by creating a special task force on self-sufficiency (Canadian Press 2007b; 2007c). As described by Donald Savoie, "self-sufficiency involve[d] not only autonomous economic growth, but also recognition that the province will no longer be able to depend on transfer payments, as it had in the past, in order to develop and maintain its infrastructure and its public services" (Savoie 2010, 46). The Graham government's self-sufficiency project was ambitious, and though not entirely realized, it did activate the province-building mechanism centred on immigration.

During that activation, the government created a Population Growth Secretariat, which began operations in 2007. Within the New Brunswick Department of Business, the secretariat was responsible for all activities related to demography. In 2007 the government established a Settlement and Multiculturalism Branch responsible for all of the province's integration and diversity management programs. The same year, a Population Growth Advisory Board was created in which the organizations providing immigrant services would play a particularly important role (New Brunswick 2008a).

In keeping with the establishment of a public service dealing with immigration cases, New Brunswick launched an immigration strategy in 2008. This strategy was the outcome of public hearings throughout the province, conducted by the Population Growth Secretariat (New Brunswick 2008a; 2008b). Titled *Be Our Future,* this document set ambitious targets: "to achieve a net population growth of 100,000 people by 2026 in order to achieve self-sufficiency"; "to increase the number of immigrants coming to the province with the goal of attracting at least 5,000 people per year by the year 2015"; and "to establish increased targets for the number of immigrants attracted under the Provincial Nominee Program through the skilled worker stream."[15] This strategy also proposed the creation of provincial services for the linguistic, economic, and social integration of new arrivals, as well as increased collaboration with the federal government in the domain. Note that immigration was not the only target of this strategy, which also proposed measures to keep New Brunswickers home and to lure them back to the province if they had left it. In practice, however, immigration was the cornerstone of Graham government's proposed approach, a reflection of the executive's clear interest in this question.

With the publication of the strategy in 2008, the key elements of a new consensus on the role of immigration in New Brunswick became clear. This new consensus saw human capital as a demographic and economic resource that was key to the province's survival. In the government's own words, "[t]he Government of New Brunswick recognizes the important role people play in creating a self-sufficient future for the province" (New Brunswick 2009, 36). The discourses also reinforced the idea that the province should be proactive in attracting and retaining its human resources and assigned the provincial government a key role in the area. They also argued that any population growth strategy needed to be based in large part on increased immigration to the province (New Brunswick 2008b). Immigrants were now more than entrepreneurs or investors; they were citizen-workers and families, and they contributed to the province's autonomy. Finally, central to the consensus that was being established was the idea that immigration played a significant role in the growth of the province's economy (L.A., NB, 17 November 2009, 4).

The spread of that consensus was obvious in the parties' platforms during the 2010 election. In 2006 the Liberal platform had set itself apart with its proposals in the area of immigration (Liberal Party of New Brunswick 2006); in the 2010 election, all the parties made proposals regarding immigration and population support.[16] Even the NDP, until then not much focused on the issue, promised to table an immigration strategy if elected (New Democratic Party of the New Brunswick 2010). The Conservative Party was elected, but the change of government did not put the consensus at risk. In fact, the Speech from the Throne declared that "your government will show focused leadership by boosting immigration to New Brunswick. More immigrants are needed to help our province address labour shortages, create prosperity and grow our population" (L.A., NB, 10 November 2010, 10).

Following activation, and in line with the consensus emerging in the province, interventions directly related to immigration in New Brunswick expanded, as did the resources allocated to them (Canadian Press 2007b). Provincial interventions focused on internal promotion, which was aimed at provincial public opinion and, in particular, at employers and organizations providing integration services (New Brunswick 2008a; 2009). These policies and programs became institutionalized in a way that consolidated the key principles of the attraction–retention mode of intervention: interventions in the area of broad-spectrum recruitment, efforts to retain new arrivals, and policies aimed at developing the province's capacities for reception and integration.

The province's main efforts were in recruitment, which can be explained in part by the ambitious targets presented in the provincial strategy. The government maintained its PNP throughout the period and attempted to increase its numerical targets. It also invested substantial human and financial resources in promotion abroad, especially in the United States and Europe, although the targets changed and expanded over time. These efforts also targeted potential francophone immigrants, in line with various federal initiatives in the domain (Paquet and Andrew 2013). The efforts related to francophone immigrants were extended to integration, as evidenced by the creation of a strategic plan for the immigration and settlement of francophones in the province (New Brunswick Advisory Council on Youth 2008). In 2009 the province launched a website on immigration in New Brunswick (New Brunswick 2010, 41–3).

In the area of integration, the province's interventions were in line with the objectives of retention and integration into the labour market. To retain immigrants in the province the government invested in capacity-building for organizations providing services and in the community sector more generally. In 2008 the government established a funding program to support settlement – the first dedicated provincial program of general integration in New Brunswick – in order to improve the delivery of new services (New Brunswick 2009). This program was aimed at filling the gaps in federal services and at ensuring that services were provided throughout the province. New Brunswick was also active in economic integration, producing guides and information tools creating a mentorship program for newcomers. Over the same period there was an increase in funding for multicultural activities (New Brunswick 2008a; 2009).

By 2007, immigration had been raised to the status of an indispensable resource for the survival and self-sufficiency of New Brunswick. In activating a province-building mechanism, New Brunswick transitioned from an investment-seeking approach to a population growth approach. The fact that so many of the Graham government's interventions were maintained and advanced under the PC government elected in 2010 confirms that the consensus around province-building centred on immigration had been institutionalized in New Brunswick.

Province-Building in Nova Scotia

In Nova Scotia, province-building centred on immigration was set in motion in the early 2000s. The Progressive Conservative government of John Hamm came to power in 1999 after six years of Liberal rule. During its first term his government barely mentioned immigration, preferring, as the Lord government had in New Brunswick, to focus on the province's public finances (Nova Scotia 2002; 2000). In his second term, however, Hamm became convinced that immigration contributed to the province. He began to introduce ideas that would lead to the institutionalization of the attraction–retention mode of intervention in Nova Scotia.

After negotiations with the federal government, Nova Scotia signed a five-year immigration agreement in 2002 (Arthur 2002). This agreement did not, strictly speaking, activate the province-building mechanism centred on immigration. It did, however, provide the province with new tools and resources for provincial intervention in immigration.

The following year the province implemented a nomination program, though without really giving it substantial attention or visibility and without trying to expand it (Jackson 2003). The program's administration was devolved to a private company – Cornwallis – and the province did not invest in the development of administrative capacity related to the program.[17]

Elite interest in immigration did not become clearly visible until 2003. Having secured a second term, Nova Scotia's Liberal government promised to use "the recently signed Provincial Nominee Program as a catalyst for developing a comprehensive immigration policy for Nova Scotia" (Liberal Party of Nova Scotia 2003, 14). This surge in interest can be explained by three factors. First of all, there was a considerable decline in the number of immigrants to the province following a boom in the 1990s (Akbari et al. 2007; Boomer 2001; Flemming 2001; Bales 2004). Second, starting in the 2000s there was a timid mobilization of settlement and economic actors that aimed to increase the government's awareness of immigration questions (Bornais 2000; Flemming 2000; Jackson 2000a; MacKinley 2000; confidential interview, 2012; Clow 2000). Third, criticisms emerged directed at the government's interventions in investment immigration (Jackson 2000b).

In this context, the province initiated a period of reflection on immigration beginning in 2003. This was especially motivated by the personal concerns of John Hamm regarding the province's population decline. Following the signing of the agreement with the federal government, the Premier's Office invited the actors in the integration sector to present basic information on immigration in Nova Scotia. In 2003 the biggest organization providing services, the Metropolitan Immigrant Settlement Association (MISA), organized a conference on immigration. Employers, governments, and immigrant settlement organizations took part (Simpson 2003). The province organized public hearings in 2004 with the objective of developing an immigration strategy and afterwards published a discussion paper: *A Framework for Immigration* (Smith 2004; Nova Scotia 2005b, 25). During this period of reflection, the province mobilized the expertise of actors in the settlement sector, while stating that it also wanted to learn from the experience of other governments (Boomer 2004; McGinnis 2004).

The government published its first immigration strategy in 2005, a clear indication that the mechanism was being activated. Launched by the new minister responsible for immigration, Rodney MacDonald (Liberal), this strategy promoted the goals of increasing the numbers and improving the retention of new arrivals. The target set was 3,600 immigrants annually until 2009. The strategy emphasized the development of new selection channels under the PNP and the reinforcement of integration services for immigrants, through new provincial initiatives but also by favouring coordination with the federal government in order to achieve a rate of retention of close to 70 per cent (Nova Scotia 2005a).

A vital element of the strategy was a commitment to strengthen the public administration responsible for this policy area. The year 2005 saw the creation of the Nova Scotia Office of Immigration, which was assigned all responsibilities related to immigration, which until then had been dispersed among several ministries, mainly the Department of Education and the Department of Economic Development. This change was presented as reflecting the salience of immigration for the government:

> In the past, immigration activities have occurred in a number of government departments, making it difficult to give it a strong profile and focus. A minister and deputy minister have been assigned responsibility for immigration, and it will have the full attention of an executive director. This will give immigration matters a stronger voice at the Cabinet table and with the federal government … This structure ensures that immigration is fully connected to all senior policy forums and with all decision-making levels within government. (Nova Scotia 2005a, 25)

This change increased the visibility of actions on immigration as well as the number of civil servants responsible for the file. It also represented a substantial change in how the province intervened in immigration – the PNP was now entirely administered by this unit rather than by a private corporation (Nova Scotia 2005b).

The 2005 strategy was an indicator that Nova Scotia now saw immigration as a resource for preserving and developing the province. In the preamble to its immigration strategy, the province emphasized how immigration contributed, both demographically and economically, to the province's future:

> Immigrants enrich the social, cultural, and economic life of Nova Scotia. And now, more than ever, immigration is essential for building Nova Scotia's future. We are facing a number of demographic and economic challenges – slow population growth, an aging population, low

birthrate, out-migration of our young people, urbanization, low immigration numbers – all of which may lead to labour shortages, slowing demand for goods and services, and increasing fiscal pressures in the years to come. (Nova Scotia 2005a, 1)

By 2006, this consensus was shared by all political actors in the province. During the 2006 election campaign, the platform of the PCs, now led by Rodney MacDonald, the former provincial immigration minister, proposed investing even more in immigration as a means to support "smart growth" (Progressive Conservative Party of Nova Scotia 2006). Even so, immigration was not discussed much during the campaign. Despite a scandal related to the administration of the first version of the PNP, no one questioned the provincial government's proactive role.[18] After being re-elected, the provincial PCs implemented an economic development policy titled *Opportunities for Sustainable Prosperity 2006* in which immigration was an important aspect (Nova Scotia 2006a). Similarly, the 2006 Speech from the Throne emphasized that immigration – as a source of diversity – was a resource that strengthened provincial society:

> My government knows the more diverse Nova Scotia becomes, the stronger it becomes. To this end, my government will continue to implement the objectives of the Immigration Strategy … including increasing the number of immigrants that are settling in Nova Scotia, helping newcomers adjust to their new lives, and supporting the vital work of our settlement organizations. (L.A., N.S., 4 May 2006, 11)

With the continued progress of the province-building mechanism, these principles would be established as a consensus shared by all societal actors.

The activation of province-building centred on immigration led to an increase in provincial spending and actions in the field of immigration (Nova Scotia 2007; 2008, 9). Starting in 2005, the government launched many internal promotion activities aimed at increasing awareness in the population – especially among employers – of its immigrant selection programs (Nova Scotia 2006b; 2010b). The province's activities were carried out in accordance with the consensus central to province-building and were institutionalized as the attraction–retention mode of intervention.

In 2006 the province reformed its PNP program by adding a selection category for family members of business owners (Nova Scotia

2007). The following year it introduced a selection category for foreign students who had studied in the province, then later a category for immigrant entrepreneurs. To enhance the program quantitatively the province expanded its promotion efforts abroad. These efforts were carried out both independently and in collaboration with other governments in the region as well as with the federal government. The province especially targeted the European market with a view to attracting skilled workers. With the federal government's financial support, Nova Scotia launched a website to promote immigration and increased its efforts to attract francophone immigrants. In 2004 the province signed a memorandum of understanding with CIC permitting international students to work off campus during their studies (Nova Scotia 2005b).

After negotiations that began in 2006, the province signed a new immigration agreement with the federal government in 2007. This open-ended agreement permitted Nova Scotia to select a much larger number of new arrivals through its PNP. At the same time, the province began discussions with Ottawa about activities involving temporary foreign workers (Nova Scotia 2008; 2007).

With regard to integration, the province-building mechanism strengthened government activities and made them more visible. There was a general increase in the budget allocated to this area, and the activities supported by the project were especially oriented towards the economic integration of newcomers (Nova Scotia 2009). In 2006 the province added to the programs already in place second-language courses focusing on the labour market, services for recognizing prior learning and experience, and support for business creation. Nova Scotia also established integration services aimed specifically at francophone new arrivals, with an emphasis on retention (Nova Scotia 2010b). Finally, it demanded an increase in funding from the federal government for settlement services on its territory.[19]

In 2009 the PCs were defeated at the polls and the NDP took power, led by Darrell Dexter. This did not curb the activity of the province-building mechanism centred on immigration in Nova Scotia. The new government's first Speech from the Throne announced a new immigration strategy for the province and reiterated that "immigration is one way to help ensure that our communities thrive and our economy grows" (L.A., NS, 17 September 2009, 11). The strategy, called *Welcome Home to Nova Scotia*, was published in 2010 as a component of the province's economic strategy (Nova Scotia 2010a; 2010c). This strategy proposed a numerical increase in the PNP and the establishment of new selection categories based on the province's labour needs. It set the objective of receiving 5,000 immigrants annually until 2015 and 7,200 immigrants annually between 2015 and 2020. Particular emphasis was to be placed on the economic integration of newcomers as well as their contributions to the labour market.

The publication of this new strategy by a government led by a party that had not expressed a serious commitment to immigration before it came to power demonstrated that the consensus central to the province-building mechanism had been institutionalized. In five years, immigration had become a key area of government intervention in Nova Scotia.

Province-Building in Newfoundland and Labrador

The activation of the province-building mechanism in Newfoundland and Labrador took place after the decentralization mechanism was set in motion in the province and, in large part, independently of it. The province signed its first immigration agreement in 1999 when the government was led by Brian Tobin (Liberal, 1996–2000). Heir to the strategy of promoting investment established by Clyde Wells (Liberal, 1989–1996), the PNP was used primarily as an extension of provincial activities intended to attract foreign capital. The Tobin government, known for its efforts to maximize revenue from natural resources (Dyck 2006, 59–60), did not place high hopes on immigration despite the emergence of new fears related to the loss of population and provincial self-sufficiency. Nor would the Grimes and Tulk governments, from 2000 to 2003, be characterized by reflection on immigration. The limited attention given to immigration in the work and report of the Royal Commission on Renewing and Strengthening Our Place in Canada, created by Roger Grimes (Liberal, 2001–3) (Newfoundland and Labrador 2003), is a good indication of this. Between 2003 and 2007 this lack of attention was replaced by keen elite interest in immigration as a tool for development. Public policies that corresponded to the attraction–retention mode of intervention would soon follow. This reversal was related to the Williams government's goal of rethinking the province's role in economic and social development.

Danny Williams was elected in 2003 after a campaign dominated by the theme of economic autonomy for Newfoundland and Labrador. The province continued to face a difficult economic situation: a high unemployment rate, significant dependence on federal transfer payments, and a substantial provincial debt. Once elected, Williams launched a program review in order to rationalize government spending as a first step towards stabilizing the provincial economy (Marland 2007). Against this backdrop of restructuring and substantial cutbacks in the activities of the provincial government, a second immigration agreement was signed in 2004. This open-ended agreement raised the limit on the number of nominees the province could select. The implementation of the program, which was limited and not very visible, was assigned to the Department of Human Resources, Labour, and Employment.

Nevertheless, during this period the political elite began to reflect on and learn about the benefits of immigration. In 2004, at the cabinet's request, the main organization providing integration services in the province and a provincial civil servant gave a presentation on immigration.[20] This presentation would have a significant impact on the government, which would decide the following year to begin developing an administrative unit responsible for immigration. Over the same period, the government conducted studies on the receptive capacity of Newfoundland and Labrador and looked into the practices of other provinces for ideas for its own programs and policies (Newfoundland and Labrador 2005a).

Immigration was clearly on the agenda of the province's PC government by 2005, and the province-building mechanism centred on immigration was activated. Three factors contributed to this change. The first of these was the province's return to fiscal health, brought about by the Williams government's reforms, revenue growth from natural resources, and an increase in federal transfers (Dunn 2005). Second was the emergence of concerns about potential labour shortages in the oil and fish-processing industries. Third was the emergence of the theme of population decline (Marland 2007). During the 2003 election campaign the potential impact of a declining and aging population on the province's economic and political position in the federation was a constant theme. In 2006 these concerns were reinforced when the province recorded more deaths than births for the first time in its history (Marland 2010). These factors would transform the reflections of the provincial political elite around immigration into a real will to act. Immigration would become a means for Newfoundland and Labrador to achieve autonomy.

The first real sign that province-building had been activated was the organization of public hearings to develop an immigration strategy in 2005 (Newfoundland and Labrador 2007a). During these hearings the government presented increasing immigration to the province as "an excellent opportunity to stimulate and enhance the economic, social, and cultural development of the province" (Newfoundland and Labrador 2005b). The consultation document made a direct link between increased immigration and economic strategies aimed at provincial autonomy, presenting immigrants as the missing piece in the province's development model (Newfoundland and Labrador 2005b).

In 2007 the government published its first provincial immigration strategy, titled *Diversity – Opportunity and Growth* (Newfoundland and Labrador 2007b). The strategy set numerical targets. The Williams government aimed to triple the number of immigrants received by the province before 2012 – that is, bring it up to 1,500 new arrivals per year – and to double the province's retention rate (Newfoundland and Labrador 2007a). This strategy underscored the importance of integration services to foster the retention of immigrants. The government placed particular emphasis on services related to economic integration. The strategy was accompanied by a significant financial commitment (L.A., NL, 15 May 2007). Starting in 2007, immigration was officially associated with the province's economic development efforts.

A basic element of the strategy was a commitment to centralize the public service responsible for immigration, which until then had been scattered among several ministries. In 2007 all programming in immigration, including the administration of the PNP, was shifted to the newly established Office of Immigration.[21] Between 2007 and 2010 that office would continue to develop, recruiting employees, creating expertise in the field, and forging links with key actors in the settlement sector, especially the Association for New Canadians, the main organization delivering settlement services in the province (Newfoundland and Labrador 2008).

The activation of the province-building mechanism centred on immigration in Newfoundland and Labrador was inextricably linked to a consensus that saw immigration as a resource supporting efforts to build prosperity in the province (Newfoundland and Labrador 2007b). Within this framework, the government took on a new role as an agent tasked with attracting workers and revitalizing the population. In 2007 the Speech from the Throne presented this clearly:

> My Government will also enrich our investment climate by encouraging those from away, not only to do business in Newfoundland and Labrador, but also to make Newfoundland and Labrador their home. My

Government this year launched a comprehensive Immigration Strategy to welcome people around the world to join us in making Newfoundland and Labrador a home second to none. Newfoundland and Labrador offers immigrants the best quality of life in Canada, freedom, security, economic opportunity and a sense of family. Immigrants, in turn, bring to Newfoundland and Labrador new ideas, new ways of thinking, strong connections to foreign markets and significant benefits for the local communities in which they establish businesses and employ their new neighbours. Our door to newcomers is open wide and our welcome is warm and sincere. (L.A., NL, 1 May 2007)

During the 2007 election the province's two main political parties explicitly mentioned immigration in their election platforms – a first for the province – and directly linked immigration with the maintenance of the provincial population at an acceptable level. The PCs viewed immigration as a means to grow and revitalize the province's population.[22] For its part, the Liberals promised to implement a vigorous immigration policy, based on Quebec's, as one of two pillars of a population growth strategy (Liberal Party of Newfoundland and Labrador 2007).

Besides being a demographic resource, immigration was presented as a human capital asset. Describing its objectives in recruitment and retention, the government of Newfoundland and Labrador underscored the importance of immigration for the province:

Recruiting workers to Newfoundland and Labrador and retaining them is a critical challenge for business, labour, communities, and government. A shrinking workforce will likely lead to labour shortages that could hamper business expansion and investments. This could negatively affect the competitiveness of employers, which in turn, may limit future employment opportunities. (Newfoundland and Labrador 2009, 15)

Immigrants, then, were seen as a resource for *all* of provincial society. The intervention of the government of Newfoundland and Labrador in immigration thus became a pillar of the general actions of the Williams government aimed at economic and political autonomy for the province (Newfoundland and Labrador 2008).

After the consensus spread, the province's activities in immigration developed in accordance with the key principles of the attraction–retention mode of intervention. They consisted of general recruitment efforts and integration policies aimed at retaining new arrivals. The

Williams government also implemented measures to increase the visibility of its actions with the population and, in particular, with employers.[23]

In the area of recruitment, Newfoundland and Labrador significantly increased its international promotion efforts.[24] Besides creating a website for the province, the government helped many municipalities expand their presence on the Web to publicize immigration opportunities (Newfoundland and Labrador 2009; 2008). The province also took part in missions abroad – especially in Europe – aimed at promoting the province as a destination.[25] In 2009 it launched recruitment efforts aimed at professions that were in especially short supply in the province – for example, nurses (Newfoundland and Labrador 2010a).

But the province's preferred policy instrument remained the PNP. Gradually but persistently, the province increased the number of nominees selected starting in 2007. From 105 in 2007, the number increased to 309 in 2010 (Newfoundland and Labrador 2010b). In 2007, to make its program more accessible, the province reduced the costs associated with filing nominee applications (Newfoundland and Labrador 2008). While maintaining the selection categories already in place (immigrant entrepreneurs, skilled immigrants), Newfoundland and Labrador implemented new selection streams starting in 2007, including one for people with family connections in the province and another for students who had graduated from an institution of advanced education in the province (Newfoundland and Labrador 2009).

Intervention in integration in the province was intended mainly to maximize the retention of immigrants. After publishing its immigration strategy the government set up a funding program for settlement and integration services, the Newfoundland and Labrador Settlement and Integration Program (NLSIP). Through this instrument, it funded organizations providing services to help them offer activities such as English classes, information services, and other services intended to address needs not filled by the federal government. In 2008 the province allocated $600,000 to this program. It was also very active in multiculturalism, launching its strategy in this area in 2008 and funding cultural activities. The same year, to ensure the presence of integration services throughout the province, the government funded the hiring of settlement program personnel in poorly served regions (Newfoundland and Labrador 2009; 2011).

In 2010 the mechanism activated by Williams was still operating. In its last Speech from the Throne, his government celebrated the change to the status of a "have" province for the first time since Confederation

(L.A., NL, 22 March 2010). Williams's surprise resignation in 2010 and the provincial election that followed, in which the PCs were re-elected under the leadership of Kathy Dunderdale, did not curtail activities in this policy area. One indication that the consensus had been consolidated was the presence of immigration in the platforms of all provincial parties in the 2011 election, and the spread of a discourse presenting immigration as a resource for the province among all political actors (Liberal Party of Newfoundland and Labrador 2011; Progressive Conservative Party of Newfoundland and Labrador 2011; New Democratic Party of Newfoundland and Labrador, 2011).

Conclusion

After years of passivity, the 2000s saw a reawakening to immigration in the Atlantic provinces. This was brought about by the idea that immigration was a resource for the development and self-sufficiency of provincial societies, as well as the activation of the province-building mechanism. Spurred by rising concerns about demography and by the promotion of intervention in immigration by the federal government and regional institutions, the elites of each of the Atlantic provinces reflected on how immigration could be a useful tool for reinventing their societies. The consensus on the importance of immigration then spread, and actions were gradually implemented that would become known as the attraction–retention mode of intervention. As in the rest of Canada, province-building centred on immigration evolved according to the interests of the political elite. However, the trajectories of these four provinces were distinct because of the importance given by the provincial elites to the building of a societal consensus. This reflected the potential political risks associated with intervention in immigration in the region, in a changing economic context.

Province-building centred on immigration in the Atlantic provinces was characterized by a comparatively lower number of demands made to the federal government. Two factors help explain this difference: the timing of the activation of the province-building mechanisms centred on immigration, and the lesser scale of the financial issues connected to immigration in these provinces before 2010. Not until later in the process of federalization did immigration became intertwined with each province's political life. By then the federal government's interests were quite different from what they had been in the early 1990s and provincial intervention in immigration was no longer a novel idea in Canada.

To understand the increasing importance of immigration for those governments, one must consider distributive issues related to regionalism and economic development at the national level, and those emerging from the increasing federalization of the institutional regime of governance of immigration and integration.

All of the Atlantic provinces signed PNP agreements at a time when the federal government was trying to disseminate that program and expressing concerns about how immigrants were distributed across Canada. The Atlantic provinces thus acquired powers, while the decentralization mechanism operated at full speed. The decentralization mechanism did not immediately activate the province-building mechanisms centred on immigration. This subsequent and autonomous activation – brought about through the political, economic, and demographic situations in those societies – did not lead to demands for additional powers from the federal government. Certainly, the provinces would have ultimately liked to raise the numerical limits set by their first agreements and to consolidate their collaborative relations with the federal government. However, the trajectory leading to the second wave of immigration agreements in the region was more administrative in nature and had less to do with an alignment of the interests of the two levels of government.

The relative weakness of the Atlantic provinces' financial demands with regard to immigrant integration can be explained in a functional way. These provinces continued to receive only a very small portion of newcomers to Canada, and therefore, pressures on provincial services and programs (education, health, etc.) remained minimal. For a large part of the period studied, the services funded by the federal government seemed to meet the settlement needs in the four provinces. The paucity of discourses on integration and the emphasis on the attraction of new arrivals are indications of this.

The effectiveness of many provincial selection programs as well as growing concerns about the retention of immigrants would come to modify the situation somewhat.[26] Until 2011 the funding allocated to the provinces for settlement and integration was calculated according to the average number of immigrants during the three preceding years. The rapid growth of the number of new arrivals in some Atlantic provinces in the space of a few years meant that the sums invested by the federal government no longer met these provinces' needs. The Atlantic provinces found themselves obligated to compensate for this shortfall from their own budgets or else face the demands of societal actors decrying the lack of services for immigrants. But only after 2010 were these dynamics felt and were political discourses on these questions heard.

Because of the belated activation of the province-building mechanisms centred on immigration in Atlantic Canada and the fact that they still received, despite a few changes, a very low proportion of immigrants, it is difficult to predict what forms their relationships with the federal government will take in the years to come. Despite their status as "have not" provinces in the area of immigration, they view themselves as full players in the contemporary governance of immigration in Canada.[27] In the four provinces discussed in this chapter, immigration became an unavoidable area of intervention, closely related to the development of the economy and the survival of provincial society. The province-building mechanism centred on immigration became the means by which the provincial political elite secured its legitimacy in the face of a changing society and an evolving Canada.

Chapter 6

The Future of the "Canadian Model"

The result of the federalization process has been simple: shared constitutional jurisdiction over immigration, which for a long time was divided only on paper, is now an embodied reality. Through an analysis of federalism focusing on the process of change – rather than on the description and the evaluation of the consequences of change – it has become clear that the transformation described in this book involved gradual institutional change. The discreet nature of that evolution – which has occurred across twenty years and resulted from a combination of bilateral and multilateral relationships among governments – was such that only at the end of the process were the actors were really able to measure its scope. A fundamental transformation has occurred in the "Canadian model" of immigration and integration, partly as a result of the changing interests of actors but also in part out of the unintended consequences of political decisions at different points in time.

The federalization process can only be understood by considering the provinces' role as agents of change in contemporary Canadian federalism. By taking an interactional approach to federalism, this book has shown that it is impossible to describe accurately this episode of Canada's political life by focusing on the federal government's decisions and actions. In this case, the provinces played a crucial role as *triggers* of federalization, and over time they contributed strongly to maintaining pressure on the federal government, thus supporting the activity of the decentralization mechanism (the role of *maintainers*). Through the province-building mechanism centred on immigration – a mobilization of elites around strategies aimed at developing provincial societies, using immigration as a resource – the provinces have seen their interest in immigration and integration develop autonomously. In the ten provinces, the identification of immigration as a resource for demographic survival and especially for economic development has contributed to distinct modes of intervention and, of course, to the growth of demands on the federal government.

As shown by the analysis of the ten provincial trajectories, province-building centred on immigration has been the mechanism through which the provincial modes of intervention have developed. The process-tracing-based comparison shows that this social mechanism operated in three stages: activation, consensualization, and institutionalization. Province-building was driven by provincial elites. The political actors who had executive power, provincial civil servants, and, in some cases, economic actors or actors in the community sector were therefore at the centre of the change in the "Canadian model" of immigration and integration. Although in some cases the activation of the mechanism coincided with changes of government in the provinces, never was the activation or the operation of province-building the result of electoral debates, social movements, or immigrant mobilization. Moreover, the presence of immigration in electoral platforms shows that, once in motion, province-building structured elite discourses around immigration. These cross-case and cross-time characteristics demonstrate that the provincial elites were capable, in this policy sector, of acting relatively independently of society. In defining problems, setting agendas, formulating policies, and making decisions, the actors at the centre of the federalization process have followed their particular interests. Though always specific to each provincial context, these interests nonetheless revolved around the objective of maintaining the centrality, the independence, and the power of provincial elites in the face of the political, economic, and structural changes affecting all of Canada. By establishing institutions and public actions, those elites intended to support the existence of their societies of reference and to define a place for their provinces within the Canadian federation. The province-building mechanism they thereby set in motion helped reshape the political, social, and economic communities of Canadian provinces.

In this regard, the interactional approach to federalism adopted in this book makes it possible to demonstrate that provincial political life remains alive and consequential in the twenty-first century. The provinces are not passive recipients of federal policies or simply victims of international economic and political dynamics. They respond instead to the pressures and opportunities created by changing contexts according to their histories and their economic situations, but also according to their internal political lives. In this sense, the mechanistic approach to revitalizing the concept has made it possible to describe *how* province-building operates, without, however, generating postulates regarding its results (e.g., increased conflict with Ottawa, or growth in provincial spending). This opens the door to comparisons between the provinces – of the type made in this book – but also to comparisons between policy areas and between time periods. It also lays the foundations for an empirical study of the interests and actions of the actors in the provincial elites in contemporary Canadian politics.[1] So it is crucial to continue to study and compare provinces rigorously in order to truly understand contemporary political life and federalism in Canada.

Federalism and Gradual Institutional Changes

The reconstitution of the federalization process over time shows the analytical power of an institutionalist approach focusing on gradual institutional changes with respect to the study of Canadian federalism (Mahoney and Thelen 2010a; Streeck and Thelen 2005). The concept of institutional regime that is central to this approach – the relationships between actors who, through formal and informal rules, organize the distribution of resources and power – makes it possible to clearly identify the underlying dynamics of the federalization process. Besides showing that actors' behavioural changes can contribute endogenously to the processes of change, this approach highlights the importance of resources when it comes to defining the interests of the actors over time.

In the case of the federalization process, these resources are the immigrants, but also the associated funding, the powers, and the autonomous capacity to act within the institutional regime that governs immigration and integration. Throughout this process, both the provinces and the federal government responded to the changes unfolding within this regime in order to restore a distribution of resources suitable to their interests. In chapter 2, three changes – the signing of the devolution agreement between Quebec and the federal government in the area of immigration, Settlement Renewal, and the creation of the Provincial Nominee Program – were situated according to their impacts on Quebec and Manitoba. The chapters that followed showed that the consequences of these changes for the redistribution of resources have strongly coloured the redefinition of elite interests in Ontario, British Columbia, Alberta, Saskatchewan, and the Atlantic provinces over time. Chapters 3, 4, and 5 have documented the ways in which federal reactions and the actions of the other provinces in the area of immigration and integration impacted the struggle for a better distribution of resources between the actors from 1990 to 2010. During those years, the federal government first tried to tilt the redistribution of resources to its advantage, then attempted to curb, as much as possible, the consequences of decisions limiting its legitimacy and its capacity to act. All of these interactions took place against a backdrop of substantial changes in the area of national public policies and fiscal federalism, as well as in the organization of partisan politics in Canada.

Part of the explanatory power of this approach to the study of federalism comes from the temporal lens used in this book. As conceptualized by Tulia Falleti (2010), analysis over the medium term makes it possible to take into account contextual changes often ignored by institutionalist studies, which focus on more wide-ranging or large-scale events. However, these contextual changes have a strong influence on the activation and operation of the mechanisms, as this book has demonstrated. Four broader changes in the federal context that affected both levels of government underscored the interaction of the mechanisms: changes in health and social services transfers to the provinces; the asymmetrical withdrawal of the federal government from labour market management policies; the renewal of the federal role in economic development; and modifications to federal practices in intergovernmental relationships, especially after the successive elections of Conservative governments in Ottawa. Over the medium term, covered by chapters 2 to 5, these changes generated significant economic, social, and ideological pressures to reposition the two levels of government. The activation and interaction of the province-building mechanisms and decentralization were therefore also the result of that repositioning, at various moments in time.

So on the whole, it is important for studies of Canadian federalism to continue exploring the potential of the institutional approach centred on gradual changes. The other applications of this approach (e.g., Papillon 2012; Benz and Broschek, 2013) show its range beyond the area of immigration. Because it emphasizes actors and the distribution of resources, and because it is capable of describing dynamics over the medium term, this approach could clarify the recent dynamics within the Canadian federal regime. To the extent that Canada seems to still resist constitutional changes, it is instead in gradual changes and in the medium-term impact of the changing interests of the provinces and the federal government that we can find the keys to understanding contemporary Canadian federalism.

Federalization after 2010

The political trajectory described in this book did not stop in 2010. Both the interactional approach to federalism and the perspective of gradual institutional changes are, in fact, rooted in a postulate of constant dynamism. Federalization has reconfigured the division of resources between the actors and made it possible for new behaviours to appear within the institutional governance regime of immigration and integration. The configuration that emerges from this is still not entirely fixed as a new equilibrium; over the medium term the actors will continue to mobilize. Federalization reached its peak in 2010, at which point all the actors began to feel its full impact. As in many other policy areas in which Ottawa has partly shed its role as the sole leader – for example, social or environmental regulation – the federal government has tried to reclaim a role, through adjustments, after the fact (Harrison 2006).

Since 2010, intergovernmental relations in immigration have been characterized by the federal government's obvious desire to take back control, following the election of a majority Conservative government led by Stephen Harper in 2011 and a return to a Liberal majority government with the election of Justin Trudeau in 2015. However, since they take place in a federalized institutional regime – in which the provinces are now institutional actors possessing a certain legitimacy and well-defined interests in immigration – these forays by Ottawa now encounter provinces that refuse, more or less successfully, to submit to federal decisions. The provinces continue, in fact, to be committed to immigration, and although the federal government has made changes limiting their influence, these adjustments have had minimal impact because of their political consequences. The federal government has responded by attempting to support new actors coming onto the scene in the institutional regime of governance, in order to limit the influence of the provinces. It has also emulated fundamental principles of provincial intervention in reforming its own immigration and integration policies. While the central features of the "Canadian model" have remained stable despite federalization, this new phase in interactions carries the risk, in the medium term, of calling into question the essential principles of Canada's distinct approach.

The Provinces: Continuity and Expansion

At the provincial level, the commitment to immigration as a resource and the modes of intervention institutionalized since the 1990s have been maintained since 2010. This continuity can be explained by the success of many provincial interventions with regard to the province-building objective, as well as by the creation of groups benefiting from provincial actions in immigration. After policies and programs were institutionalized, those groups included employers' associations, organizations providing immigrant services (which are now also funded by the provinces), and economic actors benefiting from new sources of labour and capital, as well as the whole industry of immigration consultants. As has been shown in other policy areas (Pierson 1994), these groups of beneficiaries have made it difficult and extremely costly politically to dismantle the provincial modes of intervention in immigration and integration. Thus, with the passing years, as institutions have been established, the provincial role in immigration has gone beyond the interests of the provincial elites to extend to a larger proportion of society.

This continuity can be verified in all the provinces, with a few slight variations. First of all, although the specific characteristics of the four modes of intervention – holistic, reactive, bridging, and attraction-retention – are being maintained in immigration policy, many provinces have begun taking their cue from Alberta's policies. Reflecting the influence of the provinces within the federation, some characteristics of Alberta's bridging mode of intervention are now being emulated by other provinces. This is the case in BC, which seems to want to break with its passive approach with regard to selecting and recruiting immigrants. Indeed, the provincial stakeholders we spoke to emphasized BC's desire to acquire even more powers over selection. This interest illustrates that province's tendency to favour a model that is more in line with Alberta's policies; it also confirms the content of the report of the province's immigration task force, released in 2012 (British Columbia 2012). Over time, this has also been visible in the province's use of the PNP, in relation to federal Express Entry, to select especially in-demand workers in large numbers (e.g., technology workers); and in its implementation of a tax exemption for individuals coming to BC through the PNP. When discussing these changes and the need for more federal support for the PNP, BC premier Christy Clark (Liberal) has highlighted more and more the importance of immigrants for the growth of specific economic sectors (British Columbia 2017a). At the same time, the province has been engaged in institution-building in immigration; the 2017 implementation of the Provincial Immigration Programs Act (PIPA) (British Columbia 2017b) is the most recent indicator of this trend.

Even in Quebec, despite the election of the Parti Québécois in 2012 and the proposed "Charter of Quebec Values," which led to heated debates over how to manage ethnocultural diversity (Quebec National Assembly 2013; Iacovino 2015), the consensus on immigration has been maintained. Thus in the winter of 2015, the Liberal government of Philippe Couillard launched a process to develop a new framework policy on immigration for Quebec (Richer 2015). Quebec has maintained a vision of immigration as a resource for the province, as reflected in the introduction to the consultation paper on the new policy:

> With immigration perceived as having an essential role to play in fostering its development, in particular by contributing to the growth and renewal of the working-age population, Québec is determined to distinguish itself on the international scene in order to attract the best talents and to demonstrate its international solidarity in keeping with its societal choices. (Québec 2015, 1)

Similarly, the public consultations on this new policy in the winter of 2015 did not result in a questioning of the consensus. Indeed, the stakeholders invited to those consultations urged the government to expand its actions in immigration and integration, in accordance with the standard principles of the holistic mode of intervention (Paquet, Belkhodja, and Smith-Chanona 2017).[2] The resulting policy, "Together, we are Quebec" (*Politique québécoise en matière d'immigration, de participation et d'inclusion Ensemble, nous sommes le Québec*), launched in 2016, explicitly linked immigration to prosperity (Quebec 2016). It also included policy proposals similar to those of other provinces (especially bridging programs) and a pledge to implement an immigrant selection model based on the Australian and Canadian "express entry" systems. While not yet implemented, these changes demonstrate the durability of the province's engagement with immigration.

Expansion has been visible in *all* provinces. Nova Scotia has maintained its internal mobilization towards immigration and developed policies to that end, and the premier established an immigration advisory council in 2014. That same year, New Brunswick released a Population Growth Strategy and a Francophone Immigration Action Plan (New Brunswick 2014). Newfoundland and Labrador launched a new immigration plan in 2017 that set the objective of welcoming 1,700 immigrants annually by 2022 (Newfoundland and Labrador 2017). Similarly, despite the economic downturn and the election of an

NDP government in 2015, immigration has remained a priority for the Alberta government (Alberta 2015). In Manitoba in 2016, the repatriation of settlement responsibilities and the return to government of the Progressive Conservatives did not slow the province's actions, at least in immigrant selection. Indeed, the post-2010 period has seen pro-immigrant political debates across Canada in which the provinces are the central venues. Despite changes in government, external events, and federal policy changes, the consensus institutionalized through province-building appears to be here to stay.

Growing Tensions

In all the provinces, the post-2010 period has seen ongoing demands on the federal government – and in many cases, a strengthening of those demands. But as a result of federalization, these demands are being expressed partly through new inter-governmental and inter-administrative venues (Schertzer 2015). Still growing out of the province-building mechanism, these demands usually focus on immigrants as resources and are aimed at increasing funding and powers for the provinces. The interactions between the mechanisms of province-building and decentralization are such that many provincial demands are arising in response to federal government's political and program decisions. A central and stable demand made by the provinces has been for an increase in PNP intakes (Burgmann 2016). Indeed, despite some changes in consultative practices, the provinces continue to denounce Ottawa's lack of respect for their immigration needs. As an example, in a 2015 interview, Nova Scotia's immigration minister Lena Metlege Diab summed up her approach to immigration: "We need to be equal partners with (the federal government) when we talk about immigration so that they can give us the flexibility to have a say in the system. And not only that, I want us to have more linkages in the Office of Immigration provincially with [Citizenship and Immigration Canada]" (Taylor 2015).

Ontario, offended by the federal government's apathy towards the signature of a new immigration agreement to replace the 2005–10 COIA, made immigration one of its main bones of contention with Ottawa. After 2010 the province began demanding the complete devolution of settlement services and immigrant selection processes, just as in the Quebec agreement. The federal government rejected these demands outright and abandoned the negotiations for a new immigration agreement.[3] Provincial activity then became more and more visible, with the aim of strengthening relationships between the provincial government and social groups in the area of immigration and integration. Thus the Ontario government published in 2012, after public hearings, its first-ever immigration strategy (Ontario 2012). While remaining true to the principles of the reactive mode of intervention, a new discourse about the importance for Ontario to manage immigrant selection started to appear. Since 2016 this has been embodied in the growth of Ontario's PNP, in the maintenance of demands for increased PNP allocations for the province, and in explicit efforts to generate strong links with immigration stakeholders in the province (Ontario 2017). In 2017 the province finally signed a new five-year immigration agreement that build on Ontario's demands (Canada 2017a). Thus, since 2010, Ontario has kept up its demands on the federal government and has even expanded them, adding immigrant selection to its list of perennial grievances with Ottawa.

Similar developments have been visible in Atlantic Canada. After 2007, Prince Edward Island, New Brunswick, Nova Scotia, and Newfoundland and Labrador would join the other provinces in demanding a new formula for calculating transfers for integration, as well as a general increase in the funds allocated to the provinces in that area (L.A., NL, 31 May 2007). In 2010, after Ottawa announced it would be curbing the growth of PNPs, the Atlantic provinces protested. All four provinces challenged this decision in one way or another, and the mobilization of the Atlantic provinces on this topic was in strong contrast to the apathy that prevailed in the region during the 1990s.[4] For example, in its second immigration strategy, Nova Scotia underscored the importance of convincing the federal government to reverse its decision:

> The Nominee Program is our best option for attracting international professional and skilled workers to help meet the changing needs of our economy. To meet our goal of doubling immigration, we will need to issue 1,000 nomination certificates a year by 2015 and 1,500 certificates by 2020. That will require the federal government to eliminate the cap on nomination certificates. In the fall of 2010, Premier Darrell Dexter and his Atlantic counterparts expressed concern that federal immigration policies are not taking into consideration the specific needs of the Atlantic Provinces. As a first step, the Council of Atlantic Premiers called on the federal government to remove the cap on their provincial nominee programs. Nova Scotia will leverage our existing good relationships with our federal and

provincial/territorial partners to help ensure the benefits of immigration are shared equitably across the country. (Nova Scotia 2010c, 7)

In the years that followed, this mobilization would continue through the Council of Atlantic Premiers (New Brunswick 2011). It would be maintained after the 2015 federal election, directly via premier-to-minister relationships (Huras 2016a; Huras 2016b; *Chronicle Herald* 2016). Indeed, the inclusion of the Atlantic Immigration Pilot Program in the new Atlantic Growth strategy and its implementation in 2017 was the result of Atlantic premiers' pressure on Ottawa. This employer-driven program combines three streams (high-skilled, intermediate-skilled, and international graduates) and makes selection contingent on a job offer as well as on the endorsement of the government of the province where the applicant will settle (Canada 2017b). The pilot program, active for three years, does not replace the PNP but does increase the number of applicants for which these provinces may have a say. This innovation demonstrates that the Justin Trudeau government is also affected by provincial mobilization in immigration and is likely to attempt a balance between decentralization and role reassertion.

Of relevance also are provinces' reactions to world immigration events. The implementation of the Syrian refugee initiative after the 2015 federal election demonstrated that the provinces were interested in taking part in large-scale immigration operations but remained unhappy about being treated as subordinates. In 2016 the provinces' response to the increase in irregular border crossings from the United States, especially in Quebec and Manitoba, pointed to ongoing intergovernmental tensions in immigration (Hoyce 2017; Cotter 2017; Lecavalier 2017). Though they lack the capacity to stop border crossings, the provinces have emerged as sophisticated actors capable of understanding the consequences of immigration on their areas of jurisdiction and on fiscal federalism. This episode of provincial calls for federal actions and financial support in a climate of federal inertia are reminiscent of American-style immigration federalism. Interestingly, however, Canada's provinces have not yet moved away from the consensus central to province-building centred on immigration when demanding action from the Trudeau government, even in the case of Quebec.

Thus, after 2010, the ten Canadian provinces remained involved in the trajectories outlined in chapters 2, 3, 4, and 5 of this book. Besides maintaining the key principles of the modes of intervention they began to establish in 1990, the provinces have continued to demand more powers, autonomy, and resources from the federal government. In some cases these demands have expanded in ways that distinguish them from those traditionally expressed in their modes of intervention; nevertheless, they are always rooted in the key objective of province-building centred on immigration: the establishment of strategies aimed at developing provincial society through the resource of immigration.

The Federal Government: Centralization and New Actors

The emergence of the provinces as institutional actors in the immigration and integration governance regime resulted in a loss of autonomy for the federal government. This was because its decisions with regard to immigration and integration policies and programs were now perceived by the provinces as having important distributive consequences and therefore intergovernmental impacts. But it would be too optimistic to present the provinces as really having a veto in this new configuration of the institutional regime. Ottawa still has considerable degrees of freedom to change policies, stemming from its institutional capacity and fiscal resources.

Thus, despite the recognition of the provinces' role in institutions of governance, and despite the plan to coordinate immigration policies, the post-2010 period persuasively demonstrates the maintenance of federal capacities. Faced with growing pressure from the provinces and the loss of manoeuvring room resulting from the new distribution of resources, the federal government is working to re-establish its autonomy. It is still too early to know whether its attempts to limit the influence of province-building will succeed. It is nevertheless clear that these decisions are being carried out in a federalized regime, and accordingly, traces of the provinces are visible in all federal efforts.

The federal government's most visible actions since 2010 have already been presented in these pages. They include the decision not to renew the agreements on transfers of the administration of settlement services in BC and Manitoba; the implementation of numerical limits and additional regulations for the PNP; and the abandoning of negotiations for the renewal of an immigration agreement with Ontario. These decisions show that despite the federalization of immigration, Ottawa is still able to act unilaterally and in accordance with its own interests. All of these decisions have had the objective of recovering resources – in this case autonomy and financial resources – that were becoming more and more limited by the actions and interests of the provinces.

Thus we have seen Ottawa trying to recentralize part of the governance regime since 2010, in order to re-establish its legitimacy and margin of manoeuvre in the area of immigration and integration. This strategy has not been not carried out by a single government; notwithstanding their different intergovernmental agendas, the Conservative *and* Liberal governments have acted in ways to increase their freedom within Canada's immigration and integration regime.

The strong provincial reactions to these changes show that the federalization of immigration and integration governance has increased the political costs of federal decisions. Those costs are more and more apparent in the electoral sphere and in the relations between governments. It should therefore be remembered that in the short and medium term, these policy areas will remain *federalized*: their governance will now involve the management of relations between two levels of government possessing considerable political, social, and institutional legitimacy, and both aiming to achieve their own political objectives.

One consequence of the federalization process – a subtle one for the time being, but with potentially transformative effects – is federal efforts to include new actors in the immigration and integration governance regime. This goal is being expressed in two main ways: the growth of the Temporary Foreign Worker Program, and a new system for selecting immigrants. In both cases, these decisions have created or reinforced the links between the federal government and economic actors while excluding or circumventing the provinces. Little by little, these new actors are acquiring an official role and a certain legitimacy in the governance regime, and this has the potential to dilute the influence of the provinces.

The Expansion of the Temporary Foreign Worker Program

The growth of the federal Temporary Foreign Worker Program is in part Ottawa's response to federalization. Since 2010 this program has expanded significantly in terms of numbers; also, its management has been made much more flexible, by among other things permitting the entrance of low-skilled workers on temporary visas (Worswick 2013; Islam 2013). This growth is generally disparaged, because of problems related to fraud, human rights abuses, and potential problems related to the management of the Canadian job market (Goldring and Landolt 2013). Apart from these real problems, this growth should also be seen as a federal effort to serve the interests of economic actors in the area of immigration. In effect, Ottawa is proposing a solution to labour shortages that competes with the solution offered by the provinces, that is, the PNP. By making it easier for economic actors to use the Temporary Foreign Worker Program, the federal government hopes to divert those actors from the relationships they have recently established with the provinces through the PNP. This growth has made economic actors an interest group whose needs in the area of immigration have a new transmission platform: a program administered by the federal government. This trend, started under the Harper Conservative government, has been maintained by the Trudeau Liberal government (Liberal Party of Canada 2015). Indeed, announcements related to the modernization and increased flexibility of this federal program were presented in the 2017 federal budget, which announced the Liberals' desire to expand their reach through this program (Canada 2017c). Despite party differences and amidst ideological diversity, the growth of the Temporary Foreign Worker Program should be seen as an attempt by the federal government to maintain its position as the dominant actor in immigration governance and to insert a new actor that can rival the provinces within that regime.

Federal "Express Entry"

The new federal system for selecting immigrants follows a similar logic. In place since January 2015, the "Express Entry" program is aimed at immigrants who wish to settle permanently in Canada, on the basis of economic criteria. Express Entry applies to federal programs for skilled workers, workers in skilled trades, and the Canadian experience selection category (Canada 2015a). This new system has two objectives: to modernize federal selection, and, especially, to improve the process for integrating immigrants by better matching their skills with the needs of the Canadian market. This system divides the selection process for immigrants into two stages. In the first stage, the nominees are required to present an expression of interest in immigrating to Canada through an electronic profile established with Citizenship and Immigration Canada (CIC). This expression of interest includes information related to education, work experience, and language ability, as well as, where applicable, information on job offers they have received in Canada. Using this information, the government then establishes a pool of potential candidates for immigration, according to the federal selection grid. During the second phase, the candidates in the pool are evaluated and ranked relative to the others using the Comprehensive Ranking System (CRS) (Canada 2015c). Following interdepartmental instructions, a variable number of candidates with the highest ranking in a pool will be invited to make a permanent residency application. The federal government will thus be able to extract candidates from a given pool for a period of one year; after twelve months the candidates will be asked to restart the process from the beginning, after the federal government empties its pool of potential candidates (Canada 2015a).

In three ways, the Express Entry system is a reflection of the federalization of immigration and its present-day consequences. First of all, as with the Temporary Foreign Worker Program, this new system assigns an expanded role to economic actors in the selection of immigrants. Candidates who have job offers are ranked at the top of the pool, which implies growing pressure for employers to play a proactive role in recruitment abroad. In addition, the federal government is currently working to directly connect its employability services (e.g., the federal Job Bank) to the Express Entry system and to a liaison network with employers (Canada 2015b). These two measures have increased employers' capacity to select permanent immigrants directly – a first for Canada since the establishment of the post-war "Canadian model." At the level of the governance regime, these characteristics related to Express Entry have helped integrate economic actors in the process as legitimate players. Their growing inclusion in the selection system belongs to the same logic of pluralization and competition with the provinces as the decision to expand the Temporary Foreign Worker Program.

Second, the rhetoric and the principles supporting this new system are based largely on the provincial bridging mode of intervention, institutionalized in Alberta and Saskatchewan. In the bridging mode (see chapters 1 and 4), the government's role is primarily to create bridges to facilitate quick access of new arrivals to employment, which is the main indicator of integration. To that end, the selection is done according to the economic needs expressed, and economic actors play a predominant role in formulating and managing public policies. The Express Entry system has similar characteristics. To ensure quick access to employment, the selection criteria focus strongly on matching skills with the job market's current needs, while asking candidates to take the steps necessary for the recognition of their education when they enter the selection process (Canada 2015d). Furthermore, the new system assigns a higher rank to any candidate who has a validated job offer from a Canadian employer. Clearly, in immigration, as in Canadian health and social policies, provincial innovations can be emulated by the federal government when it crafts national policies. Thus the federalization process, by opening the door to diverse provincial modes of intervention in immigration and integration, has had an impact on the general orientation of Canadian policies.

Third, the new system involves recognizing the role of the provinces in immigrant selection. The Express Entry system does not signify the end of the PNP; on the contrary, it gives the provinces another avenue for directly selecting immigrants. Except for Quebec, they will be able to select permanent immigrants from a pool of candidates established by the federal government. Indeed, since its implementation, federal Conservative and Liberal immigration ministers have strongly promoted the idea that Express Entry is a way for the provinces to influence the overall direction of the federal immigration program (e.g.: Morris 2014). In this new system, provincial preferences have a great deal of influence; being selected by a province gives any candidate 600 additional points in the Comprehensive Ranking System (CRS), in which the maximum is 1,200 points. It goes without saying that provincial nomination is equivalent to moving to the top of the ranking among the candidates in the pool. The possibility for the provinces to draw from the federal pool and the importance accorded to their decisions within the CRS ranking illustrate the federalized nature of immigration in Canada. This signals the fact that to be effective and politically viable, any general reform by the federal government must now recognize the legitimacy of the provinces as institutional actors in immigration.

Current and future changes to Canada's immigration policies and programs will greatly be affected by the federalization of immigration. Faced with more and more vociferous provincial demands, and in response to political obligations to share resources, successive federal governments have been working since 2010 to reclaim manoeuvring room within the immigration and integration governance regime. To that end, Ottawa has recentralized certain domains and has also worked, with the help of the Temporary Foreign Worker Program and the Express Entry system, to give economic actors an expanding role in the institutional regime. These facts, which also express a recognition of the actions and legitimacy of the provinces, could be the beginning of a new process of gradual institutional change. Only time will tell of its consequences for provinces, for Canada as an immigration society, and, especially, for newcomers to the country.

Appendix

An Approach Comparing Provincial Policies and Programs

Aside from this book, there have been no comprehensive comparisons of contemporary immigration and integration policies and programs in Canada's provinces. And when these policies and programs have been considered in part, the comparisons have not included all ten provinces. In Canada there have been many descriptive contributions, mostly studies of specific programs (e.g., Leo and Enns 2009; Lewis 2010) or general surveys of provincial immigration programs (e.g., Hiebert and Sherell 2010). The literature is much more abundant in the area of municipal involvement in multicultural policies and in the delivery of settlement and integration services (e.g., Good 2009; Fourot, 2009; Fourot, 2013; Tolley and Young, 2011). Where it does exist, comparative work tends to be one-dimensional (a characteristic that in no way invalidates it). Many researchers have presented research that focuses on the differences between Quebec and the other provinces. Within that framework, the analytical criterion of differentiation is sometimes the specific characteristic of the Canada–Quebec immigration agreement of 1991 (Kostov 2008; Becklumb 2008), the intercultural approach (McAndrew 2009; Bourque and Duchastel 2000) or variations in the division of responsibilities (Brown and Astravas 2009; Biles 2008). Implicitly or explicitly, what emerges from this research is the idea that variation among the provinces (with the exception of Quebec) in the area of immigration and integration policies is limited or even non-existent. More recent literature compares the provinces according to their intergovernmental immigration agreements. In those analyses, the provinces can be differentiated according to four or five types of bilateral immigration agreements (ranging from devolution to collaboration) (Seidle 2010b; Andrew and Hima 2011; Banting 2012). Some authors classify the provinces dichotomously between those that have received a substantial number of new arrivals and those that have received very few (Belkhodja and Traisnel 2011; Akbari et al. 2007). Finally, a few authors instead emphasize the strong similarities among provincial approaches (Garcea 2006) or highlight the disparate nature of provincial involvement (Tolley et al. 2011).

Comparative politics has a hard time, more generally, applying at the level of federal entities and local governments the classifications and indexes created to compare national public actions in that policy area (Helbling 2013; Koopmans 2010). Because of these limitations, the comparison of modes of intervention proposed in this book is based on an inductive perspective.

Within that framework, the concept of modes of intervention is used to take into account potential variations and similarities among the provinces in the area of provincial public policies.[1] Because it is the outcome of research on the development of the welfare state and regimes of public policies, this concept highlights the fact that combinations of policies are the result of more or less long trajectories, within which decisions and conflicts leave lasting effects. In this way, it supports the general idea that each configuration of provincial policies and programs can be the corollary of a specific political trajectory over time.

In keeping with the classifications formulated by G. Esping-Andersen, I am proposing that we go beyond describing a tendency towards the general growth of provincial interventions in immigration and integration and instead examine the qualitative variations within each policy area (Esping-Andersen 1990). As in the case of welfare state regimes, it is appropriate to base research on an inductive approach aimed at expressing the specific logic underlying each province's intervention. Similarly, the comparison of provincial actions should closely examine the roles assigned to the government and the other actors in the attainment of the objectives of public policies (e.g., Hicks and Esping-Andersen 2005; Jenson and Phillips 1996). This concern about the sharing of responsibilities is accompanied by close attention to the combination of different policy areas that affect new arrivals (Banting 2010; Freeman 2004).

Operationalization

For the purposes of operationalization, three interdependent dimensions were used to express the mode of intervention. Using these, I established a typology of provincial modes of intervention in immigration and integration (Elman 2005, Smith 2002). This typology focused on the policies put in place by the provinces from 2008 to 2010, in order to paint a picture of the provincial approaches as they emerged at the end of the federalization process.

First, I considered the interventions in two areas – recruitment and selection of immigrants, and settlement and integration of immigrants – and identified these elements:

* the definition of the objectives of policies and programs (when relevant);
* the main areas of intervention;
* the quantitative importance of provincial efforts (where applicable);
* the orientation of provincial interventions;
* the types of programs and policy instruments favoured; *and*
* the provincial discourses with respect to recruitment and selection, and to settlement and integration.

Within this framework, the analysis aimed to recognize how good the match was among public actions within these two public policy areas.

Second, qualitative analysis made it possible to identify the roles attributed to the government, to the market, and to civil society (Jenson and Phillips 1996) by each province within the framework of its intervention in immigration and integration.

Third, from these two stages the dominant logic of the provincial intervention was identified, that is, the element that seemed to dominate the action of each province, both in terms of discourse and in terms of the implementation of policies and programs.

The Data Sources

The typology was based on qualitative and financial data related to provincial action in the area of immigration and integration. The information used for the analysis included the following: (1) the annual activity reports of the provincial governments (coming from ministries and other units responsible for activities related to the targeted policy areas), (2) the intergovernmental agreements and the related interpretative documents, (3) the general publications of the provinces related to the policies implemented (official descriptions of programs, strategies publicized, websites, help documents for the preparation of funding applications, etc.), (4) program evaluations of provincial governments and the federal government, and (5) the public accounts of the provincial governments and federal government. In addition, sources of quantitative data on immigration in Canada, and secondary literature on provincial action, were used to produce the provincial portraits. Finally, some information was obtained or confirmed through informal interviews with civil servants of the provincial governments.

In accordance with the concept of mode of intervention, the analysis focused on the policies explicitly described by the provincial governments as actions in the domains of immigration and integration. That implies, among other things, that the results reported represent a rather limited vision of the overall intervention of the provincial governments in the area. In fact, as pointed out by John Biles in his portrait of the policies implemented by the three levels of government in Canada:

> To a great extent, provincial participation in integration is due to the fact that many sectors integral to the integration process are the responsibility of provincial governments, such as housing, education, and health … however, it is still difficult to ascertain the full range of integration-related policies that exist at the provincial level. For example, integration-related expenses in departments responsible for education, employment, and health remain hidden in most cases. Calculating these costs remains a challenge for provincial governments, just as it is for the other order of government. (Biles 2008, 159)

While openly recognizing these limitations, the analysis took up the challenge of conceiving the definition of the area of intervention and the explicit identification of efforts by the provincial governments as a significant datum in itself.[2]

Many of the measures used to characterize the provincial actions were estimates. This was first of all due to the fact that, as pointed out by Biles (2008), measuring provincial action remains a challenge for these governments. Second, this problem was exacerbated by the variety of the practices of financial reporting of the provincial governments. In some cases the funds allocated to each program could easily be traced, while in other cases immigration was recorded as a single budgetary unit and it was impossible to apportion the sums among operating costs, funding for integration, and so on. Faced with this problem, the assistance of provincial civil servants was necessary to produce an estimate of the allocation of spending and to help validate the scope of the action in these policy areas.

Notes

1. Provinces, Immigration, and Institutional Change

1 The concept of federalization still represents a construct in the social sciences. It is most often used to describe processes of establishing federal institutions or institutional changes (Graefe and Bourns 2009). It is also used to explain the diversification of policies established by federal entities (Moreno and Obydenkova 2013) or the opposite movement (Celis and Meier 2011).

2 Some authors maintain that there was a form of economic neo-nationalism in Newfoundland and Labrador during the government of Danny Williams (Conservative Party [CP], 2003–6). This neo-nationalism, however, had very different bases (natural resources and political alienation) than those of Quebec nationalism. See the analysis by Marland (2010).

3 The process used to compare provincial policies and programs is described in this volume's appendix.

4 These changes, it must be recognized, are added to forces affecting Canada as a whole: globalization and continental integration, the rise or fall of political and economic paradigms, the end of the transition towards service and knowledge economies, and the aging of the population. These pressures, especially globalization and the influence of neoliberal ideology, have reinforced the historically unitary relationship of the Canadian state toward immigration, and the growth of a discourse linking immigration and human capital. See Green and Green (2004), as well as Abu-Laban and Gabriel (2002) and Abu-Laban (2004).

5 In order to operationalize the context, this book uses the general definition of *context* formulated by Falleti and Lynch: "the relevant aspects of a

setting (analytical, temporal, spatial, or institutional) in which a set of initial conditions leads (probabilistically) to an outcome of a defined scope and meaning via a specified causal mechanism or set of causal mechanisms" (Falleti and Lynch 2009, 10).

6 Institutionalization explains the self-reproducing nature of the mechanism. The creation of public administrations generates a new elite that wants to maintain and expand its powers; at the same time, the implementation of public policies creates direct links among the provincial government, actors active in delivering services, and the direct or indirect beneficiaries of those policies.

2. Quebec and Manitoba: Province-Building Centred on Immigration

1 When the public administration responsible for immigration was created, political actors, more broadly, also took the view that federal policy would not serve the development objectives of the province. This is shown by the passages on immigration in the 1966 election platforms; that year was the first election in Quebec in which the parties included this question in their official documents. The platform of the Union nationale was unambiguous: "The immigration policy designed and applied by Ottawa does not take into account the economic, social, and cultural realities of Quebec. In addition, the propaganda of Canada abroad is misleading, and gives a false impression of the labour market situation. Future immigrants have their first contact with Canada through civil servants who are almost all Anglophones; their welcome to Quebec is left to volunteers. The Liberal regime still has not done anything to correct the situation. In the area of immigration, the Union nationale is committed to an energetic policy focusing on the well-being of immigrants and the needs of our economy: '1. Creation of a Ministry of Immigration and the establishment of reception services and schools to meet the needs of new Quebecers. 2. Participation of Quebec in all international commissions studying population and migration problems. 3. Creation of a national demography centre'" (Union nationale 1966, 408–409). The Liberal Party platform was also instructive: "The development of a strong Quebec, capable of ensuring the continuing improvement of the well-being of its citizens, requires that Quebec possesses and effectively carries out broad responsibilities in everything related to job assignments and occupational rehabilitation. This is why Quebec will implement: ... selective, but active immigration policy intended to favour the integration of neo-Canadians into the francophone community" (Liberal Party of Quebec 1966, 44).

2 The Union nationale government of Jean-Jacques Bertrand (1968–70) set
up the Gendron Commission in 1969, in part in reaction to the publication
of the report of the Royal Commission on Bilingualism and Biculturalism
(Laurendeau–Dunton Commission). The Gendron Commission had a
mandate to study the language question in Quebec as a whole. In 1972 it
produced a three-volume report, one volume of which dealt exclusively
with ethnic minorities and language (Daniel 2006, 49). From 1969 to 1977,
successive governments implemented more and more legislative measures
based on the report. In 1969 the Union nationale government passed
Law 63, which assigned the Ministry of Immigration responsibility for
"[mandatory] learning of French by immigrants." Then in 1974, the Liberal
government of Robert Bourassa enacted Law 22, which made French the
official language of Quebec. It also limited to students who already knew
English the right to "attend schools of that language." In 1976, there was
extensive reform of Law 22 and English schools catering to immigrants
were closed. Finally, in 1977, the first Parti Québécois government, led
by René Lévesque, adopted Law 101, also known as the Charter of the
French Language. It made French the province's official language of
communication, both in the workplace and for relations between the
citizens and the government. The law also established criteria limiting
access to education in English and created the Office québécois de la
langue française and the Conseil supérieur de la langue française (Parti
Québécois 1970, 20).
3 For example, after calling for the creation of a ministry, all of the parties
proposed in their 1970 election platforms measures related to language
as a key element concerning immigration. The Union nationale promised
to increase the number of special language classes for the children of
immigrants; the Parti Québécois said that under its government "new
immigrants will be required to pass a French exam to obtain their citizenship,
and they will have to send their children to French schools" (Parti Québécois
1970, 20); and the Liberal Party made the linguistic identity of Quebec a pillar
of future immigration policy (Liberal Party of Quebec 1970, 10).
4 The party of René Lévesque began to demand immigration powers as
part of the "Beau risque" ("good risk"), a policy of openness intended
to resolve the constitutional crisis that erupted in 1985 and to respond
to the policy of the Progressive Conservative government of Brian
Mulroney (1984–93) that was aimed at convincing Quebec to accept the
1982 constitution. According to an actor at the time, the inclusion of
immigration among the PQ government's demands was not automatic:
"In 1984, the Ministry of Immigration had to apply pressure and convince

the Quebec government that it should include immigration in those
constitutional demands. So, even in 1984 … the Quebec administration and
politicians were still not convinced … Do you know what argument finally
convinced them? You cannot ask for less in constitutional negotiations
with the federal government than what the Liberals asked for" (interview,
retired provincial civil servant, 27 August 2012).

5 Research interview, former elected official, 28 March 2012.

6 Research interview, retired provincial civil servant, 29 March 2012.

7 At the same time, the Parti Québécois was demanding that the constitutional situation be clarified, claiming that an immigration policy that
would truly serve the interests of Quebec could be realized only in the
context of a sovereign Quebec. It proposed among other things to orient
immigration policy to facilitate the integration of cultural communities,
to give priority to francophone immigrants, especially those coming from
Canada and the United States, to increase the weight given to French in
the selection of new arrivals, to increase Quebec's representation in target
countries, to make "francization" classes more accessible, to promote
integration activities and support community organizations, to establish
courses on Quebec language and culture with employers, to accelerate
the implementation of programs for access to equality and campaigns to
change mentalities in the workplace, and to promote the settlement [of
immigrants] outside Montreal (Parti Québécois 1990, 84–5).

8 Research interview, retired provincial civil servant, 5 September 2012.

9 Because of the very low popularity of Mulroney following the failure of
the Meech Lake draft constitutional accord, in 1990 the Manitoba party
decided to change its name by dropping the word "progressive"; thereafter
it was simply the Conservative Party.

10 Research interview, retired provincial civil servant, 8 November 2011.

11 Research interview, representative of a Manitoba community organization,
22 November 2012.

12 Research interview, provincial civil servant, 26 April 2012.

13 A federal civil servant who was active in the negotiations with Manitoba
long before the official creation of the province's Nominee Program
observed that the demographic imperative was strong: "I think Manitoba
was the first … was really the most aggressive to tie immigration
in with their population policy. They simply had some communities that
were [declining] … There were so many people who were leaving. And
population wasn't being replaced … communities were losing their critical
mass." And Manitoba declared: "We want to use this authority to try to
bring people." Research interview, retired federal civil servant, 1 April 2012.

14 Research interview, retired provincial civil servant, 16 March 2012.

15 It went so far as to consult other provinces on their policies and programs
(see, for example, Manitoba 1993, 35). In this regard, two senior civil
servants of the period have indicated that it was primarily Quebec,
among all the provinces, that served as a model for the development of
Manitoba's policies and demands. One of them, active in immigration
during the 1990s, recalled that senior civil servants from Manitoba had
visited their Quebec colleagues to learn more: "we actually went and
studied what was happening in Québec and we did a field trip and
we took the council and we met and they talked about their welcome
programs and how [they were] encouraging movement from countries
where they were relatively convinced that there was a good fit, where
people would come and they would stay. Because the problem they were
having was that people would come to Quebec because it was easier and
they were … quickly going to Toronto." In the course of the discussion,
this person further pointed out that "[o]ne of the key events was really our
trip to Québec and looking at what had been done there and what was
possible. That was a pretty important one … the fact that I went with the
Clerk of Council, that [it] wasn't just a casual visit." Research interview,
retired provincial civil servant, 16 March 2012.

16 The accord also opened the door to immigration agreements for other
provinces that wanted them. The provisions on immigration were the least
controversial in the draft Meech Lake Accord; public and political opinion
became very critical of other demands made by Quebec after the campaign
led by Pierre Elliott Trudeau and after Quebec passed Law 178 on the
French language and public signs (Russell 2004).

17 Research interview, retired federal civil servant, 19 October 2011.

18 Research interview, retired provincial civil servant, 27 August 2012.

19 As a symptom of the activation of the mechanism of province-building in
Manitoba, the Liberal MLAs in Manitoba, then in opposition, expressed
concern that "the clauses on immigration compromise the growth of small
provinces such as Manitoba by granting the larger provinces a higher
proportion of immigrants" (*La Presse* 1988).

20 Research interview, retired federal civil servant, 4 November 2011.

21 It should also be noted that provisions related to federal–provincial
immigration agreements were contained in the Charlottetown
constitutional proposals that were defeated in 1992.

22 Research interview, retired federal civil servant, 19 October 2011.

23 Research interview, retired provincial civil servant, 16 March 2012.

24 Research interview, federal civil servant, 18 January 2012.

25 Research interview, representative of a Manitoba community organization, 22 November 2012, and research interview, Manitoba elected official, 17 May 2012.
26 Research interview, retired federal civil servant, 19 October 2011.
27 Research interview, federal civil servant, 18 January 2012.
28 Since the 1980s, under the federal Temporary Foreign Worker Program, employers who wish to hire foreign workers are required first of all to complete an Application for a Labour Market Opinion and submit it to Service Canada. The opinion determines the impact the entry of a foreign worker would have on the Canadian labour market (Canada 2012b).
29 Research interview, provincial civil servant, 25 June 2012.
30 Research interview, retired federal civil servant, 3 November 2011.
31 Research interview, retired federal civil servant, 7 November 2011.
32 Research interview, retired federal civil servant, 5 April 2012.
33 Research interview, retired federal civil servant, 1 April 2012.
34 Research interview, retired federal civil servant, 7 December 2011.
35 Research interview, federal civil servant, 15 February 2012.
36 For example, by concluding international bilateral agreements aimed at facilitating the recruitment and immigration of particular national groups (such as the French) or particular professional groups (such as doctors) (Québec Ministry of Citizen Relations and Immigration 1997).
37 This is an important characteristic of the holistic mode of intervention. In several other provinces, as the following chapters will show, government activity was aimed almost entirely at promotion and recruitment. Only after those efforts began to bear fruit, and the number of landed immigrants increased, did a true provincial reflection on intervention in integration begin, often because of problems related to the retention or integration into the provincial labour market of these new arrivals.
38 According to official publications of the period, in addition to responsibilities in the recruitment and selection of immigrants as well as in the area of delivery of services to new arrivals, "the new ministry has the mission of promoting the rights and freedoms of the person and encouraging citizens to exercise their civic and social responsibilities. It favours equality among persons and their participation in collective life and the development of society. It is responsible for promoting solidarity between the generations and ensuring that the needs of seniors are taken into account. It is also called upon, through its initiatives, to promote openness to pluralism and intercultural rapprochement, thus favouring a sense of belonging to the Quebec people" (Québec 1997, 9). Although the language used in reference to this reorganization indicates an objective

of competitive nation-building, the policies put forward by the ministry starting in 1996 had the specific aim of improving the integration of immigrants of all origins as well as racial minorities. The objective therefore was both to ensure the allegiance of new arrivals to Quebec *rather than* to Canada, and to ensure full integration and complete participation of new arrivals in Quebec society. In this regard, the mobilization of a discourse on citizenship and the increase in the number of "citizenship" policies after the Parti Québécois came to power need to be linked to the objective of societal development through immigration, by endeavouring to increase participation, one possible indication of the level of retention and economic integration. See also Danielle Juteau's (2002) analysis.

39 Research interview, community organization, 26 July 2012.
40 Research interview, federal civil servant, 17 January 2012.
41 Research interview, provincial civil servant, 26 April 2012.
42 Research interview, provincial civil servant, 28 March 2012.
43 Research interview, community organization, 4 July 2012.
44 Research interview, Manitoba elected official, 17 May 2012.

3. Ontario and British Columbia: Expansion and Contraction

1 The CHST was created by the federal government following the abolition of two other transfer programs (Established Programs Financing and the Canada Assistance Plan), which up to that point had been used to fund social policies and health care.

2 The "Common Sense Revolution," the election program that Harris would implement during his first term, reflected a particular ideological orientation. It included (1) the fight against the budget deficit, (2) limiting the size of the provincial government (supporting cuts to the Ontario public service as well as decentralization in the form of the transfer of responsibilities to municipal governments), (3) minimal taxation, (4) a central role for the market and individuals, and (5) a limited role for the civil society and "special interests" in decision-making and the development of policies (Progressive Conservative Party of Ontario 1994). When it was re-elected in 1999, the government put forward a new platform – the Blueprint – which was in keeping with the same principles (Progressive Conservative Party of Ontario 1999).

3 Around the same time in Canada, the concept of groups representing "special interests" began to be extensively used by political actors. As pointed out by Brodie (2008), the demands identified as coming from "special interests" were presented as being intrinsically opposed to

the interests of "ordinary citizens." The label was used in this way to marginalize and delegitimize groups and their demands (Dobrowolsky 1998).

4 Research interview, retired provincial civil servant, 11 January 2012.

5 Research interview, community organization, 18 April 2012.

6 Research interview, retired provincial civil servant, 11 January 2012.

7 Research interview, retired federal civil servant, 19 October 2011.

8 Research interview, provincial civil servant, 23 March 2012.

9 Research interview, provincial civil servant, 23 March 2012.

10 Research interview, retired federal civil servant, 7 December 2011.

11 Research interview, community organization, 24 February 2012.

12 Research interview, retired provincial civil servant, 11 January 2012.

13 Research interview, federal civil servant, 15 February 2012.

14 Research interview, federal civil servant, 1 February 2012.

15 Research interview, retired provincial civil servant, 11 January 2012.

16 Research interview, federal civil servant, 1 April 2012.

17 Research interview, provincial civil servant, 23 March 2012.

18 Research interview, provincial civil servant, 5 July 2012.

19 Research interview, federal civil servant, 1 April 2012.

20 Research interview, provincial civil servant, 5 July 2012.

21 Research interviews, community organizations, 3 April 2012 and 18 April 2012.

22 Research interview, retired federal civil servant, 1 April 2012.

23 Research interview, civil servant Ontario, 11 January 2012.

24 Research interview, retired Ontario civil servant, 5 February 2012.

25 Research interview, federal civil servant, 16 January 2012.

26 A civil servant active at the time remembers this period: "What happened is I think that BC started to … really started to get concerned about human capital and skill shortage and having the right skill people, the right skills coming, they started to see it as part of its society-building" (Research interview, retired provincial civil servant, 1 April 2012).

27 Research interview, provincial civil servant, 23 May 2012.

28 In 2002 and 2003, responsibilities were divided between the Ministry of Community, Aboriginal and Women's Services and the Ministry of Competition, Science and Enterprise. Between 2003 and 2005, responsibility for integration and selection came under the Ministry of Aboriginal Affairs and the Ministry of Multiculturalism and Immigration. Between 2005 and 2008, these responsibilities would finally be divided between the Ministry of Attorney General and the Ministry of Economic Development.

29 Research interview, provincial civil servant, 19 April 2012.

30 Research interview, provincial civil servant, 28 March 2012.

31 Research interview, provincial civil servant, 19 April 2012.
32 Research interview, retired federal civil servant, 3 April 2011.
33 Research interview, federal civil servant, 16 January 2012.
34 Research interview, retired provincial civil servant, 5 February 2012.
35 Research interview, federal civil servant, 1 February 2012.
36 Research interview, federal civil servant, 23 December 2011.
37 Research interview, provincial civil servant, 11 January 2012 and research interview, federal civil servant, 16 January 2012.
38 Research interview, federal civil servant, 15 February 2012.
39 Research interview, provincial civil servant, 5 July 2012.
40 There was, however, a certain discomfort with respect to the allocation of the monies transferred to the province. In fact, under the first agreement, the provincial government paid part of the funds directly into the settlement program and another portion into a general fund. This practice raised fears that the province might use the sums transferred for settlement services for other purposes, including to fund tax cuts implemented during Gordon Campbell's first term (Leo and August 2009, 93–116).
41 Research interview, provincial civil servant, 28 March 2012.
42 The NDP, in a very marginal position during those elections, did not take a position on immigration in its platform and did not criticize the immigration policies of the outgoing government (Ontario New Democratic Party 2007).
43 Research interview, Ontario civil servant, 11 January 2012.
44 Research interviews, Ontario community organizations, 10 May 2012 and 6 July 2012.
45 Research interview, Ontario civil servant, 11 January 2012.
46 Research interview, provincial civil servant, 19 April 2012.
47 Research interview, provincial civil servant, 19 April 2012.
48 Research interview, provincial civil servant, 28 March 2012.
49 For example, having a say in the decision to exempt an occupational domain from the obligation to obtain an evaluation of local labour market conditions for the employment of temporary foreign workers (British Columbia 2007, 9).
50 Research interview, provincial civil servant, 28 March 2012.

4. Alberta and Saskatchewan: Immigrants as "Natural Resources"

1 Alberta and Saskatchewan signed bilateral immigration agreements with the federal government in the 1950s. Saskatchewan also signed a general cooperation agreement with the federal government in 1978. This

agreement was the result of efforts by the federal government to respond to criticisms following the signing of the Cullen–Couture Agreement with Quebec (Hawkins 1991, 44–5).

2 Research interview, retired federal civil servant, 5 April 2012.

3 Research interview, retired provincial civil servant, 2 May 2012.

4 Research interview, former elected official, 10 April 2012.

5 Research interview, provincial civil servant, 20 June 2012.

6 Research interview, retired federal civil servant, 5 April 2012.

7 Research interview, federal civil servant, 1 February 2012.

8 Research interview, federal civil servant, 18 January 2012.

9 Research interview, federal civil servant, 1 February 2012.

10 Research interview, former elected official, 10 April 2012.

11 Research interview, retired provincial civil servant, 2 May 2012.

12 Anecdotally, a federal negotiator maintained that at the time of the signing of the agreement on the Provincial Nominee Program, Saskatchewan showed interest in the recruitment of pork producers from Europe: "I know that Saskatchewan had a very specific interest in pig farmers from Europe, where they were paying very high manure taxes. And so in Europe, pig farms were not a very pleasant thing to live by … And so in Europe, pig farms … had to pay a tax that was based on the amount of manure that was produced by their stock. And so, Saskatchewan was able to say 'Come to Northern Saskatchewan and your pigs can poop as much as they want. We won't charge you a diamond' [*sic*]." Research interview, federal civil servant, 18 January 2012. This anecdote shows to what extent the province was facing substantial demands from individuals and businesses that wanted to do business in Saskatchewan, which presented itself above all as a destination for business immigrants.

13 Research interview, provincial civil servant, 28 May 2012.

14 François Rocher and Christian Rouillard emphasized the crucial difference between decentralization and deconcentration: "As a general rule, decentralization is associated with a growing influence of the provincial governments to the detriment of the capacity for intervention of the federal government. It is a zero-sum game … In a process of decentralization, the federal government loses all its authority over the transferred competencies. If the federal government continues to participate in the establishment of restrictive mechanisms for the design, assessment, orientation, and/or control to which the provinces were subordinated, we are dealing less with a dynamic of decentralization than with another … qualified as deconcentration" (Rocher and Rouillard 1998, 239).

15 Research interview, provincial civil servant, 12 July 2012.

16 Research interview, provincial civil servant, 14 July 2012.

17 Research interview, provincial civil servant, 20 June 2012.

18 Communications with the Alberta government, August 2011.

19 Research interview, provincial civil servant, 28 May 2012.

20 Research interview, former elected official, 10 April 2012.

21 Research interview, provincial civil servant, 28 May 2012.

22 Research interview, provincial civil servant, 28 May 2012. "The only program … that was ahead of us was Manitoba and yes we borrowed things from Manitoba … But there were also things that Manitoba was doing that didn't fit our needs. For example, … when their program first came in, there was huge demand in the clothing industry and [they used a network of people in the Philippines to recruit there] that is something we never looked at that but some of their process we did, some of their criteria … I met with them twice and others met with me several times." Research interview, retired provincial civil servant, 2 May 2012.

23 Research interview, retired provincial civil servant, 2 May 2012.

24 Research interview, federal civil servant, 15 February 2002.

25 Research interview, provincial civil servant, 28 May 2012.

26 Research interviews, provincial civil servants, 20 June 2012 and 12 July 2012.

27 Research interview, federal civil servant, 17 January 2012.

28 Research interviews, federal civil servants, 23 December 2011 and 18 January 2012.

29 Research interview, community organization, 30 April 2012.

30 Research interview, federal civil servant, 1 February 2012.

31 Research interview, federal civil servant, 18 January 2012.

32 Research interview, federal civil servant, 17 January 2012.

33 Research interview, federal civil servant, 17 January 2012.

34 Research interview, provincial civil servant, 19 April 2012.

5. Atlantic Canada: Immigration for the Survival of Provincial Societies

1 Confidential interviews, community organizations, 2 May 2012 and 4 May 2012.

2 Confidential interview, retired federal civil servant, 26 October 2011.

3 Confidential interview, retired federal civil servant, 19 October 2011.

4 Confidential interview, retired federal civil servant, 1 April 2012.

5 Confidential interview, retired federal civil servant, 7 December 2011.

6 Established in 1987, ACOA "works to create opportunities for economic growth in Atlantic Canada by helping small and medium-sized enterprises

(SMEs) to become more competitive, innovative and productive; by
working with communities to develop and diversify local economies;
and by championing the region's strengths in partnership with Atlantic
Canadians. It plays an important role in developing and supporting
policies and programs that strengthen the region's economy" (Atlantic
Canada Opportunities Agency 2013, 5). In practice, this federal agency
maintains offices in the four Atlantic provinces as well as in Ottawa, and
works to improve the productivity, growth, and competitiveness of those
economies. The means and priorities identified for this purpose have
varied over time.

7　"The Council of Atlantic Premiers (CAP) was established in May 2000,
with the signing of a Memorandum of Understanding on Regional
Cooperation by Premiers Bernard Lord, New Brunswick; Brian
Tobin, Newfoundland and Labrador; John Hamm, Nova Scotia; and
Patrick Binns, Prince Edward Island … The goals of the Council of
Atlantic Premiers are to: – cooperate for the benefit of the residents of
Atlantic Canada; – enhance existing mechanisms for cooperation and
communication between the provinces; and commit to establishing a
framework for joint development of an Atlantic Canada approach to
national issues" (Council of Atlantic Premiers 2003, 1).

8　This table was an official partnership between ACOA and the four
governments and was funded by the two levels of government. Created
in 2005 to meet the challenges related to the region's demographics,
it permits the sharing of efforts and knowledge of groups active in
immigration through sub-committees (attraction and promotion, retention,
repatriation, working with international students, and research) (Prince
Edward Island 2007a).

9　Confidential interview, federal civil servant, 15 January 2012.

10　Confidential interview, retired provincial civil servant, 6 June 2012.

11　Confidential interview, retired provincial civil servant, 18 April 2012.

12　Confidential interview, provincial civil servant, 11 April 2012.

13　Confidential interview, retired provincial civil servant, 6 June 2012.

14　The key tool for the attraction efforts was the expansion of the Provincial
Nominee Program. In 2005 it was still the responsibility of an independent
agency, Island Development Incorporated. In addition to efforts at
numerical expansion, a new selection category was created, "Immigrant
Connections." Through this category, the province favoured the
recruitment of individuals who already had connections, since selection
depended, among other things, on the fact that the candidate had been
sponsored during his or her integration by a "champion" (Prince Edward
Island 2006, 11).

15 The goal was to achieve a ratio of 60% skilled workers and 40% immigrant entrepreneurs (New Brunswick 2008b, 11).

16 With the exception of the Green Party and the People's Alliance, two parties still very marginal in the province in 2010.

17 The first version of the Nova Scotia Provincial Nominee Program had three selection categories: skilled workers, economic nominees, and community-identified nominees (Dobrowolsky 2012). In 2004 the province signed a memorandum of understanding with Citizenship and Immigration Canada (CIC) permitting foreign students to work off campus during their studies (Nova Scotia 2005b, 25).

18 This scandal concerned in particular the administration of the business nominees category. The business nominees were very often not able to obtain the promised support to achieve their objectives of attaining high-level positions in Nova Scotia companies. In addition, as recalled by Alexandra Dobrowolsky: "Issues surfaced in relation to Cornwallis Corporation as well, from the fact that its contract had been untendered (and it had made substantial financial contributions to the party in government awarding the contract), to newspaper reports alleging that: 'Cornwallis had raked in almost $4 million without much to show for its efforts'" (Dobrowolsky 2012, 206). Accordingly, the government of the province stopped accepting applications for the economic category of its program in 2007 and did not renew its contract in 2006 (Auditor General of Nova Scotia 2008a; 2008b).

19 Confidential interview, community organization, 3 August 2012.

20 Confidential interview, community organization, 2 May 2012.

21 The creation of this public service was greatly inspired by practices in other provinces. The strategy acknowledges this influence by pointing out that "a review of 'best practices' in other provinces indicate [*sic*] that those experiencing the greatest success have consolidated their efforts relating to immigration into one 'administrative unit'" (Newfoundland and Labrador 2007b, 26; 2007a, 27).

22 In association with a family policy: "With progressive family growth and immigration policies, we will begin the process of reversing the decline, rebuilding our population and strengthening our communities" (Progressive Conservative Party of Newfoundland and Labrador, 2007, 19).

23 For example, in 2006 the government published an information bulletin and magazine, organized during the following years a wide range of symposiums bringing together government, economic, and social actors, and published guides for employers on the hiring of immigrants and foreign students (Newfoundland and Labrador 2007a, 13).

24 The province also put in place, in collaboration with other provinces,
   promotion efforts within Canada (Brautigam, 2007).
25 The 2007 immigration strategy identified target countries for recruitment,
   mainly European countries, and in particular the United Kingdom
   and Ireland. Those two countries were favourites for the following
   reasons: "The province has a rich history of immigration from this
   area […], Close proximity […] English speaking […] High probability
   of successful integration and retention […] Build on Irish Business
   Partnerships initiative" (Newfoundland and Labrador 2007b, 33). In order
   of importance, the countries and regions targeted by the strategy were
   the United Kingdom, Ireland, France and Saint-Pierre and Miquelon, the
   United States, South America, India, Korea, China, and finally Africa.
26 Confidential interview, federal civil servant, 20 January 2012.
27 Confidential interviews, federal civil servants, 20 January 2012 and 12 June
   2012.

6. The Future of the "Canadian Model"

1 Beyond recognizing the objective of the elites to maintain their centrality
   and their power, the conception of province-building as a social
   mechanism makes no assumptions regarding the interests of those
   elites. In this respect, this epistemological and theoretical repositioning
   is compatible with the socio-institutional variants of the concept as
   well as with the variants arising from the Canadian political economy
   (Paquet 2014). It also makes it possible to go beyond a simplistic reading
   of interests (e.g., re-election), to consider the processes through which
   interests are developed (e.g., social learning or emulation), and to
   conceptualize the capacity of actors to develop their interests in the short,
   medium, and long term. While recognizing the current limitations of the
   concept – in particular, its potential to overestimate the independence or
   the importance of the elite with respect to society – I nevertheless propose
   that only through empirical studies of mobilizations at the provincial level
   will it be possible to refine this conceptual tool for the study of the political
   life of the provinces and federalism in Canada.
2 In Quebec, as in the other provinces, this continuity underscores a
   general characteristic of the mechanism of province-building and clarifies
   many elements related to its functioning in the field of immigration
   and integration. First of all, it is primarily directed by the political elites
   and then becomes institutionalized. The policy of the Quebec Liberal
   government, elected in 2014, does not, in fact, reflect the major trends

in public discourses and public opinion that call into question the place
of immigration in Quebec and show growing intolerance for certain
groups seen as immigrants, rightly or wrongly. Second, the political
dynamics related to these fields after 2010 show to what extent diversity
management policies responded to considerations other than those related
to immigration and integration. Both in the case of the "Charter of Quebec
Values," starting in 2012, and in the case of the "crisis" over reasonable
accommodation, starting in 2006, as in the case of religious arbitration
in Ontario between 2004 and 2006 (Lépinard, 2010), the divisive public
debates did not overturn the consensuses on the concept of immigration
as a resource for the provincial societies concerned. What is more, these
conflicts mobilized actors different from those typically active in the
mechanism of province-building – for example, social movements, the
legal sector, researchers and, above all, the groups targeted by public
policies. It is important therefore to continue to explore the potential
differences between the "modes" of policies related to immigration and
integration, and the "modes" of policies related to diversity management
(Freeman, 1995). This book has initiated that work by showing that these
two areas, often related rightly or wrongly in public debates, can move
forward in relatively independent ways.
3 Research interview, federal civil servant, 15 February 2012.
4 Research interview, federal civil servant, 12 June 2012.

Appendix

1 That is, the configuration of institutions, strategies, public policies, and
policy instruments that are mobilized by a government to intervene in a
given policy area.
2 The difficulties in precisely delimiting all provincial actions related to
immigration are heightened by the fact that (1) many programs are co-
managed and it is difficult to gauge precisely the influence of the province
on their governance without carrying out fieldwork, and (2) many
federal transfers – beyond transfers officially allocated to immigration,
and to settlement and integration services – can be allocated indirectly
to objectives related to the integration of immigrants. The agreements on
labour market development are an example of this (e.g., Klassen, 2000).

Bibliography

Abu-Laban, Y. 2004. "Jean Chrétien's Immigration Legacy." *Review of Constitutional Studies* 9 (1): 133–49.

Abu-Laban, Y., and C. Gabriel. 2002. *Selling Diversity: Immigration, Multiculturalism, Employment Equity, and Globalization.* Peterborough: Broadview Press.

Abu-Laban, Y., and J.A. Garber. 2005. "The Construction of the Geography of Immigration as a Policy Problem: The United States and Canada Compared." *Urban Affairs Review* 40 (4): 520–61. https://doi.org/10.1177/1078087404273443.

Adam, C. 2008. *Politics in Manitoba: Parties, Leaders, and Voters.* Winnipeg: University of Manitoba Press.

Akbari, S., A. Hussain, S. Lynch, J.T. McDonald, and W. Rankaduwa. 2007. *Socioeconomic and Demographic Profiles of Immigrants in Atlantic Canada.* Halifax: Atlantic Metropolis Centre.

Alberta. 2001. *Prepared for Growth: Building Alberta's Labour Supply.* Edmonton: Labour Force Planning Committee, Alberta Human Resources and Employment.

–. 2004a. *Integrating Skilled Immigrants into the Alberta Economy.* Edmonton: Alberta Learning and Alberta Human Resources and Employment.

–. 2004b. *Today's Opportunities, Tomorrow's Promise: A Strategic Plan for the Government of Alberta.* Edmonton: Government of Alberta.

–. 2005a. *Human Resources and Employment Ministry Annual Report 2004–2005.* Edmonton: Department of Alberta Human Resources and Employment.

–. 2005b. *Supporting Immigrants and Immigration to Alberta.* Edmonton: Employment and Immigration.

–. 2006a. *Alberta Economic Development 2005–2006 Annual Report.* Edmonton: Alberta Economic Development.

–. 2006b. *Building and Educating Tomorrow's Workforce: Alberta's 10 Years Strategy*. Edmonton: Alberta Human Resources and Employment.

–. 2006c. *Human Resources and Employment Ministry Annual Report 2005–2006*. Edmonton: Alberta Economic Development.

–. 2007. *Employment, Immigration and Industry Annual Report 2006–2007*. Edmonton: Employment, Immigration and Industry.

–. 2008. *Employment, Immigration and Industry Annual Report 2007–2008*. Edmonton: Department of Alberta Employment and Immigration.

–. 2009. *Employment and Immigration Annual Report 2008–2009*. Edmonton: Employment and Immigration.

–. 2010. *Employment and Immigration Annual Report 2009–2010*. Edmonton: Employment and Immigration.

–. 2015. *Jobs, Skills, Training and Labour: Business Plan 2015–2018*. Edmonton: Department of Jobs, Skills, Training and Labour.

Alberta Liberals. 2007. *It's Time: A Real Action Plan for Alberta*. Calgary: Alberta Liberals.

Alberta Social Credit Party. 2006. *Our Social Credit Policies*. Edmonton: Alberta Social Credit Party.

Amin, N. 1987. "A Preliminary History of Settlement Work in Ontario 1900-Present." Ministry of Citizenship, Citizenship Development Branch. http://ceris.ca/wp-content/uploads/virtual-library/Amin_1987.pdf (accessed 31 August 2017).

Andrew, C., and N. Bradford. 2011. "The Harper Immigration Agenda: Policy and Politics in Historical Context." In *How Ottawa Spends, 2011–2012: Life under the Knife (Again!)*, ed. Christopher Stoney and Bruce G. Doern, 262–79. Montreal and Kingston: McGill–Queen's University Press.

Andrew, C., and R.A. Hima. 2011. "Federal Policies on Immigrant Settlement." In *Immigrant Settlement Policy in Canadian Municipalities*, ed. Erin Tolley and Robert A. Young, 49–72. Montreal and Kingston: McGill–Queen's University Press.

Arsenault, K. 2000. *Toward a Comprehensive Immigration and Settlement Strategy for Prince Edward Island*. Charlottetown: Kevin J. Arsenault Consulting.

Arthur, R. 2002. "Immigrant deal a first step: Provincial nomination agreement should be welcomed, but it is only part of bigger picture." *Daily News*, 7 September 2002, 17.

–. 2003. "Coderre seeks toolbox: Inclusive immigration strategy would include community." *Daily News*, 19 April, 2.

Atlantic Canada Opportunities Agency. 2013. *Reports on Plans and Priorities 2012–2013*. Ottawa: Treasury Board of Canada.

Atlantic Provinces Economic Council 2004. *An Agenda for Growth and Prosperity in Atlantic Canada*.

Aucoin, P., and L. Turnbull. 2003. "The Democratic Deficit: Paul Martin and Parliamentary Reform." *Canadian Public Administration* 46 (4): 427–49. https://doi.org/10.1111/j.1754-7121.2003.tb01586.x.

Auditor General of Nova Scotia. 2008a. *Special Report to the House of Assembly on the Office of Immigration Economic Stream of the Nova Scotia Nominee Program. Phase I (5 June)*. Halifax: Office of the Auditor General of Nova Scotia.

–. 2008b. *Special Report to the House of Assembly on the Office of Immigration: Economic Stream of the Nova Scotia Nominee Program. Phase II (25 September)*. Halifax: Office of the Auditor General of Nova Scotia.

Baglay, S., and D. Nakache, eds. 2014. *Immigration Regulation in Federal States: Challenges and Responses in Comparative Perspective*. Dordrecht: Springer.

Bakvis, H., G. Baier, and D. Brown, eds. 2009. *Contested Federalism: Certainty and Ambiguity in the Canadian Federation*. Oxford: Oxford University Press.

Bakvis, H., and D. Brown. 2010. "Policy Coordination in Federal Systems: Comparing Intergovernmental Processes and Outcomes in Canada and the United States." *Publius* 40 (3): 484–507. https://doi.org/10.1093/publius/pjq011.

Baldacchino, G. 2011. "Breaking into a Clannish Society: The Settlement and Integration Experiences of Immigrants on Prince Edward Island." In *The Integration and Inclusion of Newcomers and Minorities across Canada*, ed. Erin Tolley, John Biles, Robert Vineberg, Meyer Burstein, and James Frideres, 355–72. Montreal and Kingston: McGill–Queen's University Press.

Bales, S. 2004. "Immigrants key to N.S. prosperity – Fage: Gov't struggling to reverse 10-year decline in immigration numbers." *Amherst Daily News*, 5 November, A3.

Banting, K. 1995. "The Welfare State as Statecraft: Territorial Politics and Canadian Social Policy." In *European Social Policy: Between Fragmentation and Integration*, ed. Stephan Leibfried and Paul Pierson, 269–300. Washington: The Brookings Institution.

–. 2010. "Is There a Progressive's Dilemma in Canada? Immigration, Multiculturalism and the Welfare State." *Canadian Journal of Political Science* 43 (4): 797–820. https://doi.org/10.1017/S0008423910000983.

–. 2012. "Remaking Immigration: Asymmetric Decentralization and Canadian Federalism." In *Canadian Federalism: Performance, Effectiveness and Legitimacy*, ed. Herman Bakvis and Grace Skogstad, 261–81. Toronto: Oxford University Press.

Banting, K., R. Gibbins, P.M. Leslie, A. Noël, R. Simeon, and R. Young, eds. 2006. *Open Federalism: Interpretations, Significance*. Kingston: Institute for Intergovernmental Relations.

Barker, F. 2015. *Nationalism, Diversity, and the Politics of Identity: Old Politics, New Arrivals*. New York: Palgrave Macmillan.

Barnetson, B., and J. Foster. 2013. "The Political Justification of Migrant Workers in Alberta, Canada." *Journal of International Migration and Integration* 15 (2): 1–22.

Bassler, G.P. 1994. "Deemed Undesirable: Newfoundland's Immigration Policy, 1900–1949." In *Twentieth Century Newfoundland*, ed. J. Hiller and P. Neary, 153–77. St John's: Breakwater Books.

Battle, K. 1998. "Transformation: Canadian Social Policy since 1985." *Social Policy and Administration* 32 (4): 321–40. https://doi.org/10.1111/1467-9515.00119.

Beach, D., and R.B. Pedersen. 2012. *Process-Tracing Methods: Foundations and Guidelines*. Ann Arbor: University of Michigan Press.

Becklumb, P. 2008. *Immigration: The Canada–Quebec Accord*. Ottawa: Library of Parliament.

Behiels, M.D. 1991. *Le Québec et la question de l'immigration: de l'ethnocentrisme au pluralisme ethnique, 1990–1985*. Ottawa: Canadian Historical Association.

Béland, D., and A. Lecours. 2007. "Federalism, Nationalism and Social Policy Decentralization in Canada and Belgium." *Regional & Federal Studies* 17 (4): 405–19. https://doi.org/10.1080/13597560701712643.

Bélanger, É. 2006. "La langue française et la politique d'immigration." In *Le Parti libéral: Enquête sur les réalisations du gouvernement Charest*, ed. F. Pétry, É. Bélanger, and L.M. Imbeau, 257–72. Québec: Presses de l'Université Laval.

Belkhodja, C., and C. Traisnel. 2011. "Immigration and Diversity in New Brunswick." In *The Integration and Inclusion of Newcomers and Minorities across Canada*, ed. E. Tolley, J. Biles, R. Vineberg, M. Burstein, and J. Frideres, 277–99. Montreal and Kingston: McGill–Queen's University Press.

Bennett, A., and C. Elman. 2006. "Qualitative Research: Recent Developments in Case Study Methods." *Annual Review of Political Science* 9 (1): 455–76. https://doi.org/10.1146/annurev.polisci.8.082103.104918.

Benz, A., and J. Broschek, eds. 2013. *Federal Dynamics: Continuity, Change, and the Varieties of Federalism*. New York: Oxford University Press. https://doi.org/10.1093/acprof:oso/9780199652990.001.0001.

Bickerton, J. 2001. "Nova Scotia: The Political Economy of Regime Change." In *The Provincial State in Canada: Politics in the Provinces and Territories*, ed. K. Brownsey and M. Howlett, 49–74. Peterborough: Broadview Press.

–. 2010. "Deconstructing the New Federalism." *Canadian Political Science Review* 4 (2–3): 56–72.

Biles, J. 2008. "Integration Policies in English-Speaking Canada." In *Immigration and Integration in Canada in the Twenty-first Century*, ed. J. Biles,

M. Burstein, and J. Frieders, 139–86. Montreal and Kingston: McGill–Queen's University Press.

Biles, J., E. Tolley, C. Andrew, V. Esses, and M. Burstein. 2011. "Integration and Inclusion in Ontario: The Sleeping Giant Stirs." In *Integration and Inclusion of Newcomers and Minorities across Canada*, ed. E. Tolley, J. Biles, R. Vineberg, M. Burstein, and J. Frideres, 195–246. Montreal and Kingston: McGill–Queen's University Press.

Bilodeau, A., L. Turgeon, and E. Karakoç. 2012. "Small Worlds of Diversity: Views toward Immigration and Racial Minorities in Canadian Provinces." *Canadian Journal of Political Science* 45 (3): 579–605. https://doi.org/10.1017/S0008423912000728.

Black, E.R., and A.C. Cairns. 1966. "A Different Perspective on Canadian Federalism." *Canadian Public Administration* 9 (1): 27–44. https://doi.org/10.1111/j.1754-7121.1966.tb00919.x.

Black, J.H., and D. Hagen. 1994. "Québec Immigration Politics and Policy: Historical and Contemporary Perspectives." In *Québec: State and Society*, 2nd ed., ed. Alain-G. Gagnon, 280–303. Toronto: Nelson.

Bloemraad, I. 2006. *Becoming a Citizen: Incorporating Immigrants and Refugees in the United States and Canada*. Berkeley: University of Califormia Press.

Bodhan, K. 2011. "Assessing the Multiculturalism/Immigration Policy Nexus in Saskatchewan." In *New Directions in Saskatchewan Public Policy*, ed. D. McGrane, 53–71. Edmonton: Canadian Plains Research Center Press.

Boismenu, G., and P. Graefe. 2004. "The New Federal Tool Belt: Attempts to Rebuild Social Policy Leadership." *Canadian Public Policy* 30 (1): 71–89. https://doi.org/10.2307/3552581.

Boomer, R. 2001. "Immigrants bypass N.S.: Bluenose province only one with falling number of newcomers." *Daily News*, 11 November, 9.

–. 2004. "Province looks to Winkler, Man., for inspiration: Tiny town getting as many immigrants per capita as T.O." *Daily News*, 19 November, 4.

Bornais, S. 2000. "Attract more immigrants, report says," *Daily News*, 26 September, 23.

Bourgon, J. 2009. *Program Review, the Government of Canada's Experience Eliminating the Deficit, 1994–1999: A Canadian Case Study*. Waterloo: Centre for International Governance Innovation.

Bourque, G., and J. Duchastel. 2000. "Multiculturalisme, pluralisme et communauté politique: le Canada et le Québec." In *Mondialisation, citoyenneté et multiculturalisme*, ed. Mikhaël Elbaz and Denise Helly, 147–69. Ste-Foy: Presses de l'Université Laval.

Bourque, G.L. 2000. *Le modèle québécois de développement: De l'émergence au renouvellement*. Québec: Presses de l'Université du Québec.

Boychuk, G. 1998. *Patchwork of Purpose: The Development of Provincial Social Assistance Regimes in Canada*. Montreal and Kingston: McGill–Queen's University Press.

Brautigam, T. 2007. "Atlantic premiers head to Alberta in hopes of stemming tide of outmigration." *Canadian Press*, 27 January 2007, 15.

British Columbia. 1998. *Ministry of Employment and Investment 1997/1998 Annual Report*. Victoria: Ministry of Employment and Investment.

–. 1999. *Ministry of Employment and Investment 1998/1999 Annual Report*. Victoria: Ministry of Employment and Investment.

–. 2001a. *Ministry of Employment and Investment Annual Performance Report 2000–2001*. Victoria: Ministry of Employment and Investment, 2001.

–. 2001b. *Ministry of Multiculturalism and Immigration 2000–2001 Annual Performance Report*. Victoria: Ministry of Multiculturalism and Immigration.

–. 2004. *Ministry of Community, Aboriginal and Women's Services. 2003/04 Annual Service Plan Report*. Victoria: Ministry of Community, Aboriginal and Women's Services.

–. 2005. *Ministry of Community, Aboriginal and Women's Services. 2004/05 Annual Service Plan Report*. Victoria: Ministry of Community, Aboriginal and Women's Services.

–. 2006. *Ministry of Economic Development 2005/06 Annual Service Plan Report*. Victoria: Ministry of Economic Developmemt.

–. 2007. *Ministry of Attorney General: Annual Service Report Plan 2006/07*. Victoria: Ministry of Attorney General.

–. 2008. *Ministry of Economic Development: 2007/08 Annual Service Report Plan*. Victoria: Ministry of Economic Development.

–. 2009. *Ministry of Advanced Education and Labour Market Development: 2008/09 Annual Service Plan Report*. Victoria: Ministry of Advanced Education and Labour Market Development.

–. 2012. *British Columbia Immigration Task Force*. Victoria: Minister of State for Multiculturalism.

–. 2017a. "Additional property transfer tax exemptions will help grow economy, create jobs." Victoria: Office of the Premier. Accessed 20 September 2017. https://news.gov.bc.ca/releases/2017PREM0037-000677.

–. 2017b. "Provincial Immigration Programs Act regulation comes into effect." Victoria: Government of British Columbia. Accessed 20 September 2017. https://news.gov.bc.ca/releases/2017JTST0015-000210.

Brock, K.L. 2008. "The Politics of Asymmetrical Federalism: Reconsidering the Role and Responsibilities of Ottawa." *Canadian Public Policy* 34 (2): 143–61. https://doi.org/10.3138/cpp.34.2.143.

Brodie, J. 1990. *The Political Economy of Canadian Regionalism*. Toronto: Hancourt Brave Jovanovich Canada.

–. 2008. "We Are All Equal Now: Contemporary Gender Politics in Canada." *Feminist Theory* 9 (2): 145–64. https://doi.org/10.1177/1464700108090408.

Brown, M., and R. Astravas. 2009. "The Governance of Immigration in Canada: the Evolution of Federal, Provincial/Territorial, and Municipal Roles." In *The Migration Policy Puzzle: Sharing Responsibilities for Managing Immigration and Integration*, ed. A. Zavos, 48–60. Athens: Hellenic Migration Policy Institute.

Burgmann, T. 2016. "Fort Mac fire losses underscore import of resources to Canadian economy: Clark." *Canadian Press*, 6 May 2016.

Cairns, A.C. 1977. "The Governments and Societies of Canadian Federalism." *Canadian Journal of Political Science* 10 (4): 695–725. https://doi.org/10.1017/S0008423900050861.

Cameron, D.R., and J.D. Krikorian. 2002. "The Study of Federalism, 1960–1999: A Content Review of Several Leading Canadian Academic Journals." *Canadian Public Administration* 45 (3): 328–63. https://doi.org/10.1111/j.1754-7121.2002.tb01161.x.

Cameron, D., and R. Simeon. 2002. "Intergovernmental Relations in Canada: The Emergence of Collaborative Federalism." *Publius* 32 (2): 49–72. https://doi.org/10.1093/oxfordjournals.pubjof.a004947.

Canada. 1987. *Constitutional Accord: First Ministers' Conference on the Constitution*. Ottawa: Federal–Provincial Conference of First Ministers on the Constitution.

–. 1994. *Settlement Renewal: A New Direction for Newcomer Integration*. Ottawa: Immigration and Citizenship Canada.

–. 2002. *Competing for Immigrants. House of Commons Standing Committee on Citizenship and Immigration*. Ottawa: Queen's Printer.

–. 2003a. *The Provincial Nominee Program: A Partnership to Attract Immigrants to All Parts of Canada. House of Commons Standing Committee on Citizenship and Immigration*. Ottawa: Queen's Printer.

–. 2003b. "Roundtable discusses ways to attract newcomers to Nova Scotia." *Canada Newswire*, 6 November.

–. 2008. "Canada's government and Saskatchewan working together to improve the Temporary Foreign Worker Program." Ottawa: Human Resources and Social Development. https://www.canada.ca/en/news/archive/2008/08/canada-government-saskatchewan-working-together-improve-temporary-foreign-worker-program.html (consultée le 13 mai 2012).

–. 2011a. *Evaluation of the Provincial Nominee Program*. Ottawa: Evaluation Division, Citizenship and Immigration Canada.

–. 2011b. *Facts and Figures 2010: Immigration Overview – Permanent and Temporary Residents*. Ottawa: Evaluation Division, Citizenship and Immigration Canada.

–. 2012a. *Evaluation of the Grant to Quebec*. Ottawa: Evaluation Division, Citizenship and Immigration Canada.

–. 2012b. *Application for a Labour Market Opinion*. Ottawa: Human Resources and Skills Development Canada.

–. 2015a. "How Express Entry works." Ottawa: Immigration and Citizenship Canada. https://www.canada.ca/en/immigration-refugees-citizenship/services/immigrate-canada/express-entry/works.html (accessed 2 September 2017).

–. 2015b. "Employer Liaison Network." Ottawa: Immigration and Citizenship Canada. https://www.canada.ca/en/immigration-refugees-citizenship/services/work-canada/hire-foreign-worker/employer-liaison-network.html (accessed on 2 September 2017).

–. 2015c. "Entry criteria and the Comprehensive Ranking System." Ottawa: Immigration and Citizenship Canada. https://www.canada.ca/en/immigration-refugees-citizenship/services/immigrate-canada/express-entry/become-candidate/criteria-comprehensive-ranking-system.html (accessed 2 September 2017).

–. 2015d. "Fill out your profile: Skilled immigrants (Express Entry)." https://www.canada.ca/en/immigration-refugees-citizenship/services/immigrate-canada/express-entry/become-candidate/fill-profile.html (accessed 2 September 2017).

–. 2017a. "Canada-Ontario Immigration Agreement – General Provisions 2017." Ottawa: Immigration, Refugee and Citizenship Canada. https://www.canada.ca/en/immigration-refugees-citizenship/corporate/mandate/policies-operational-instructions-agreements/agreements/federal-provincial-territorial/ontario/immigration-agreement-2017.html (accessed 25 November 2017).

–. 2017b. "Atlantic Immigration Pilot." Ottawa: Immigration, Refugee and Citizenship Canada. https://www.canada.ca/en/immigration-refugees-citizenship/services/immigrate-canada/atlantic-immigration-pilot.html.

–. 2017c. *Budget 2017: Building a Strong Middle Class*. Ottawa: Department of Finance.

Canadian Press. 2003. "Immigration program in Nova Scotia attracts only 26 applicants." 15 September, 20:34.

–. 2005a. "Après l'Ontario, l'Alberta réclame des fonds fédéraux accrus." 4 September.

–. 2005b. "P.E.I. joining with university to study immigration to Island." 10 October.

–. 2006a. "Alberta Tory leadership candidate talks about immigration policy."
27 July.

–. 2006b. "N.B. Liberal leader pledges to turn province from a have-not to a
have." 16 August.

–. 2006c. "N.B. Liberals unveil plan to bring more New Brunswickers back
home." 11 September.

–. 2007a. "Alberta minister says new immigration deal with Ottawa not
coming soon." 2 February.

–. 2007b. "New Brunswick nearly doubles population growth budget to $3
Million." 11 May.

–. 2007c. "Task force sets aggressive time line to achieve N.B. self-sufficiency."
7 May.

Caponio, Tiziana, and Michael Jones-Correa. 2017. "Theorising
Migration Policy in Multilevel States: The Multilevel Governance
Perspective." *Journal of Ethnic and Migration Studies,* Online first. DOI:
10.1080/1369183X.2017.1341705.

Caron, J.-F., and G. Laforest. 2009. "Canada and Multinational Federalism:
From the Spirit of 1982 to Stephen Harper's Open Federalism." *Nationalism &
Ethnic Politics* 15 (1): 27–55. https://doi.org/10.1080/13537110802672370.

Carroll, W.K., and R.S. Ratner. 2005. "The NDP Regime in British Columbia,
1991–2001: A Post-Mortem." *Canadian Review of Sociology* 42 (2): 167–96.
https://doi.org/10.1111/j.1755-618X.2005.tb02460.x.

Carter, T., and B. Amoyaw. 2011. "Manitoba: The Struggle to Attract and
Retain Immigrants." In *The Integration and Inclusion of Newcomers and
Minorities across Canada,* ed. E. Tolley, J. Biles, R. Vineberg, M. Burstein, and
J. Frideres, 1–55. Montreal and Kingston: McGill–Queen's University Press.

CBC. Calgary. 2007. "Alberta edging closer to immigration deal with Ottawa."
4 May.

CBC Edmonton. 2006. "Look at Ed Stelmach's campaign promises."
4 December.

Celis, K., and P. Meier. 2011. "Convergence and Divergence: The
Federalization of Belgian Equality Policies." *Regional & Federal Studies* 21 (1):
55–71. https://doi.org/10.1080/13597566.2010.507403.

Chowdhari Tremblay, R., and A. Bittner. 2011. "Newfoundland and Labrador:
Creating Change in the 21st Century." In *The Integration and Inclusion of
Newcomers and Minorities across Canada,* ed. E. Tolley, J. Biles, R. Vineberg, M.
Burstein, and J. Frideres, 325–53. Montreal and Kingston: McGill–Queen's
University Press.

Chronicle Herald. 2016. "N.S. is being punished on immigration numbers:
premier McNeil." 10 March.

Clement, G.L. 2003. "The Manitoba Experience." In *Canadian Immigration Policy for the 21st Century*, ed. Charles M. Beach, Alan G. Green, and Jeffrey G. Reitz, 197–201. Montreal and Kingston: McGill–Queen's University Press.

Clow, J. 2000. "Fresh blood needed: Immigration helped shape our economy: Now, our prosperity depends on it." *Daily News*, 3 December, 4.

Cody, H. 2008. "Minority Government in Canada: The Stephen Harper Experience." *American Review of Canadian Studies* 38 (1): 27–42. https://doi.org/10.1080/02722010809481819.

Conservative Party of British Columbia. 2009. *Be a Part of the Change*. Victoria: BC Conservative.

Conservative Party of Ontario. John Tory. 2007. *For a Better Ontario, Leadership Matters*. Toronto: Ontario PC Party.

Cornellier, M. 2005. "McGuinty persiste et signe. Malgré l'irritation des 'cousins fédéraux,' l'Ontario continuera de lutter pour obtenir sa juste part des fonds d'Ottawa." *Le Devoir*, 21 April, A1.

Cotter, John. 2017. "Alberta willing to accept more refugees: Premier Rachel Notley." *Global News*. https://globalnews.ca/news/3221245/alberta-willing-to-accept-more-refugees-premier-rachel-notley/.

Council of Atlantic Premiers. 2003. *Report for 2001–2003*. Halifax: Secretariat of the Council of Atlantic Premiers.

Courchene, Thomas J. 2005. "Vertical and Horizontal Fiscal Imbalances: An Ontario Perspective." Ottawa: Presentation at the Standing Committee on Finance, House of Commons, Parliament of Canada. http://irpp.org/research-studies/presentation-2005-05-04/ (accessed 1 November 2017).

Daily Herald. 2000. "Input sought on Sask. immigration policy." 24 August, 3.

Daniel, Dominique. 2006. "La politique d'immigration du Québec." In *Politiques publiques: le Québec comparé*, ed. Jean Crête, 43–69. Québec: Presses de l'Université Laval.

Davies, Philip H.J. 2001. "Spies as Informants: Triangulation and the Interpretation of Elite Interview Data in the Study of the Intelligence and Security Services." *Politics* 21 (1): 73–80. https://doi.org/10.1111/1467-9256.00138.

de Clercy, C. 2005. "Leadership and Uncertainty in Fiscal Restructuring: Ralph Klein and Roy Romanow." *Canadian Journal of Political Science* 38 (1): 175–202. https://doi.org/10.1017/S0008423905050092.

Deloitte & Touche. 1992. *Summary Report & Recommendations on the Immigrant Investor Program Review, December 30, 1992*. Winnipeg: Department of Industry, Trade and Tourism.

Denis, C. 1995. "'Government Can Do Whatever It Wants': Moral Regulation in Ralph Klein's Alberta." *Canadian Review of Sociology* 32 (3): 365–83. https://doi.org/10.1111/j.1755-618X.1995.tb00777.x.

Desserud, D.A. 2008. "The 2006 Provincial Election in New Brunswick." *Canadian Political Science Review* 2 (1): 51–63.

Dobrowolsky, Alexandra. 1998. "Of 'Special Interest': Interest, Identity and Feminist Constitutional Activism in Canada." *Canadian Journal of Political Science* 31 (4): 707–42. https://doi.org/10.1017/S0008423900009616.

–. 2012. "Nuancing Neoliberalism: Lessons Learned from a Failed Immigration Experiment." *Journal of International Migration and Integration* 14 (2): 197–218.

Dufour, F.G., and M. Forcier. 2015. "Immigration, néoconservatisme et néolibéralisme après la crise de 2008: le nouveau régime de citoyenneté canadien à la lumière des trajectoires européennes." *Revue interventions économiques* 52: 1–20.

Dunn, C. 2001. "Comparative Provincial Politics: A Review." In *The Provincial State in Canada: Politics in the Provinces and Territories*, ed. Keith Brownsey and Michael Howlett, 441–78. Peterborough: Broadview Press.

–. 2005. "Why Williams Walked, Why Martin Balked: The Atlantic Accord Dispute in Perspective." *Options politiques* 9 (February): 9–14.

Dyck, R. 2006. "Provincial Politics in the Modern Era." In *Provinces: Canadian Provincial Politics*, ed. Christopher Dunn, 57–94. Peterborough: Broadview Press.

Elman, C. 2005. "Explanatory Typologies in Qualitative Studies of International Politics." *International Organization* 59 (2): 293–326. https://doi.org/10.1017/S0020818305050101.

Esping-Andersen, G. 1990. *The Three Worlds of Welfare Capitalism*. Princeton: Princeton University Press.

Fafard, P., and F. Rocher. 2009. "The Evolution of Federalism Studies in Canada: From Centre to Periphery." *Canadian Public Administration* 52 (2): 291–311. https://doi.org/10.1111/j.1754-7121.2009.00076.x.

Falleti, T.G. 2010. *Decentralization and Subnational Politics in Latin America*. Cambridge: Cambridge University Press. https://doi.org/10.1017/CBO9780511777813.

Falleti, T.G., and J.F. Lynch. 2009. "Context and Causal Mechanisms in Political Analysis." *Comparative Political Studies* 42 (9): 1143–66. https://doi.org/10.1177/0010414009331724.

Finbow, R. 1994. "Dependents or Dissidents? The Atlantic Provinces in Canada's Constitutional Reform Process, 1967–1992." *Canadian Journal of Political Science* 27 (3): 465–91.

Fine-Meyer, R. 2002. "Unique Refugees: The Sponsorship and Resettlement of Vietnamese 'Boat People' in Ontario, 1978–1980." MA thesis, Toronto: University of Toronto.

Flemming, B. 2000. "Let's attract brain gain: Nova Scotia could benefit by increasing appeal to immigrants." *Daily News*, 4 October, 20.

–. 2001. "People a hot commodity: Population forecasts paint a bleak picture for provinces like Nova Scotia." *Daily News*, 28 March, 13.

Fontaine, L. 1993. *Un labyrinthe carré comme un cercle: Enquête sur le ministère des communautés culturelles et de l'immigration du Québec et sur ces acteurs réels et imaginés*. Montréal: L'Étincelle éditeur.

Fourot, A.-C. 2009. "Gestions du nouveau pluralisme religieux dans les villes canadiennes. Établissement de mosquées et mécanismes de personnalisation des canaux de médiation à Montréal et à Laval." *Canadian Journal of Political Science* 42 (3): 637–55. https://doi.org/10.1017/S0008423909990096.

–. 2013. *L'intégration des immigrants: Cinquante ans d'action publique locale*. Montréal: Presses de l'Université de Montréal.

Freeman, Gary P. 1995. "Modes of Immigration Politics in Liberal Democratic States." *International Migration Review* 29 (4): 881–902. https://doi.org/10.2307/2547729.

–. 2004. "Immigrant Incorporation in Western Democracies." *International Migration Review* 38 (3): 945–69. https://doi.org/10.1111/j.1747-7379.2004.tb00225.x.

Frideres, J. 2011. "Alberta: Four Strong Winds – Immigration without Direction." In *The Integration and Inclusion of Newcomers and Minorities across Canada*, ed. E. Tolley, J. Biles, R. Vineberg, M. Burstein, and J. Frideres, 103–32. Montreal and Kingston: McGill–Queen's University Press.

Gagnon, A.-G. 2001. *The Moral Foundations of Asymmetrical Federalism: A Normative Exploration of the Case of Quebec and Canada*. Cambridge: Cambridge University Press.

–. 2006. "Les effets du nationalisme majoritaire au Canada." In *Le fédéralisme canadien contemporain: fondements, traditions, institutions*, ed. A.-G. Gagnon, 151–78. Montréal: Presses de l'Université de Montréal.

Gagnon, A.-G., and R. Iacovino. 2003. "Le projet interculturel québécois et l'élargissement des frontières de la citoyenneté." In *Québec: État et société*, vol. 2, ed. A.-G. Gagnon, 413–36. Montréal: Québec Amérique.

Garcea, J. 1991. "The Immigration Clause in the Meech Lake Accord." *Manitoba Law Journal* 21: 274–300.

–. 1994. *Federal–Provincial Relations in Immigration, 1971–1991: A Case Study of Asymmetrical Federalism*. PhD diss., Department of Political Science, Carleton University.

–. 2006. "Provincial Multiculturalism Policies in Canada, 1974–2004: A Content Analysis." *Canadian Ethnic Studies* 38 (3): 1–20.

Gazso, A., and H. Krahn. 2008. "Out of Step or Leading the Parade? Public Opinion about Income Support Policy in Alberta, 1995 and 2004." *Journal of Canadian Studies / Revue d'Etudes Canadiennes* 42 (1): 154–78. https://doi.org/10.3138/jcs.42.1.154.

Goldring, L., and P. Landolt. 2013. *Producing and Negotiating Non-Citizenship: Precarious Legal Status in Canada.* Toronto: University of Toronto Press.

Good, K.R. 2009. *Municipalities and Multiculturalism: The Politics of Immigration in Toronto and Vancouver.* Toronto: University of Toronto Press. https://doi.org/10.3138/9781442690417.

Graefe, P. 2006. "State Restructuring, Social Assistance, and Canadian Intergovernmental Relations in Canada: Same Scales, New Tunes." *Studies in Political Economy* 7 (8): 97–113.

Graefe, P., and A. Bourns. 2009. "The Gradual Defederalization of Canadian Health Policy." *Publius* 39 (1): 187–209. https://doi.org/10.1093/publius/pjn029.

Green, A.G., and D.A. Green. 2004. "The Goals of Canada's Immigration Policy: A Historical Perspective." *Canadian Journal of Urban Research* 13 (1): 102–39.

Haddow, Rodney. 2015. *Comparing Quebec and Ontario – Political Economy and Public Policy at the Turn of the Millennium.* Toronto: University of Toronto Press.

Haddow, R., and T.R. Klassen. 2006. *Partisanship, Globalization, and Canadian Labour Market Policy: Four Provinces in Comparative Perspective.* Toronto: University of Toronto Press. https://doi.org/10.3138/9781442678279.

Hainmueller, J., and D.J. Hopkins. 2014. "Public Attitudes toward Immigration." *PS: Political Science* 17 (1): 225.

Hall, A. 2012. "Ottawa lauds gov't immigration changes; Minister mum on numbers." *Saskatoon Star Phoenix*, 19 May, A1.

Hardcastle, L., A. Parkin, A. Simmons, and N. Suyama. 1994. "The Making of Immigration and Refugee Policy: Politicians, Bureaucrats and Citizens." In *Immigration and Refugee Policy: Australia and Canada Compared*, ed. H. Adelman, A. Borowski, M. Burnstein, and L. Foster, 95–124. Carlton: Melbourne University Press.

Harmes, A. 2007. "The Political Economy of Open Federalism." *Canadian Journal of Political Science* 40 (2): 417–37. https://doi.org/10.1017/S0008423907070114.

Harrison, K. 2006. *Racing to the Bottom?: Provincial Interdependence in the Canadian Federation.* Vancouver: UBC Press.

Harrison, T. 1996. "Class, Citizenship, and Global Migration: The Case of the Canadian Business Immigration Program, 1978–1992." *Canadian Public Policy* 22 (1): 7–23. https://doi.org/10.2307/3551746.

Hawkins, F. 1988. *Canada and Immigration: Public Policy and Public Concern.* 2nd ed. Kingston and Montreal: McGill–Queen's University Press.

–. 1991. *Critical Years in Immigration: Canada and Australia Compared.* Montreal and Kingston: McGill–Queen's University Press.

Helbling, M. 2013. "Validating Integration and Citizenship Policy Indices." *Comparative European Politics* 11 (5): 555–76. https://doi.org/10.1057/cep.2013.11.

Helly, D. 1996. *Le Québec face à la pluralité culturelle, 1977–1994: Un bilan documentaire des politiques*, ch. 2. Ste-Foy: Institut québécois de recherche sur la culture.

Hepburn, E., and R. Zapata-Barrero, eds. 2014. *The Politics of Immigration in Multi-Level States: Governance and Political Parties*. New York: Palgrave Macmillan.

Hicks, A., and G. Esping-Andersen. 2005. "Comparative and Historical Studies of Public Policy and the Welfare State." In *The Handbook of Political Sociology: States, Civil Societies, and Globalization*, ed. T. Janoski, R. Alford, A. Hicks, and M.A. Schwartz, 509–25. New York: Cambridge University Press.

Hiebert, D., and K. Sherell. 2010. "The Integration and Inclusion of Newcomers in Canada: The Case of British Columbia." *Willy Brandt Series of Working Papers in International Migrations and Ethnic Relations*, 1, 1–33.

–. 2011. "The Integration and Inclusion of Newcomers in British Columbia." In *Integration and Inclusion of Newcomers and Minorities across Canada*, ed. E. Tolley, J. Biles, R. Vineberg, M. Burstein, and J. Frideres, 77–101. Montreal and Kingston: McGill–Queen's University Press.

Hiller, H.H. 2009. *Second Promised Land: Migration to Alberta and the Transformation of Canadian Society*. Montreal and Kingston: McGill–Queen's University Press.

Howlett, M., and K. Brownsey. 2001. "British Columbia: Politics in a Post-Staples Political Economy." In *The Provincial State in Canada: Politics in the Provinces and Territories*, ed. Keith Brownsey and Michael Howlett, 309–34. Toronto: University of Toronto Press.

Hoyce, B. 2017. "Manitoba boosts funds for asylum seekers, calls on feds to step up." *CBC News*. http://www.cbc.ca/news/canada/manitoba/manitoba-refugees-border-1.3995642 (accessed 22 August 2017).

Huras, A. 2016a. "Immigration minister says feds ready to aid province." *Telegraph-Journal* 10 October, A1.

–. 2016b. "Ottawa rejects province's immigrant wish list." *Telegraph-Journal*, 9 March.

Iacovino, R. 2015. "Contextualizing the Quebec Charter of Values: Belonging without Citizenship in Quebec." *Canadian Ethnic Studies* 47 (1): 41–60. https://doi.org/10.1353/ces.2015.0004.

Imbeau, Louis, Réjean Landry, Henri Milner, François Pétry, Jean Crête, Pierre G. Forest, and Vincent Lemieux. 2000. "Comparative Provincial Policy Analysis: A Research Agenda." *Canadian Journal of Political Science* 33 (4): 779–804.

Institute of Island Studies. 2000. *A Place to Stay? Report of the PEI Population Strategy '99 Panel*. Charlottetown: University of Prince Edward Island.

Islam, M.K. 2013. "Levels and Trends of Temporary Foreign Workers in Canada: A Sociological Analysis." *American Journal of Sociological Research* 3 (4): 90–100.

Jackson, David. 2000a. "Chamber lobbies N.S. to increase immigration; Move would address shortage of skilled workers." *Chronicle Herald*, 26 September 2000, C10.

–. 2000b. "N.S. plans to make good to investors; Failed fund used for one project." *Chronicle Herald*, 15 April 2000, A12.

–. 2003. "Provincial immigrants program has few applications OK'd to date." *Chronicle Herald*, 26 November 2003, A5.

Jenson, J. 1997. "Fated to Live in Interesting Times: Canada's Changing Citizenship Regimes." *Canadian Journal of Political Science* 30 (4): 627–44. https://doi.org/10.1017/S0008423900016450.

–. 1998. "Reconnaître les différences: sociétés distinctes, régimes de citoyennetés et partenariats." In *Sortir de l'impasse: les voix de la réconciliation*, ed. Guy Laforest and Roger Gibbins, 235–62. Montréal: IRPP.

Jenson, J., and S.D. Phillips. 1996. "Regime Shift: New Citizenship Practices in Canada." *International Journal of Canadian Studies* 14 (Fall): 111–36.

Jones, B.D., and F.R. Baumgartner. 2012. "From There to Here: Punctuated Equilibrium to the General Punctuation Thesis to a Theory of Government Information Processing." *Policy Studies Journal* 40 (1): 1–20. https://doi.org/10.1111/j.1541-0072.2011.00431.x.

Juteau, D. 2002. "The Citizen Makes an Entrée: Redefining the National Community in Quebec." *Citizenship Studies* 6 (4): 441–58. https://doi.org/10.1080/1362102022000041268a.

Kataoka, S., and W. Magnusson. 2011. "Immigrant Settlement Policy in British Columbia." In *Immigrant Settlement Policy in Canadian Municipalities*, ed. Erin Tolley and Robert Young, 291–94. Montreal and Kingston: McGill–Queen's University Press.

Kelley, N., and M. Trebilcock. 2010. *The Making of the Mosaic: A History of Canadian Immigration Policy*. 2nd ed. Toronto: University of Toronto Press.

Klassen, T.R. 2000. "The Federal–Provincial Labour Market Development Agreements: Brave New Model of Collaboration?" In *Federalism, Democracy and Labour Market Policy in Canada*, ed. Tom McIntosh, 159–203. Montreal and Kingston: McGill–Queen's University Press.

Koopmans, R. 2010. "Trade-Offs between Equality and Difference: Immigrant Integration, Multiculturalism and the Welfare State in Cross-National Perspective." *Journal of Ethnic and Migration Studies* 36 (1): 1–26. https://doi.org/10.1080/13691830903250881.

Kostov, C. 2008. "Canada–Quebec Immigration Agreements (1971–1991) and Their Impact on Federalism." *American Review of Canadian Studies* 38 (1): 91–103. https://doi.org/10.1080/02722010809481822.

Kymlicka, W. 2003. "Canadian Multiculturalism in Historical and Comparative Perspective: Is Canada Unique." *Constitutional Forum* 13: 1–8.

Labelle, M., and J.-C. Icart. 2007. "Lecture du débat sur les accommodements raisonnables." *GLOBE: Revue Internationale d'Etudes Quebecoises* 10 (1): 121–36. https://doi.org/10.7202/1000082ar.

Laflamme, L. 2002. "Reaction to Proposed Immigration Policy." *CTV – Canada AM*, 17 October.

La Presse. 1988. "Mme [Sharon] Carstairs espère encore faire fléchir Ottawa et Québec." 15 décembre, B6.

–. 1990. "Immigration: Québec et Ottawa sont tout près de conclure une entente." *La Presse*, 11 August, A6.

Lebrun, D., and S. Rebelo. 2006. *The Role of Universities in the Economic Development of Atlantic Canada: A Focus on Immigration.* Moncton: Atlantic Canada Opportunities Agency.

Lecavalier, C. 2017. "L'opposition croit que c'est à Ottawa de payer pour l'immigration." *Le Journal de Montréal*, 29 August 2017.

Lecours, A. 2017. "Dynamic De/Centralization in Canada, 1867– 2010." *Publius: The Journal of Federalism*. Online first. Pjx046, https://doi. org/10.1093/publius/pjx046.

Legislative Assembly of Saskatchewan. 2008. Standing Committee on Human Services, Hansard Verbatim Report, no. 15, 12 May.

Lemieux, V. 2008. *Le Parti libéral du Québec: Alliances, rivalités et neutralités. Deuxième édition revue et augmentée.* Québec: Presses de l'Université Laval.

–. 2012. "Le Parti libéral du Québec et la formulation des politiques." In *Les partis politiques québécois dans la tourmente: Mieux comprendre et évaluer leur rôle*, ed. Réjean Pelletier, 249–71. Québec: Presses de l'Université Laval.

Leo, C., and M. August. 2009. "The Multilevel Governance of Immigration and Settlement: Making Deep Federalism Work." *Canadian Journal of Political Science* 42 (2): 491–510. https://doi.org/10.1017/S0008423909090337.

Leo, C., and J. Enns. 2009. "Multi-Level Governance and Ideological Rigidity: The Failure of Deep Federalism." *Canadian Journal of Political Science* 42 (1): 93–116. https://doi.org/10.1017/S0008423909090040.

Lépinard, E. 2010. "In the Name of Equality? The Missing Intersection in Canadian Feminists' Legal Mobilization against Multiculturalism." *American Behavioral Scientist* 53 (12): 1763–87. https://doi. org/10.1177/0002764210368096.

Leslie, K. 2005. "McGuinty takes swipe at Nfld. as he again demands more federal money for Ont." *Canadian Press*, 16 February.

Lewis, N.M. 2010. "A Decade Later: Assessing Successes and Challenges in Manitoba's Provincial Immigrant Nominee Program." *Canadian Public Policy* 36 (2): 241–64.

Liberal Party of British Columbia. 2001. *A New Era for British Columbia: A Vision for Hope & Prosperity for the Next Decade and Beyond.* Vancouver: BC Liberals.

–. 2006. *Real Leadership, Real Progress for British Columbia*. Vancouver: BC Liberals.

Liberal Party of Canada. 2015. *A New Plan for a Strong Middle Class*. Ottawa.

Liberal Party of Nova Scotia. 2003. *Believe in Better*. Halifax.

Liberal Party of New Brunswick. 2006. *Charter for Change: The Liberal Plan for a Better New Brunswick*.

Liberal Party of Newfoundland and Labrador. 2007. *People … Progress … Prosperity! Gerry Reid's New Liberalism: A Plan to Develop Newfoundland and Labrador for the Benefit of its People*. St John's.

–. 2011. *People's Platform*. St John's.

Liberal Party of Ontario. 2003. *Growing Strong Communities: The Ontario Liberal Plan for Clean, Safe Communities that Work*. Toronto: Ontario Liberal Party.

Liberal Party of Quebec. 1966. *Québec en Marche: Plateforme du Parti libéral du Québec*. Québec: Conseil général de la Fédération libérale du Québec.

–. 1970. *Québec: au travail!* Montreal.

–. 1985. *Synthèse du programme libéral*. Montréal: politique du Parti libéral.

–. 1988. *S'ouvrir à demain: document thématique du 24e Congrès des membres: un aperçu*. Montréal: Service de la recherche, du Développement et des communications du Parti libéral du Québec.

Linz, J.J. 1993. "State Building and Nation Building." *European Review* 1 (4): 355–69. https://doi.org/10.1017/S1062798700000776.

Linz, J.J., M.S. Darviche, and W. Genieys. 1997. "Construction étatique et construction nationale." *Pôle Sud* 7 (1): 5–26. https://doi.org/10.3406/pole.1997.977.

Lorjé, P. 2003. *OPEN UP Saskatchewan! A Report on International Immigration and Inter-Provincial In-Migration Initiatives to Increase the Population of the Province of Saskatchewan*. Saskatoon: Government of Saskatchewan.

MacDonald, M. 1998. "The Impact of a Restructured Canadian Welfare State on Atlantic Canada." *Social Policy and Administration* 32 (4): 389–400. https://doi.org/10.1111/1467-9515.00122.

MacKinley, S. 2000. "Worker shortage becoming critical, biz leaders warn: Skilled immigrants in demand." *Daily News*, 12 October, 12.

MacKinnon, W. 2007. "The 2007 Provincial Election in Prince Edward Island." *Canadian Political Science Review* 1 (2): 69–74.

Maclure, J. 2005. *Beyond Recognition and Asymmetry*. Kingston: Institute of Intergovernmental Relations, Queen's University. https://www.queensu.ca/iigr/sites/webpublish.queensu.ca.iigrwww/files/files/WorkingPapers/asymmetricfederalism/Maclure2005.pdf (accessed 13 August 2016).

Maddren, J. 2003. "Immigration as an election issue – a federal immigration minister is accusing Ontario Premier Ernie Eves of playing politics with immigrants. The Conservative leader has made immigration part of his election campaign." *CBC Radio – World Report*, 12 September.

Mahoney, J., and K. Thelen, eds. 2010a. *Explaining Institutional Change: Ambiguity, Agency, and Power*. New York: Cambridge University Press.

–. 2010b. "A Theory of Gradual Institutional Change." In *Explaining Institutional Change: Ambiguity, Agency, and Power*, ed. J. Mahoney and K. Thelen, 1–37. New York: Cambridge University Press.

Mailhot, P. 2007. "Le Canada et l'Alberta ratifient un nouvel accord en matière d'immigration." *CCN Matthews/Marketwire*, 11 May.

Manitoba. Immigration and Settlement Branch. 1986. *Manitoba Immigration Information Bulletin*. Winnipeg: Immigration and Settlement Branch, Employment Services and Economic Security.

Manitoba. Department of Manitoba Family Services. 1990. *Annual Report 1989–1990*. Winnipeg: Department of Family Services.

Manitoba. Department of Culture, Heritage and Citizenship. 1992. *Manitoba Immigration Information Bulletin, 1987–1990*. Winnipeg: Immigration and Settlement Branch.

–. 1993. *Annual Report 1992–1993*. Winnipeg: Department of Culture, Heritage and Citizenship.

–. 1994. *Annual Report 1993–1994*. Winnipeg: Department of Culture, Heritage and Citizenship.

–. 1995. *Annual Report 1994–1995*. Winnipeg: Department of Culture, Heritage and Citizenship.

–. 1997. *Annual Report 1996–1997*. Winnipeg: Department of Culture, Heritage and Citizenship.

–. 1999. *Annual Report 1998–1999*. Winnipeg: Department of Culture, Heritage and Citizenship.

Manitoba Finance. 2003. *Manitoba's Action Strategy for Economic Growth: Building for the Future*. Winnipeg: Department of Finance.

Manitoba Labour. 2000. *Manitoba Labour Annual Report 1999–2000*. Winnipeg: Department of Labour.

Manitoba Labour and Immigration. 2007. *Labour and Immigration Annual Report 2006–2007*. Winnipeg: Department of Labour and Immigration.

–. 2008. "Manitoba, Philippines Agree to Facilitate Worker Recruitment." Winnipeg: Department of Labour and Immigration.

–. 2009. *Labour and Immigration Annual Report 2008–2009*. Winnipeg: Department of Labour and Immigration.

–. 2010a. *Department of Labour and Immigration 2009–2010*. Winnipeg: Department of Labour and Immigration.

–. 2010b. *Manitoba Growth Strategy*. Winnipeg: Department of Labour and Immigration.

Manitoba Progressive Conservative Association. 1977. *The Challenges Ahead for Manitoba.* Winnipeg: Progressive Conservative Association of Manitoba.

Marland, A. 2007. "The 2007 Provincial Election in Newfoundland and Labrador." *Canadian Political Science Review* 1 (2): 75–85.

–. 2010. "Masters of Our Own Destiny: The Nationalist Evolution of Newfoundland Premier Danny Williams." *Revue internationale d'études canadiennes* 42: 155–81.

Marquez, T., and S. Schraufnagel. 2013. "Hispanic Population Growth and State Immigration Policy: An Analysis of Restriction (2008–12)." *Publius* 43 (3): 347–67. https://doi.org/10.1093/publius/pjt008.

Marquis, G. 2008. "New Brunswick's Population Growth Strategy in Historical Perspective." Paper presented at the Atlantic Studies Research and Development Centre conference "Exploring the Dimensions of Self-Sufficiency for New Brunswick." St Thomas University, 9–10 May.

McAndrew, M. 2009. "Quebec Interculturalism Policy: Convergence and Divergence with the Canadian Model." In *Multiculturalism: Public Policy and Problem Areas in Canada and India,* ed. Christopher Raj and Marie McAndrew, 204–21. Delhi: Manak.

McBride, S. 1996. "The Continuing Crisis of Social Democracy: Ontario's Social Contract in Perspective." *Studies in Political Economy* 50 (1): 65–93. https://doi.org/10.1080/19187033.1996.11675337.

McBride, S., and K. McNutt. 2007. "Devolution and Neoliberalism in the Canadian Welfare State: Ideology, National and International Conditioning Frameworks, and Policy Change in British Columbia." *Global Social Policy* 7 (2): 177–201. https://doi.org/10.1177/1468018107078161.

McCarten, J. 2003. "Experts wary of Ont. Tory motives for promise to redistribute new immigrants." *Canadian Press,* 23 September.

McGinnis, S. 2004. "N.S.'s Immigration Strategy Ambitious." *New Brunswick Telegraph-Journal,* 7 December, A4.

McGrane, D.P. 2008. "The 2007 Provincial Election in Saskatchewan." *Canadian Political Science Review* 2 (1): 64–71.

McIntosh, T. 2004. "Intergovernmental Relations, Social Policy and Federal Transfers after Romanow." *Canadian Public Administration* 47 (1): 27–51. https://doi.org/10.1111/j.1754-7121.2004.tb01969.x.

McLaughlin, P. 1997. "War of words: Metro's burgeoning immigrant community has overwhelmed ESL programs, leaving children losers in the linguistic battle, educators say." *Daily News,* 30 March, 4.

McLeod, J. 1991. "N.S. losing immigrant dollars." *Daily News,* 18 September, 21.

–. 2002. "Forced immigration a bad plan for Atlantic Region." *Daily News,* 25 June, 21.

–. 2006. "Nova Scotia Politics: Clientelism and John Savage." *Canadian Journal of Political Science* 39 (3): 553–70.

McRoberts, K. 1999. *Un pays à refaire: l'échec des politiques constitutionnelles canadiennes*. Montréal: Boréal.

–. 2001. "Canada and the Multinational State." *Canadian Journal of Political Science* 34 (4): 683–713. https://doi.org/10.1017/S0008423901778055.

Mitchell, K. 2001. "Transnationalism, Neo-Liberalism, and the Rise of the Shadow State." *Economy and Society* 30 (2): 165–89. https://doi.org/10.1080/03085140120042262.

Money, J. 1997. "No Vacancy: The Political Geography of Immigration Control in Advanced Industrial Countries." *International Organization* 51 (4): 685–720. https://doi.org/10.1162/002081897550492.

Montpetit, É. 2007. *Le fédéralisme d'ouverture: la recherche d'une légitimité canadienne au Québec*. Québec: Septentrion.

Moreno, L., and A. Obydenkova. 2013. "Federalization in Russia and Spain: The Puzzle of Reversible and Irreversible Outcomes." *Regional & Federal Studies* 23 (2): 151–68. https://doi.org/10.1080/13597566.2012.742071.

Morris, C. 2014. "Minister promotes fast-track immigration for province." *Fredericton Daily Gleaner*, 14 November.

Morrison, C. 1991. "N.S. Declines to pick favorites for immigration; Province opts out of fed program." *Daily News*, 20 May, 6.

Netherton, A. 2001. "Paradigm and Shift: A Sketch of Manitoba Politics." In *The Provincial State in Canada: Politics in the Provinces and Territories*, ed. Keith Brownsey and Michael Howlett, 203–39. Peterborough: Broadview Press.

New Brunswick. 1990. *Commerce and Technology, Annual Report 1989–1990*. Fredericton: Department of Commerce and Technology.

–. 1993. *Annual Report 1992–1993: Advanced Education and Labour*. Fredericton: Department of Advanced Education and Labour.

–. 1997. *Annual Report 1996–1997: Advanced Education and Labour*. Fredericton: Department of Advanced Education and Labour.

–. 1999a. *Annual Report 1998–1999: Department of Labour*. Fredericton: Department of Labour.

–. 1999b. *Annual Report 1998–1999: Department of Economic Development, Tourism and Culture*. Fredericton: Department of Economic Development, Tourism and Culture.

–. 2000. *Annual Report 1999–2000: Department of Labour*. Fredericton: Department of Labour.

–. 2002. *Greater Opportunity: New Brunswick's Prosperity Plan, 2002–2012*. Fredericton.

–. 2005. *Annual Report 2004–2005: Department of Business, New Brunswick*. Fredericton: Business New Brunswick.

–. 2008a. *2007–2008, Annual Report: Department of Business, New Brunswick.* Fredericton: Department of Business.

–. 2008b. *Be Our Future: New Brunswick's Population Growth Strategy.* Fredericton: Population Growth Secretariat.

–. 2009. *2008–2009, Annual Report: Department of Business, New Brunswick.* Fredericton: Business New Brunswick.

–. 2010. *2009–2010, Annual Report: Department of Business, New Brunswick.* Fredericton: Business New Brunswick.

–. 2011. "Atlantic premiers act to strengthen regional collaboration." Office of the Premier. http://www2.gnb.ca/content/gnb/en/news/news_release.2011.05.0542.html (accessed 27 September 2017).

–. 2014. *Putting Our Resources to Work: New Brunswick Population Growth Strategy.* Fredericton: Department of Post-Secondary Education, Training and Labour.

New Brunswick Advisory Council on Youth. 2008. *Rock the Boat – Here Today, Here to Stay.* Fredericton: Government of New Brunswick.

New Democratic Party of British Columbia. 2006. *Carole James Leader: BC NDP Because Everyone Matters.* Burnaby: BC New Democrats.

–. 2009. *Take Back Your BC. Because Everyone Matters.* Burnaby: BC New Democrats.

New Democratic Party of Newfoundland and Labrador. 2011. *Five Pledges for the First Year.* St John's: NL New Democratic Party.

New Democratic Party of New Brunswick. 2010. *NDP 2010: Practical, Responsible Change: The Voice for the Middle Class in Your Legislature.* Dieppe: NB New Democratic Party.

Newfoundland and Labrador. 2003. *Our Place in Canada: Final Report of the Newfoundland Royal Commission on Renewing and Strengthening Our Place in Canada.* St John's: Queen's Printer.

–. 2005a. *Department of Human Resources, Labour and Employment Annual Report 2004–2005.* St John's: Queen's Printer.

–. 2005b. *An Immigration Strategy for Newfoundland and Labrador: Opportunity for Growth.* Discussion Paper, June 2005. St John's: Queen's Printer.

–. 2007a. *Department of Human Resources, Labour and Employment Annual Report 2006–2007.* St John's: Queen's Printer.

–. 2007b. *Diversity – Opportunity and Growth: An Immigration Strategy for Newfoundland and Labrador.* St John's: Queen's Printer.

–. 2008. *Department of Human Resources, Labour and Employment Annual Report 2007–2008.* St John's: Queen's Printer.

–. 2009. *Department of Human Resources, Labour and Employment Annual Report 2008–2009.* St John's: Queen's Printer.

–. 2010a. *Department of Human Resources, Labour and Employment Annual Report 2009–2010.* St John's: Queen's Printer.

–. 2010b. *Provincial Nominee Program Fact Sheet, September 2010*. St John's: Office of Immigration and Multiculturalism, Department of Human Resources, Labour and Employment.

–. 2011. Newfoundland and Labrador Settlement & Integration Program (NLSIP) Funding Guidelines 2011–2012. St John's: Office of Immigration and Multiculturalism, Department of Human Resources, Labour and Employment.

–. 2017. *The Way Forward on Immigration in Newfoundland and Labrador*. St John's: Advanced Education, Skills and Labour, Government of Newfoundland and Labrador.

Newswire. 2004. "Enhanced Language Training Agreement Helps Saskatchewan Immigrants." 29 November.

Newton, L., and B.E. Adams. 2009. "State Immigration Policies: Innovation, Cooperation or Conflict?" *Publius* 39 (3): 408–31. https://doi.org/10.1093/publius/pjp005.

Noël, A. 2007. "When Fiscal Imbalance Becomes a Federal Problem." In *The 2006 Federal Budget: Re-thinking Fiscal Priorities*, ed. Charles M. Beach, Michael Smart, and Thomas A. Wilson, 127–43. Montreal and Kingston: McGill–Queen's University Press.

Nova Scotia. 2000. *Opportunities for Prosperity. A New Economic Growth Strategy for Nova Scotians*. Halifax: Nova Scotia Economic Development.

–. 2002. *Skills Nova Scotia Framework and 2002–2003 Action Plan*. Halifax: Department of Education.

–. 2004. *Nova Scotia Department of Education Annual Accountability Report for the Fiscal Year 2003–2004*. Halifax: Department of Education.

–. 2005a. *Nova Scotia's Immigration Strategy*. Halifax: Nova Scotia Office of Immigration.

–. 2005b. *Skills Nova Scotia Annual Progress Report 2004–2005*. Halifax: Department of Education.

–. 2006a. *Opportunities for Sustainable Prosperity 2006: An Updated Economic Growth Strategy for Nova Scotia*. Halifax: Department of Economic Development.

–. 2006b. *Skills Nova Scotia Annual Progress Report 2005–2006*. Halifax: Department of Education.

–. 2007. *Nova Scotia Office of Immigration Annual Accountability Report for the Fiscal Year 2006–2007*. Halifax: Nova Scotia Office of Immigration.

–. 2008. *Nova Scotia Office of Immigration Annual Accountability Report for the Fiscal Year 2007–2008*. Halifax: Nova Scotia Office of Immigration.

–. 2009. *Nova Scotia Office of Immigration Annual Accountability Report for the Fiscal Year 2008–2009*. Halifax: Nova Scotia Office of Immigration.

–. 2010a. *Jobs Here: The Plan to Grow Our Economy*. Halifax: Department of Transportation and Infrastructure Renewal.

–. 2010b. *Nova Scotia Office of Immigration Annual Accountability Report for the Fiscal Year 2009–2010*. Halifax.

–. 2010c. *Welcome Home to Nova Scotia: A Strategy for Immigration*. Halifax: Nova Scotia Office of Immigration.

Oliver, C., and J. Ibbitson. 2003. "Interview with Dalton McGuinty." CTV – Question Period, 5 October, 2003.

Ontario. 1996. *Business Plan*. Toronto: Ministry of Citizenship, Culture and Recreation.

–. 1997. *Business Plan 1997–1998. Ministry of Citizenship, Culture and Recreation*. Toronto.

–. 2004a. *Ministry of Citizenship Annual Reports 2002–2003 and 2003–2004*. Toronto.

–. 2004b. *Results-Based Plan Briefing Book 2004–2005. Ministry of Citizenship and Immigration*. Toronto.

–. 2007. *Results-Based Plan Briefing Book 2006–2007. Ministry of Citizenship and Immigration*. Toronto.

–. 2010. *Results-Based Plan Briefing Book 2009–2010. Ministry of Citizenship and Immigration*. Toronto.

–. 2011. *Results-Based Plan Briefing Book 2010–2011. Ministry of Citizenship and Immigration*. Toronto.

–. 2012. "Ontario Developing 'First-Ever' Immigration Strategy." Ministry of Citizenship and Immigration. https://news.ontario.ca/mci/en/2012/03/ontario-developing-first-ever-immigration-strategy.html (accessed 27 September 2017).

–. 2017. *A New Direction: Ontario's Immigration Strategy 2016 Progress Report*. Toronto: Ministry of Citizenship and Immigration.

Ontario New Democratic Party. 2007. Howard Hampton's Fair Deal for Today's Working Families. Toronto: Ontario New Democrats.

Ouellette, R. 2012. "1 800 MCKENNA." *Options politiques* (June 2012): 49–53.

Papillon, M. 2012. "Adapting Federalism: Indigenous Multilevel Governance in Canada and the United States." *Publius* 42 (2): 289–312. https://doi.org/10.1093/publius/pjr032.

Pâquet, M. 2005. *Aux marges de la cité: Étranger, Immigrant et État au Québec, 1621–1981*. Montréal: Boréal.

Paquet, M. 2012. "Beyond Appearances: Citizenship Tests in Canada and the UK." *Journal of International Migration and Integration* 13 (2): 243–60.

–. 2014. "La construction provinciale comme mécanisme: le cas de l'immigration au Manitoba." *Politique et Sociétés* 33 (3): 101–30. https://doi.org/10.7202/1027942ar.

–. 2015. "Bureaucrats as Immigration Policy-makers: The Case of Subnational Immigration Activism in Canada, 1990–2010." *Journal of

Ethnic and Migration Studies 41 (11): 1815–35. https://doi.org/10.1080/136 9183X.2015.1023185.

Paquet, M., and C. Andrew. 2013. "Les réseaux de soutien à l'immigration francophone de l'Ontario: résultats, adaptations et points de tensions d'une expérience de gouvernance communautaire." In *Gouvernance communautaire et innovation au sein de la francophonie néobrunswickoise et ontarienne*, ed. Linda Cardinal and Eric Forgues, 69–96. Québec: Presses de l'Université Laval.

Paquet, M., C. Belkhodja, and S.-M. Smith-Chanona. 2017. *La transformation du "modèle québécois": premier portrait des impacts. Pathways to Prosperity Project Report.* http://p2pcanada.ca/wp-content/blogs.dir/1/files/2017/05/ La-transformation-du--modele-quebecois--premier-portait-des-impacts1. pdf (accessed 3 Jul7 2017).

Paquet, M., and J. Broschek. 2017. "This Is Not a Turn: Canadian Political Science and Social Mechanisms." *Canadian Journal of Political Science* 50 (1): 295–310. https://doi.org/10.1017/S0008423917000038.

Parti Québécois. 1970. *Oui, le Parti Québécois vous offre la solution*. Montréal.

–. 1990. *Programme du Parti Québécois*. Montréal.

Pedwell, T. 2003. "Eves Wants 'Made-in-Ontario' Plan for Immigration in the Province." *Canadian Press*, 4 September.

PEI Population Strategy '99 Panel. 1999. *Backgrounder: Population and Demographic Trends on Prince Edward Island*. Charlottetown: Institute of Island Studies.

Pelletier, R. 2002. *Intergovernmental Cooperation Mechanisms: Factors for Change? Discusssion paper no. 29*. Ottawa: Commission on the Future of Health Care in Canada.

–. 2008. *Le Québec et le fédéralisme canadien: un regard critique*. Québec: Presses de l'Université Laval.

Perrella, A.M.L., S.D. Brown, B.J. Kay, and D.C. Docherty. 2007. "The 2007 Provincial Election and Electoral System Referendum in Ontario." *Canadian Political Science Review* 2 (1): 78–81.

Phillips, P. 1998. "Whither Saskatchewan?" *Canadian Business Economics* 6 (4): 36–49.

Pierson, P. 1994. *Dismantling the Welfare State? Reagan, Thatcher, and the Politics of Retrenchment*. Cambridge: Cambridge University Press. https://doi. org/10.1017/CBO9780511805288.

–. 1995. "Fragmented Welfare States: Federal Institutions and the Development of Social Policy." *Governance: An International Journal of Policy, Administration and Institutions* 8 (4): 449–78. https://doi. org/10.1111/j.1468-0491.1995.tb00223.x.

–. 2004. *Politics in Time: History, Institutions and Social Analysis*. Princeton: Princeton University Press.

Pitsula, J.M., and K. Rasmussen. 1990. *Privatizing a Province: The New Right in Saskatchewan*. Vancouver: New Star Books.

Poirier, C. 2006. "Ethnocultural Diversity, Democracy, and Intergovernmental Relations in Canadian Cities." In *Canada: The State of the Federation: Municipal–Federal–Provincial Relations in Canada*, ed. R. Young and C. Leuprecht, 201–19. Montreal and Kingston: McGill–Queen's University Press.

Policy Committee of the Liberal Party of Quebec. 1989. *Une richesse à renouveler: programme politique*. Montreal: Liberal Party of Quebec.

Prince Edward Island. 2002. *PEI Department of Development and Technology Annual Report 2001–2002*. Charlottetown.

–. 2003. *Annual Report 2002–2003, Department of Development and Technology*. Charlottetown: Department of Development and Technology.

–. 2005a. Standing Committee on Community Affairs and Economic Development. "First Report of the Third Session Sixty-second General Assembly: Attracting New Immigrants to Prince Edward Island." Charlottetown: Prince Edward Island Legislative Assembly.

–. 2005b. "Second Report of the Second Session Sixty-second General Assembly: Attracting New Immigrants to Prince Edward Island." Charlottetown: Prince Edward Island Legislative Assembly.

–. 2006. *Department of Development and Technology Annual Report 2005–2006*. Charlottetown: Department of Development and Technology.

–. 2007a. *Development and Technology Annual Report 2006–2007*. Charlottetown: Department of Development and Technology.

–. 2007b. *Prince Edward Island. Island Prosperity – a Focus for Change Island*. Charlottetown: Department of Innovation and Advanced Learning.

–. 2008. *Department of Development and Technology Annual Report 2007–2008*. Charlottetown: Department of Development and Technology.

–. 2009. *Innovation and Advanced Learning: Annual Report 2008–2009*. Charlottetown: Department of Innovation and Advanced Learning.

–. 2010a. *Island Investment Development Incorporated Annual Report 2009/2010*. Charlottetown: Department of Economic Development and Tourism.

–. 2010b. *Prince Edward Island Settlement Strategy*. Charlottetown: Department of Innovation and Advanced Learning.

Progressive Conservative Party of Alberta. 2008. *Ed Stelmach: Change That Works for Albertans: Platform Book*. Edmonton: PC Alberta.

Progressive Conservative Party of Newfoundland and Labrador. 2007. *Proud, Strong, Determined: The Future is Ours*. St John's: PC Party of Newfoundland and Labrador.

–. 2011. *New Energy: 2011 Policy Blue Book*. St John's: PC Party of Newfoundland and Labrador.

Progressive Conservative Party of Nova Scotia. 2006. *Building for Families: Building for the Future: Plan for a Stronger Nova Scotia*. Halifax: PC Party of Nova Scotia.

Progressive Conservative Party of Ontario. 1994. *The Common Sense Revolution*. Toronto: PC Party of Ontario.

–. 1999. *Blueprint: Mike Harris' Plan to Keep Ontario on the Right Track*. Toronto: PC Party of Ontario.

Québec. Ministry of Immigration and Cultural Communities. 1981. *Quebecers Each and Every One: The Government of Québec's Plan of Action for Cultural Communities*. Québec: Les Publications du Québec.

–. 1990a. *Let's Build Québec Together: Policy Statement on Immigration and Integration*. Québec: Les Publications du Québec.

–. 1990b. *Annual Report 1989–1990 du ministère des Communautés culturelles et de l'Immigration*. Québec: Les publications du Québec.

–. 1991a. *Canada–Quebec Accord Relating to Immigration and Temporary Admission of Aliens (Gagnon-Tremblay-McDougall Agreement)*. Montréal.

–. 1991b. *Rapport annuel 1990–1991 du ministère des Communautés culturelles et de l'Immigration*. Québec: Les Publications du Québec.

–. 1992. *Rapport annuel 1991–1992 du ministère de l'Immigration et des Communautés culturelles*. Québec: Les publications du Québec.

Québec. Ministry of Citizen Relations and Immigration. 1997. *Rapport Annuel 1996–1997 du ministère des Relations avec les citoyens et de l'immigration*. Québec: Les publications du Québec.

–. 2015. *Towards a New Québec Policy on Immigration, Diversity and Inclusion: Consultation Paper*. Montréal: Ministry of Immigration, Diversity and Inclusion.

–. 2016. *Together, We Are Québec: Québec Policy on Immigration, Participation, and Inclusion*. Montréal: Ministry of Immigration, Diversity and Inclusion.

Quebec National Assembly. 2013. *Bill no. 60: Charter affirming the values of State secularism and religious neutrality and of equality between women and men, and providing a framework for accommodation requests*. Québec: Éditeur Officiel du Québec.

Ramakrishnan, K., and P. Gulasekaram. 2013. "The Importance of the Political in Immigration Federalism." *Arizona State Law Journal* 44 (1431): 4–13.

Rasmussen, K. 2001. "Saskatchewan: From Entrepreneurial State to Embedded State." In *The Provincial State in Canada: Politics in the Provinces and Territories*, ed. K. Brownsey and M. Howlett, 241–75. Peterborough: Broadview.

Rayner, J., and T.L. Beaudry-Mellor. 2009. "Hope and Fear Revisited: Did the Provincial Election of 2007 Mark the Transition to a Stable Two-Party System in Saskatchewan?" *Canadian Political Science Review* 3 (1): 17–33.

Richer, J. 2015. "Immigration au Québec: réforme majeure en vue." *Le Devoir*, 25 January, 1.

Rocher, F. 2006. "La dynamique Québec-Canada ou le refus de l'idéal fédéral." In *Le fédéralisme Contemporain*, ed. Gagnon Alain-G., 93–146. Montréal: Les Presses de l'Université de Montréal.

Rocher, F., and M. Labelle. 2010. "L'interculturalisme comme modèle d'aménagement de la diversité: Compréhension et incompréhension dans l'espace public québécois." In *La Diversité québécoise en débat: Bouchard, Taylor et les autres*, ed. Bernard Gagnon, 179–203. Montréal: Québec Amérique.

Rocher, F., and C. Rouillard. 1998. "Décentralisation, subsidiarité et néo-libéralisme au Canada: lorsque l'arbre cache la forêt." *Canadian Public Policy* 24 (2): 233–58. https://doi.org/10.2307/3551775.

Rouillard, C., I. Fortier, É. Montpetit, and A.-G. Gagnon. 2008. *De la réingénérie à la modernisation de l'État québécois*. Québec: Presses de l'Université Laval.

Roy, P.E. 1990. *A White Man's Province: British Columbia Politicians and Chinese and Japanese Immigrants, 1858–1914*. Vancouver: UBC Press.

Ruff, N. 1996. "An Ambivalent Electorate: A Review of the British Columbia General Election of 1996." *BC Studies* 110: 5–23.

Ruggeri, G.C. 1998. "Vertical Fiscal Imbalances and Renewed Federalism." *Policy Options* 19 (November): 47–49.

Russell, P.H. 2004. *Constitutional Odyssey: Can Canadians Become a Sovereign People?* 3rd ed. Toronto: University of Toronto Press.

Sancton, A., and R. Young. 2003. "Paul Martin and Cities: Show Us the Money." *Options politiques* (December–January): 29–34.

Saskatchewan. 1992. *Annual Report 1991–1992: Saskatchewan Economic Diversification and Trade*. Saskatoon: Department of Economic Diversification and Trade.

–. 1995. *Annual Report 1994–1995: Saskatchewan Economic Development*. Saskatoon: Department of Economic Development.

–. 2001. *Annual Report 2000–2001: Saskatchewan Intergovernmental and Aboriginal Affairs*. Regina: Department of Intergovernmental and Aboriginal Affairs.

–. 2002a. *2001–2002 Annual Report of Intergovernmental and Aboriginal Affairs*. Regina: Department of Intergovernmental and Aboriginal Affairs.

–. 2002b. *Meeting Needs and Making Connections: A Report on the Saskatchewan Immigrant and Refugee Settlement Needs and Retention Study*. Saskatoon: Saskatchewan Immigration Branch, Government Relations and Aboriginal Affairs.

–. 2004. *Annual Report 2003–2004: Saskatchewan Government Relations and Aboriginal Affairs*. Regina: Department of Intergovernmental and Aboriginal Affairs.

–. 2005. *Saskatchewan Action Plan for the Economy*. Saskatoon: Saskatchewan Economy and Resources.

–. 2006. *2005–2006 Annual Report: Saskatchewan Industry and Resources*. Regina: Department of Industry and Resources.

–. 2007a. *2006–2007 Annual Report: Saskatchewan Advanced Education and Employment*. Regina: Department of Advanced Education and Employment.

–. 2007b. *2006–2007 Annual Report: Saskatchewan Industry and Resources*. Regina: Department of Industry and Resources.

–. 2008. *2007–2008 Annual Report: Ministry of Advanced Education, Employment and Labour*. Regina: Department of Advanced Education, Employment and Labour.

–. 2009a. *2008–2009 Annual Report: Advanced Education, Employment and Labour*. Regina: Department of Advanced Education, Employment and Labour.

–. 2009b. *Saskatchewan Immigration Strategy: Strenghtening Our Communities and Economy*. Regina: Ministry of Advanced Education, Employment and Labour.

–. 2010a. *2009–2010 Annual Report: Advanced Education, Employment and Labour*. Regina: Department of Advanced Education, Employment and Labour.

–. 2010b. "Agreement Signed between Saskatchewan and Vietnam." Regina: Department of Advanced Education, Employment and Labour. http://www.asiapacific.ca/news/agreement-signed-between-saskatchewan-and-vietnam (accessed 27 September 2017).

Saskatchewan Liberal Party. 2003. *ReEnergizing Saskatchewan. Platform Document*. Saskatoon: Saskatchewan Liberal Party.

Saskatchewan New Democratic Party. 2003. *Building the Future for Saskatchewan Families*. Saskatoon: Saskatchewan New Democratic Party.

–. 2007. *Moving Forward Together: Making Life Better for Saskatchewan Families*. Saskatoon: Saskatchewan New Democratic Party.

Saskatchewan Party. 2011. *Brad Wall: Moving Saskatchewan Forward*. Saskatoon: SK Party.

Savoie, D.J. 2004. "Regional Economic Development in Atlantic Canada: The Next Step." In *Regionalism in a Global Society: Persistence and Change in Atlantic Canada and New England*, ed. S.G. Thomblin and C.S. Colgan, 107–47. Peterborough: Broadview.

–. 2006. *Visiting Grandchildren: Economic Development in the Maritimes*. Toronto: University of Toronto Press.

–. 2010. "Le Nouveau-Brunswick: Pour que cette crise serve à quelque chose." *Revue d'études sur le Nouveau-Brunswick* 1: 42–53.

Schertzer, R. 2015. "Intergovernmental Relations in Canada's Immigration System: From Bilateralism towards Multilateral Collaboration." *Canadian Journal of Political Science* 48 (2): 383–412. https://doi.org/10.1017/S0008423915000027X.

Seidle, L. 2010a. "The Canada Ontario Immigration Agreement: Assessment and Options for Renewal." Toronto: Mowat Centre for Policy Innovation.

–. 2010b. "Intergovernmental Immigration Agreements and Public Accountability." *Policy Options* (July–August): 49–53.

Siemiatycki, M., and T. Triadafilopoulos. 2010. *International Perspectives on Immigrant Service Provision*. Toronto: Mowat Centre for Policy Innovation.

Simeon, R. 2006. *Federal–Provincial Diplomacy: The Making of Recent Policy in Canada*. Toronto: University of Toronto Press. https://doi.org/10.3138/9781442674820.

Simpson, E. 2003. "Forum to Probe Immigrants' Short Stay in Province." *Chronicle Herald*, 5 December, A3.

Skocpol, T. 1979. *States and Social Revolutions: A Comparative Analysis of France, Russia, and China*. Cambridge: Cambridge University Press. https://doi.org/10.1017/CBO9780511815805.

Smith, A. 2004. "Province Seeks Open Door; Government Hopes to Lure Thousands of New Immigrants." *Chronicle Herald*, 1 September, B6.

Smith, K.B. 2002. "Typologies, Taxonomies, and the Benefits of Policy Classification." *Policy Studies Journal: The Journal of the Policy Studies Organization* 30 (3): 379–95. https://doi.org/10.1111/j.1541-0072.2002.tb02153.x.

Smith, M. 2009. "Diversity and Canadian Political Development: Presidential Address to the Canadian Political Science Association, Ottawa, May 27, 2009." *Canadian Journal of Political Science* 42 (4): 831–54. https://doi.org/10.1017/S0008423909990692.

Smith, P.J. 2001. "Alberta: Experiments in Governance – from Social Credit to the Klein Revolution." In *The Provincial State in Canada: Politics in the Provinces and Territories*, ed. Keith Brownsey and Michael Howlett, 277–308. Peterborough: Broadview.

Spiro, P.J. 2001. "Federalism and Immigration: Models and Trends." *International Social Science Journal* 53 (167): 67–73. https://doi.org/10.1111/1468-2451.00294.

Steel, H. 2006. "Where's the Policy? Immigration to New Brunswick, 1945–1971." *Acadiensis* 35 (2): 85–105.

Stevenson, Garth. 1980. "Political Constraints and the Province-Building Objective." *Canadian Public Policy* 6 (Supplement 1980): 265–74. https://doi.org/10.2307/3549928.

–. 1989. "The Origins of Co-operative Federalism." In *Federalism and Political Community: Essays in Honour of Donald Smiley*, ed. David P. Shugarman and Reg Whitaker, 7–31. Peterborough: Broadview.

Streeck, W., and K. Thelen. 2005. *Beyond Continuity: Institutional Change in Advanced Political Economies*. Oxford: Oxford University Press.

Tansey, O. 2007. "Process Tracing and Elite Interviewing: A Case for Non-Probability Sampling." *PS, Political Science & Politics* 40 (4): 765–72. https://doi.org/10.1017/S1049096507071211.

Taylor, R. 2015. "Province seeks flexibility with immigration strategy." *Chronicle Herald,* 26 October 2015.

Tellier, G. 2011. "L'étude comparée des politiques publiques provinciales: un laboratoire à explorer." *Politique et Sociétés* 30 (1): 95–115. https://doi.org/10.7202/1006061ar.

Tessier, K. 1995. "Immigration and the Crisis of Federalism: A Comparison of the United States and Canada." *Indiana Journal of Global Legal Studies* 3 (1995–96): 211–44.

Thelen, K. 1999. "Historical Institutionalism in Comparative Politics." *Annual Review of Political Science* 2 (1): 369–404. https://doi.org/10.1146/annurev.polisci.2.1.369.

Thomas, P.G. 2010. "Leading from the Middle: Manitoba's Role in the Intergovernmental and Transnational Arenas." In *Manitoba Politics and Government: Issues, Institutions, Traditions,* ed. Paul G. Thomas and Curtis Brown, 265–90. Winnipeg: University of Manitoba Press.

Tolley, E., J. Biles, R. Vineberg, M. Burstein, and J. Frideres. 2011. "Introduction." In *The Integration and Inclusion of Newcomers and Minorities across Canada,* ed. J. Biles, M. Burstein, J. Frideres, E. Tolley, and R. Vineberg, 1–22. Montreal and Kingston: McGill–Queen's University Press.

Tolley, E., and R. Young, eds. 2011. *Immigrant Settlement in Canadian Municipalities.* Montreal and Kingston: McGill–Queen's University Press.

Triadafilopoulos, T. 2012. *Becoming Multicultural: Immigration and the Politics of Membership in Canada and Germany.* Vancouver: UBC Press.

Turgeon, L., and J. Wallner. 2013. "Adaptability and Change in Federations: Centralization, Political Parties, and Taxation Authority in Australia and Canada." In *The Global Promise of Federalism,* ed. G. Skogstad, D. Cameron, M. Papillon, and K. Banting, 188–213. Toronto: University of Toronto Press. https://doi.org/10.3138/9781442619197-009.

Union nationale. 1966. *Objectifs 1966 de l'Union nationale: un programme d'action pour une jeune nation.* Montréal: L. Davignon, agent officiel de l'Union nationale.

Vanstone, M. 1999. *The Evolution and Impact of Manitoba's Immigration Initiatives.* Winnipeg: Manitoba Legislative Assembly.

Veugelers, J. 2000. "State–Society Relations in the Making of Canadian Immigration Policy during the Mulroney Era." *Canadian Review of Sociology* 37 (1): 95–110. https://doi.org/10.1111/j.1755-618X.2000.tb00588.x.

Vineberg, R. 1987. "Federal–Provincial Relations in Canadian Immigration." *Canadian Public Administration* 30 (2): 299–317. https://doi.org/10.1111/j.1754-7121.1987.tb00085.x.

–. 2012. *Responding to Immigrants' Settlement Needs: The Canadian Experience.* New York: Springer.

Wallner, J. 2008. "Empirical Evidence and Pragmatic Explanations: Canada's Contributions to Comparative Federalism." In *The Comparative Turn in Canadian Political Science*, ed. L.A. White, R. Simeon, R. Vipond, and J. Wallner, 158–74. Toronto: University of Toronto Press.

Wallner, J., and G.W. Boychuck. 2014. "Comparing Federations: Testing the Model of Market-Preserving Federalism on Canada, Australia, and the United States." In *Comparing Canada: Methods and Perspectives on Canadian Politics*, ed. L. Turgeon, M. Papillon, J. Wallner, and S. White, 198–221. Vancouver: UBC Press.

Walsh, J. 2008. "Navigating Globalization: Immigration Policy in Canada and Australia, 1945–2007." *Sociological Forum* 23 (4): 786–813. https://doi.org/10.1111/j.1573-7861.2008.00094.x.

Ward, P. 2002. *White Canada Forever: Popular Attitudes and Public Policy toward Orientals in British Columbia*. Montreal and Kingston: McGill–Queen's University Press.

Watts, R. 1989. *Executive Federalism: A Comparative Analysis*. Kingston: Institute of Intergovernmental Relations, Queen's University.

Wesley, J. 2011. *Code Politics: Campaigns and Cultures on the Canadian Prairies*. Vancouver: UBC Press.

White, N. 2006. "Immigration Policy 'Needs to Get beyond the Welcome': Retention Greater Moncton Immigration Board Joins Similar Group in Saint John Trying to Keep New Immigrants in N.B." *Telegraph-Journal*, 26 October, A4.

Whitehorse Star. 2007. "Alta. Minister Says Immigration Deal with Ottawa Not Coming Soon." 2 February, 27.

Wilder, M., and M. Howlett. 2015. "Bringing the Provinces Back in: Re-evaluating the Relevance of Province-Building to Theories of Canadian Federalism and Multi-Level Governance." *Canadian Political Science Review* 9 (3): 1–34.

Winter, E. 2014. *Becoming Canadian: Making Sense of Recent Changes to Citizenship Rules*. Montreal: Institute for Research on Public Policy.

Wood, D., and T.R. Klassen. 2008. "Intergovernmental Relations Post-Devolution: Active Labour Market Policy in Canada and the United Kingdom 1996–2006." *Regional and Federal Studies* 18 (4): 331–51. https://doi.org/10.1080/13597560802223912.

–. 2009. "Bilateral Federalism and Workforce Development Policy in Canada." *Canadian Public Administration* 522: 249–70.

Worswick, C. 2013. "Economic Implications of Recent Changes to the Temporary Foreign Worker Program." *IRPP Insight* 4: 1–18.

Young, R.A., P. Faucher, and A. Blais. 1984. "The Concept of Province-Building: A Critique." *Canadian Journal of Political Science* 17 (4): 783–818. https://doi.org/10.1017/S0008423900052586.
Zicone, G., and T. Caponio. 2006. "The Multilevel Governance of Migration." In *The Dynamics of International Migration and Settlement in Europe*, ed. R. Penninx, M. Berger, and K. Kraal, 269–304. Amsterdam: Amsterdam University Press.

Index